Selected Essays on Corporate Reputation and Social Media

Markus Kick

Selected Essays on Corporate Reputation and Social Media

Collection of Empirical Evidence

With a preface by Prof. Dr. Manfred Schwaiger

Markus Kick
München, Germany

Dissertation Universität München, 2014

D 19

ISBN 978-3-658-08836-1   ISBN 978-3-658-08837-8 (eBook)
DOI 10.1007/978-3-658-08837-8

Library of Congress Control Number: 2015932770

Springer Gabler
© Springer Fachmedien Wiesbaden 2015

Printed on acid-free paper

Springer Gabler is a brand of Springer Fachmedien Wiesbaden
Springer Fachmedien Wiesbaden is part of Springer Science+Business Media
(www.springer.com)

Preface

Nach allgemeinem Erkenntnisstand in Theorie und Praxis stiften immaterielle Wirtschaftsgüter wie die Corporate Reputation Unternehmen einen nachhaltigen Wertzuwachs. Im Fokus entsprechender wissenschaftlicher Untersuchungen stand allerdings bisher meist das klassische „Unternehmen", das auf Wettbewerbsmärkten agiert. Herr Kick betritt mit seiner Dissertation insofern Neuland, als er im ersten Teil seiner Dissertation der Frage nachgeht, ob die Unternehmensreputation auch in regulierten (Non-Profit-)Märkten - wie dem der gesetzlichen Krankenversicherung - eine Signalwirkung ausübt und somit Nutzen stiftet.

Die Verbindung zum zweiten Teil der Dissertation ergibt sich indirekt aus der Bedeutung einer strategisch aufgebauten integrierten Unternehmenskommunikation: Nachdem die Fakten selbst in aller Regel weit weniger entscheidend sind als die subjektive Wahrnehmung derselben, ist das Reputationsmanagement auf geeignete Maßnahmen der Unternehmenskommunikation angewiesen. Forschungsarbeiten zur integrierten Unternehmenskommunikation haben seit jeher Fragen der Orchestrierung unterschiedlicher Kommunikationskanäle behandelt, und in jüngerer Vergangenheit hat sich der Blickwinkel zunehmend auf die Integration sozialer Medien gerichtet. In diesem Forschungsfeld sind die beiden Beiträge im zweiten Teil der vorliegenden Dissertation angesiedelt, in denen Herr Kick sich mit der Frage befasst, wie Unternehmen in den Social Media auftreten und ihre Produkte bzw. Marken kommunikativ begleiten sollen.

Die **erste Studie** geht der Frage nach, ob die Reputation einer gesetzlichen Krankenversicherung Einfluss auf die betreffenden Auswahlentscheidungen der gesetzlich Versicherten hat. Hintergrund der Arbeit ist die Annahme, dass sich Versicherungsnehmer nicht nur durch die tatsächlichen Versicherungsleistungen beeinflussen lassen, sondern dass sie auch Surrogate wie die Reputation der Krankenkasse als Qualitätssignal in ihren Entscheidungsprozessen berücksichtigen. Die durchgeführte Choice-Based Conjoint Analyse zeigt nicht nur, dass in einem sehr preissensitiven Markt Reputation einen nennenswerten Einfluss auf die Wahlentscheidungen hat; sie belegt zudem, dass die aus vielen Konsumbereichen bekannte „Jagd nach dem gleichen Service zu einem günstigeren Preis" hier abgelöst worden ist durch eine „Jagd nach mehr Leistung für gleichen Preis".

Der **zweite Beitrag** stellt eine (erweiterte) Replikation der ersten Studie dar, die Zusatzbeiträge als weitere Variable in die Conjoint-Analyse einbezieht und ferner untersucht, ob die verwendeten Variablen den der Wahl einer gesetzlichen Krankenversicherung vorausgehenden Entscheidungsprozess tatsächlich umfassend abbilden können. Die Erweiterung der Variablenliste um Zusatzbeiträge erlaubt nun zu prüfen, inwieweit sich Reputationsvorteile einer direkten Zahlungsbereitschaft gegenüberstellen lassen. Es zeigt sich, dass die Bedeutung der Reputation zwar etwas zurückgegangen ist, insgesamt aber immer noch eine Rolle spielt und für rund 11% des gesamten Nutzens verantwortlich zeichnet.

Dass nicht wesentliche „kaufrelevante" Kriterien aus der Analyse ausgeschlossen wurden und keine konfundierenden Effekte zwischen Reputation und Produktqualität existieren, klärt Herr Kick im Rahmen einer zweiten Studie. Er belegt die oben erwähnte Relevanz subjektiver Wahrnehmungen: Während die Leistungen der gesetzlichen Krankenkassen weitgehend identisch sind, werden selbst dann der Techniker-Krankenkasse „Leistungsvorteile" zugeschrieben, wenn für die tatsächlich bestehenden Versicherungsbeziehungen kontrolliert wird. Diesem belastbaren Resultat ist auch eine hohe praktische Relevanz zuzumessen.

Der **dritte Beitrag** strukturiert die vorhandene Literatur zur Frage, welche Erkenntnisse hinsichtlich der Marken- und Produktkommunikation in Social Media – insbesondere im Hinblick auf deren Wirkung – bisher vorgelegt wurden. Das ist insofern relevant, als in jüngerer Vergangenheit ein Paradigmenwechsel in der Markenkommunikation offensichtlich wurde, der durch Social Media ausgelöst wurde: Marketingverantwortliche registrieren, dass die senderzentrierte Kommunikation nicht länger aufrechterhalten werden kann und in zunehmendem Maße einer nutzergetriebenen Kommunikation über Produkte und Marken gewichen ist. Es hat sich die Auffassung durchgesetzt, dass Social Media nicht lediglich als ein weiterer Kommunikationskanal zu betrachten sind, sondern eine neue Form der Markenkommunikation erfordern. Entlang der Social Media Value Chain analysiert Herr Kick die Effekte von eWOM auf *Consumer Mindset Metrics, Product and Market Performance* und *Financial Performance*. Nachdem auch in diesem Forschungsfeld nur sehr selten ein Nachweis von Main Effects geführt werden kann, kommt der Systematisierung der Arbeiten, in denen mit Moderatoren gearbeitet wurde, besondere Bedeutung zu. Herr Kick präsentiert eine ansprechende Form der Zusammenstellung der moderierenden Befunde und vermittelt so einen guten Überblick über den ohne Zweifel stark fragmentierten Bestand an Forschungsergebnissen im Bereich Social-Media-Kommunikation, aus dem zielgerichtete Handlungsanleitungen für weitere Forschungsaktivitäten abzuleiten sind.

In der **vierten Studie** bringt Herr Kick ein Experimentaldesign zur Anwendung, mit dessen Hilfe er die Rolle von Interaktivität und Grad der Lebendigkeit eines Facebook-Posts auf die Zielkategorien Recall, Einstellung zur Marke und Kaufabsicht untersucht. Als zusätzlichen Moderator nimmt Herr Kick das zugrundeliegende Involvement auf. Für sein Experiment entwickelt er Facebook-Posts unterschiedlicher Interaktivität und Lebendigkeit für ein Modelabel und einen Fahrrad-Hersteller. Herr Kick bestätigt mit seinem Feldexperiment frühere Forschungsarbeiten und zeigt, dass ein hoher Grad an Lebendigkeit und Interaktivität die Einstellung zur Marke stärker treibt als ein geringer Grad an Interaktivität und Lebendigkeit.

In der Gesamtschau erweitert Herr Kick mit dem vorliegenden Werk nicht nur den Stand der Forschung, sondern liefert auch Praktikern Anhaltspunkte zur gezielten Weiterentwicklung ihrer Geschäftsaktivitäten. Ich wünsche der Arbeit, dass sie eine breite Leserschaft in Theorie und Praxis findet, Diskussionen anzustoßen und damit weitere Forschungsarbeiten in diesem Kontext auszulösen vermag.

Prof. Dr. Manfred Schwaiger

Acknowledgements

Die vorliegende Dissertation entstand während meiner Zeit als wissenschaftlicher Mitarbeiter am Institut für Marktorientierte Unternehmensführung der Ludwig-Maximilians-Universität München. Ohne eine Vielzahl von Personen aus meinem beruflichen und privaten Umfeld, wäre es mir nicht möglich gewesen, diese Arbeit zu verfassen. Ich möchte diese Gelegenheit nutzen und mich für die Unterstützung bedanken.

Meinem Doktorvater Herrn Prof. Dr. Manfred Schwaiger danke ich zu allererst für die Möglichkeit zur Erstellung dieser Dissertation. Ich danke ihm für seine Unterstützung, seine wertvollen fachlichen und persönlichen Ratschläge, sowie für das mir entgegengebrachte Vertrauen und die mir gewährten Freiheiten während meiner Zeit am IMM. Dies alles hat maßgeblich zu meiner persönlichen und akademischen Entwicklung beigetragen. Weiterhin möchte ich mich bei Herrn Prof. Dr. Anton Meyer für die Übernahme des Korreferats, sein Interesse an meiner Arbeit und seine wertvollen Anmerkungen bedanken.

Ein besonderer Dank gilt Frau Gabriela Latinjak, die mich bei allen Hochs und Tiefs im Rahmen der Dissertation immer freundschaftlich unterstützte und gerade in der Endphase als Lektorin einen großen Beitrag zum Gelingen dieses Projektes geleistet hat. Des Weiteren bedanke ich mich bei meiner Co-Autorin Dr. Martina Panico (geb. Littich) für die gewinnbringende Zusammenarbeit. Allen Kolleginnen und Kollegen danke ich für das freundschaftliche Miteinander, die anregenden Diskussionen und viele unbezahlbare Momente. Besonders bedanken möchte ich mich bei meinem Zimmerkollegen Dr. Felix Kessel, der mich gerade zu Beginn meiner Dissertation immer wieder hilfsbereit unterstützt hat. Herrn Benjamin Pfister danke ich für seine fachliche und persönliche Unterstützung, viele Stunden Proof-Reading, sein immer ehrliches Feedback und seine Freundschaft. Maximilian Hausmann danke ich für die Vielzahl an lebhaften Forschungsgesprächen und dem damit verbundenen Anteil an dieser Dissertation.

Des Weiteren bedanke ich mich bei Matthias Hofmuth für sein offenes Ohr, die Bereicherung außerhalb des Lehrstuhls, sein fachliches Feedback und für seine wertvolle Freundschaft. Ferner möchte ich Familie Forstmeier danken, ohne die ich im wahrsten Sinne des Wortes die Zeit der Promotion nicht überlebt hätte.

Ohne die Unterstützung im privaten Umfeld wäre das Gelingen dieser Arbeit nicht möglich gewesen. Besonders bedanken möchte ich mich hier bei meinen Eltern Klara und Sebastian. Sie haben mich auf meinem gesamten Lebens- und Bildungsweg jederzeit bedingungslos unterstützt und mir immer wieder Zuspruch und Sicherheit gegeben, um die mir gesteckten Ziele verfolgen und erreichen zu können.

Meiner Frau Katrin danke ich für ihre Liebe, für ihr Verständnis, für ihr Vertrauen, für ihre nicht enden wollende Unterstützung, für ihr Interesse an dieser Arbeit sowie die unzähligen Stunden des Korrekturlesens. Ihr ist diese Arbeit gewidmet. Danke, dass es Dich gibt!

Table of Contents

Introduction

The thesis at hand contains four essays of the broader area of market-based management. Aligned along the main headline of this dissertation, the first two essays focus on corporate reputation, whereas the latter analyze key concepts in the area of social media.

Essays on Corporate Reputation

By awarding corporate reputation with the label "ubiquitous", FOMBRUN and VAN RIEL (1997, p. 5) acknowledge its enormous spread over a variety of scientific disciplines. Pushed by practitioners in the 1980s, reputational research arose out of a shift in thinking away from a pure focus on tangible assets to the realization of intangible resources' value (HALL, 1992, p. 135). Since then, corporate reputation has been applied in many different areas "[…], yet existing research has rarely been integrative" (DACIN and BROWN, 2006, p. 95). Even though today's research is lacking a universal definition for corporate reputation, its importance and numbers of studies is constantly growing (GOTSI and WILSON, 2001, p. 25, SCHWAIGER, 2004, p. 47). Under the light of an increasingly complex, ubiquitous, and uncertain economic environment, sources for competitive advantages, more independent from product-related aspects are needed (REIBSTEIN et al., 2009, p. 1). As a logical consequence, there are plenty of measuring concepts that aim to operationalize corporate reputation (e.g., SCHWAIGER, 2004, FOMBRUN et al., 2000, HELM, 2006, NEWELL and GOLDSMITH, 2001).

Academia agrees that corporate reputation is a key source of strategic and competitive advantage (RINDOVA et al., 2005), one of the most important intangible values and differentiation resources (e.g., FOMBRUN, 2001, RAITHEL and SCHWAIGER, 2014, HALL, 1993), and a key marketing metric (HANSSENS et al., 2009, p. 116). Reputation comprises cognitive knowledge about and affective emotional feelings toward a company from its multiple stakeholder groups (e.g., WEIGELT and CAMERER, 1988, FERGUSON et al., 2000, RAITHEL and SCHWAIGER, 2014). Developed over a long period of time, it is a scarce resource that is difficult to imitate but very fragile as it can be can be destroyed overnight (HALL, 1993, HUNT and MORGAN, 1995, RAITHEL et al., 2010). Positive effects of a favorable corporate reputation are shown across many different stakeholder groups. For example, a favorable corporate reputation helps to create higher trust in advertising campaigns (e.g., FOMBRUN and VAN RIEL, 1997), positively influences customer satisfaction and loyalty measures (e.g., WALSH and BEATTY,

2007), and helps to increase employer motivation and to attract and retain talent (SCHWAIGER et al., 2009, TYMON et al., 2010). Further, these beneficial aspects also positively transfer into shareholder value and a superior financial performance (e.g., EBERL and SCHWAIGER, 2005, RAITHEL and SCHWAIGER, 2014, ROBERTS and DOWLING, 2002).

Taking a closer look at the effects of corporate reputation on the consumer market reveals that consumers' purchase decisions are highly influenced by corporate reputation measures. FISHBEIN and AJZEN (1975, pp. 301-315) state that attitudinal constructs like corporate reputation play a major role when making consumption decisions. The subconscious activation of summarized cognitive and emotional aspects about a firm is able to drive purchase intention and triggers the actual purchasing act. It is able to reduce cognitive dissonance, inherent choice complexity (FOMBRUN and VAN RIEL, 1997), and perceived risk of the actual purchase (KOTHA et al., 2001). As a result, highly reputable companies gain sales advantages and are even able to charge price premiums from their customers (FOMBRUN and VAN RIEL, 1997). Reputational effects on purchase behavior have been shown across a variety of industries and settings (e.g., PREECE et al., 1995, EBERL, 2006, EBERL and SCHWAIGER, 2008, YOON et al., 1993). However, the majority of studies focus on open markets with a vivid competitive landscape. Evidence on the effects of quality signals like corporate reputation on regulated markets is scarce.

Study I, titled "The Effect of Corporate Reputation on Health Insurance Choices in a Public-Policy-Shaped Environment of Premium Equality", picks up this thought and investigates the influence of the quality signal corporate reputation on the highly regulated market of statutory health insurance. The underlying laws and regulations are utterly complex and restrict competitive forces in terms of benefit and coverage options. Thus, statutory health insurance companies lack distinct differentiation criteria. This indicates an important influence of intangible quality signals like corporate reputation. As the German statutory health insurance system has been extremely price driven, the government drastically altered the market by introducing premium equality in 2009, in order to foster a new competition based on quality rather than price. The statutory health insurance funds reacted quickly by offering new benefits and services in order to differentiate again. Regulatory forces only allow differentiating in a very small range. It can, therefore, be assumed that consumers are influenced not only by product attributes but also by signals of quality, such as those delivered by corporate reputation. The results of a choice-based conjoint experiment conducted in 2010 show that benefits such as elective tariffs, bonus programs, complementary insurance offers, voluntary coverage, and extended services significantly influence consumer choice of statutory health insurance. These findings argue for the success of the public policy strategy of the German government. Reputation is found to be fairly important in product choice when compared with product-based attributes. As a consequence of these findings, funds should not only adapt their offerings with regard to the benefits that insurants value the most but also place emphasis on corporate reputation management. An earlier version of this paper, co-authored by Martina Panico (née Littich), was presented at the 31st Association for Marketing and Health Care Research Conference in Park City — Utah, USA where it has won the *Best Paper Award.*

Along with the introduction of premium equality in 2009, the German government also opened up the possibility to deviate from the premium equality system. In case funds are no longer able to cover their costs, they are legitimated to charge additional contributions directly from their insurants. This option has only rarely been used in the first years after introduction. Thus, premium equality is still status quo on the statutory health insurance market. However, research clearly predicts that this current state of premium equality is soon to be changed (PFISTER, 2009, EIBICH et al., 2011). Further, additional contributions have been widely discussed in media coverage. **Study II**, named "The Effects of Additional Contributions on Statutory Health Insurance Choices in Germany", uses this natural, experimental constellation to revisit the thoughts of the previous study. The choice-based conjoint experiment conducted in 2012 includes the new pricing signal of additional contributions. Contrary to preliminary expectations, price is not the dominating criterion on the current market, but equally important to voluntary coverage options. Corporate reputation and a provider's brand name lose importance, but are still a major quality signal within consumer's choice decisions. The brand name TK (i.e., Technical Health Insurance Fund), as reputational leader, provides additional value for insurants. TK is able to charge up to €1.46 additional contributions from each insurant per month without falling behind their competitors. Compared to the general contribution rate of 15.5% of each insurant's gross income, of course, €1.46 seems rather low. However, the statutory health insurance funds that already charged additional contributions from their members collected between €5 and €16 per month and head. This reveals that TK is able to charge close to 10% of the additional contribution range simply due to their reputational advantage. Thus, corporate reputation proves to enhance a fund's bargaining position towards its potential insurants, as it allows charging and justifying price premiums. A second empirical study reveals that people tremendously lack knowledge about funds' benefit and coverage portfolios and the SHI system in general. Insurants consistently overestimate funds with comparably higher corporate reputation regarding their benefit and coverage details of selected performance categories. Although slightly attenuated through the reintroduction of a price signal on the statutory health insurance market, corporate reputation remains one of the most important differentiators on the market and has to be put on the agenda of fund's marketing managers. The intention of the German government to induce a quality driven competition rather than a pure price focus shows its first successes. However, about 30% of an insurant's choice decision can still be traced back to the effect of additional contributions. Opening up differentiation possibilities within the strictly regulated benefit, service, and coverage catalogue might be a more promising way to a quality driven statutory health insurance landscape. An earlier version of this manuscript was presented at the 32nd Association for Marketing and Health Care Research Conference in Big Sky — Montana, USA.

Concluding the first part of this thesis, it can be noticed that managing the quality signal corporate reputation is closely related to corporate communication efforts and their respective roles (HUTTON et al., 2001, p. 255). In their operational model, GRAY and BALMER (1998, pp. 695-696) summarize that corporate communication is the vehicle that transfers a company's corporate identity over to their respective stakeholders. Thus, it creates reputational perceptions and forms the most important tool to manage corporate reputation. HUTTON et al. (2001) further confirm that corporate communication efforts are inseparably linked to reputational management and the executive tool to influence and shape corporate reputation within and across different stakeholder groups. However, managing and orchestrating the multitude of communication channels is getting more and more complex. Especially in the last decades, new media developments offer multifarious ways to reach stakeholders and communicate with them (HENNIG-THURAU et al., 2010, p. 312). Next to the traditional vehicles like press releases, advertising efforts, or journalism, corporate communication departments now also face an immeasurable number of social media sites like Facebook, YouTube, Twitter, and a vast amount of discussion forums and blogs (JAHN and KUNZ, 2011, pp. 96-97) that all have to be included into an overall, consistent, and credible communication mix.

Essays on Social Media

Moreover, Social Media has triggered a major shift in the marketing landscape. Consumers are no longer passive receivers of brand related communication efforts. They actively create content, share experiences, write product reviews, and provide feedback on products and services offered (CHEN et al., 2011). Omnipresent connectivity in the web 2.0 environment amplifies the voice of consumers across the globe to anyone willing to listen (LABRECQUE et al., 2013). Whereas traditional social influences were limited to strong tie relationships like family and close friends, those boundaries are broken up and extended to an innumerable group of unrelated participants (SMITH et al., 2005, HENNIG-THURAU et al., 2010). The new form of traditional word-of-mouth (i.e., user-generated content, electronic word-of-mouth, online engagement, or simply buzz) contains all positive and negative statements made by any potential, actual, or former customer about a company with its related products and services via the internet (HENNIG-THURAU and WALSH, 2004). The fact that roughly 90% of consumers state that they consult product reviews, blogs, or any other kind of user-generated source on the web before purchasing a product or service exhibits the power of the new marketing force (CHANNELADVISOR, 2011).

Recent years showed an explosion of literature focusing on the effectiveness of electronic word-of-mouth and their conceptual relatives. The internet's accessibility, reach, and transparency, as well as the almost unlimited access to archived consumer interactions have provided research with valuable data resources (KOZINETS et al., 2010). However, published studies on the effectiveness of electronic word-of-mouth are fragmented, use a multitude of different research approaches, and lack a conclusive overall picture of the current state-of-the-art (CHEUNG and THADANI, 2012). Consequently, research calls for more integrative research that provides a more generalizable picture (LABRECQUE et al., 2013).

Study III, entitled "Social Media Effects along the Value Chain - A Narrative Review" provides a systematic overview of top-tier social media research with a main focus on empirical works that investigate the effects of user-generated content on measurable corporate performance indicators. Aligned along the proposed framework of the "social media value chain", 102 articles up to the end of 2013 are used as input for the conducted narrative review. By moving along the value chain, the paper presents and aggregates the effects of electronic word-of-mouth communication on consumer mindset metrics, product and market performance indicators, and financial performance measures. Next to the main effects, the paper extracts the inherent moderators and provides a suitable framework for discussion. In addition, the dual role of companies as moderators and content stimulator is also dissected. Social media conversations are a powerful force that shows effect along the whole value chain. Pure volume measures show the strongest effect. Even though valence measures contain a high degree of information, inconsistent results can be observed depending on valence operationalization and empirical methods used. Research needs to develop a better and deeper understanding of valence measures. Further, experimental field studies provide a good starting point for future empirical work. The multitude of moderator effects reveals that the impact of electronic word-of-mouth is not generalizable across industries, product categories, and social media platforms. Nevertheless, social media conversations contain rich information that has to be utilized by the marketing profession. An earlier version of this manuscript was presented in 2013 at the 35th ISMS Marketing Science Conference, Istanbul.

Social media research agrees that simply observing and learning from consumer discussions falls short. As GODES et al. (2005) already mention, a company's role in the social media environment goes way beyond observing and moderating. The need to interact with their customer base and the necessity for a constant dialogue between company and consumers is claimed by many related studies (cf. e.g., HENNIG-THURAU et al., 2010, CULNAN et al., 2010). Companies and brands more and more realize this opportunity and engage on social network sites. Platforms like Facebook, YouTube, or Twitter enable marketers to communicate and interact with their customers on special brand fan pages (DE VRIES et al., 2012). However, research about brand fan pages is scarce (HOFFMANN and FODOR, 2010, JAHN and KUNZ, 2012). Hence, the prevalent corporate communication strategy on social network sites seems to be trial and error (SHANKAR and BATRA, 2009).

Study IV, titled "Corporate Brand Posts on Facebook - The Role of Interactivity, Vividness, and Involvement" takes this research gap as starting point. By means of a two-week field experimental study on the Facebook platform, the effect of corporate brand posts on brand fans' post recall capability, attitude toward the brand, and purchase intention is studied. By posting on two different brand fan pages, the degree of brand post interactivity and vividness and the underlying degree of product involvement is manipulated. Results indicate that Facebook brand posts are able to positively influence brand fans' attitude toward the brand. The degree of interactivity and vividness positively moderates the main effect as posts with a high degree of interactivity and vividness cause a higher change in attitudinal measures than low interactive and vivid posts. Further, Facebook brand fans are able to better recall posts from high involvement brands due to selective perception effects in the distractive Facebook environment. However, posts are more effective on fans' attitude toward the brand when posted from a fan page with a comparably lower involvement level. Facebook brand posts activate peripheral routes of information processing which are in favor for communication needs of low involvement products. Additionally, a significant interaction effect between the level of involvement and the degree of interactivity and vividness is found. Highly interactive and vivid brand posts are more successful when posted by a low involvement product or brand. For marketers dealing with a high involvement product this essentially means that it does not always have to be a highly interactive and vivid brand post to keep Facebook fans content. On the contrary, it is important for low involvement products to keep the interactivity and vividness-level of posts as high as possible to get the most out of Facebook posts regarding an optimal increase in attitude toward the brand. This paper was presented at the 2014 Global Marketing Conference at Singapore.

References

CHANNELADVISOR. 2011. *2011 Consumer Survey - Global Consumer Shopping Habits* [Online]. Available: http://go.channeladvisor.com/rs/channeladvisor/images/us-ebook-consumer-survey-2011.pdf [Accessed 2014-03-09].

CHEN, J., XU, H. & WHINSTON, A. B. 2011. Moderated Online Communities and Quality of User-Generated Content. *Journal of Management Information Systems,* 28(2), 237-268.

CHEUNG, C. M. K. & THADANI, D. R. 2012. The Impact of Electronic Word-of-Mouth Communication: A Literature Analysis and Integrative Model. *Decision Support Systems,* 54(1), 461-470.

CULNAN, M. J., MCHUGH, P. J. & ZUBILLAGA, J. I. 2010. How Large U.S. Companies Can Use Twitter and other Social Media to Gain Business Value. *MIS Quarterly Executive,* 9(4), 243-260.

DACIN, P. A. & BROWN, T. J. 2006. Corporate Branding, Identity, and Customer Response. *Journal of the Academy of Marketing Science,* 34(2), 95-98.

DE VRIES, L., GENSLER, S. & LEEFLANG, P. S. H. H. 2012. Popularity of Brand Posts on Brand Fan Pages: An Investigation of the Effects of Social Media Marketing. *Journal of Interactive Marketing,* 26(2), 83-91.

EBERL, M. 2006. *Unternehmensreputation und Kaufverhalten - Methodische Aspekte komplexer Strukturmodelle,* Inaugural-Dissertation an der LMU München, Wiesbaden: Gabler.

EBERL, M. & SCHWAIGER, M. 2005. Corporate Reputation: Disentangling the Effects on Financial Performance. *European Journal of Marketing,* 39(7/8), 838-854.

EBERL, M. & SCHWAIGER, M. 2008. Die Bedeutung der Unternehmensreputation für die Zahlungsbereitschaft von Privatkunden. *Kredit und Kapital,* 41(3), 355-394.

EIBICH, P., SCHMITZ, H. & ZIEBARTH, N. R. 2011. Zusatzbeiträge erhöhen die Preistransparenz: mehr Versicherte wechseln die Krankenkasse. *Wochenbericht,* 78(51/52), 3-12.

FERGUSON, T. D., DEEPHOUSE, D. L. & FERGUSON, W. L. 2000. Do Strategic Groups Differ in Reputation? *Strategic Management Journal,* 21(12), 1195-1214.

FISHBEIN, M. & AJZEN, I. 1975. *Belief, Attitude, Intention, and Behavior : An Introduction to Theory and Research,* Reading: Addison-Wesley Pub. Co.

FOMBRUN, C. J. 2001. Corporate Reputation - Its Measurement and Management. *Thexis,* 2001(4), 23-26.

FOMBRUN, C. J., GARDBERG, N. A. & SEVER, J. M. 2000. The Reputation Quotient^{SM}: A Multi-Stakeholder Measure of Corporate Reputation. *Journal of Brand Management,* 7(4), 241-255.

FOMBRUN, C. J. & VAN RIEL, C. 1997. The Reputational Landscape. *Corporate Reputation Review,* 1(1;2), 5-13.

GODES, D., MAYZLIN, D., CHEN, Y., DAS, S., DELLAROCAS, C., PFEIFFER, B., LIBAI, B., SEN, S., SHI, M. & VERLEGH, P. 2005. The Firm's Management of Social Interactions. *Marketing Letters,* 16(3/4), 415-428.

GOTSI, M. & WILSON, A. M. 2001. Corporate Reputation: Seeking a Definition. *Corporate Communications: An International Journal,* 6(1), 24-30.

GRAY, E. R. & BALMER J. M. T. 1998. Managing Corporate Image and Corporate Reputation. *Long Range Planning,* 31(5), 695-702.

HALL, R. 1992. The Strategic Analysis of Intangible Resources. *Strategic Management Journal,* 13(2), 135-144.

HALL, R. 1993. A Framework Linking Intangible Resources and Capabilities to Sustainable Competitive Advantage. *Strategic Management Journal,* 14(8), 607-618.

HANSSENS, D., RUST, R. T. & SRIVASTAVA, R. K. 2009. Marketing Strategy and Wall Street: Nailing Down Marketing's Impact. *Journal of Marketing,* 73(6), 115-118.

HELM, S. 2006. Designing a Formative Measure for Corporate Reputation. *Corporate Reputation Review,* 8(2), 95-109.

HENNIG-THURAU, T. & WALSH, G. 2004. Electronic Word-of-Mouth : Motives for and Consequences of Reading Customer Articulations on the Internet. *International Journal of Electronic Commerce,* 8(2), 51-74.

HENNIG-THURAU, T., MALTHOUSE, E. C., FRIEGE, C., GENSLER, S., LOBSCHAT, L., RANGASWAMY, A. & SKIERA, B. 2010. The Impact of New Media on Customer Relationships. *Journal of Service Research,* 13(3), 311-330.

HOFFMANN, D. L. & FODOR, M. 2010. Can You Measure the ROI of Your Social Media Marketing? *MIT Sloan Management Review,* 52(1), 40-49.

HUNT, S. D. & MORGAN, R. M. 1995. The Comparative Advantage Theory of Competition. *Journal of Marketing,* 59(2), 1-15.

HUTTON, J. G., GOODMAN, M. B., ALEXANDER, J. B. & GENEST, C. M. 2001. Reputation Management: the New Face of Corporate Public Relations? *Public Relations Review,* 27(3), 247-261.

JAHN, B. & KUNZ, W. 2012. How to Transform Consumers into Fans of your Brand. *Journal of Service Management,* 23(3), 344-361.

KOTHA, S., RAJGOPAL, S. & RINDOVA, V. 2001. Reputation Building and Performance: An Empirical Analysis of the Top-50 Pure Internet Firms. *European Management Journal,* 19(6), 571-586.

KOZINETS, R. V., DE VALCK, K., WOJNICKI, A. C. & WILNER, S. J. S. 2010. Networked Narratives: Understanding Word-of-Mouth Marketing in Online Communities. *Journal of Marketing,* 74(2), 71-89.

LABRECQUE, L. I., VOR DEM ESCHE, J., MATHWICK, C., NOVAK, T. P. & HOFACKER, C. F. 2013. Consumer Power: Evolution in the Digital Age. *Journal of Interactive Marketing,* 27(4), 257-269.

NEWELL, S. J. & GOLDSMITH, R. 2001. The Development of a Scale to Measure Perceived Corporate Credibility. *Journal of Business Research,* 52(3), 235-247.

PFISTER, F. 2009. Der Gesundheitsfonds: Eine Analyse. *Orientierungen zur Wirtschafts- und Gesellschaftspolitik,* 120(120), 39-44.

PREECE, S., FLEISHER, C. & TOCCACELLI, J. 1995. Building a Reputation along the Value Chain at Levi Strauss. *Long Range Planning,* 28(6), 88-98.

RAITHEL, S. & SCHWAIGER, M. 2014. The Effects of Corporate Reputation Perceptions of the General Public on Shareholder Value. *Strategic Management Journal,* forthcoming.

RAITHEL, S., WILCZYNSKI, P., SCHLODERER, M. P. & SCHWAIGER, M. 2010. The Value-Relevance of Corporate Reputation during Financial Crisis. *Journal of Product and Brand Management,* 19(6), 389-400.

REIBSTEIN, D. J., DAY, G. & WIND, J. 2009. Guest Editorial: Is Marketing Academia Losing Its Way? *Journal of Marketing,* 73(4), 1-3.

RINDOVA, V. P., WILLIAMSON, I. O., PETKOVA, A. P. & SEVER, J. M. 2005. Being Good or Being Known: An Empirical Examination of the Dimesnions, Antecedents, and Consequences of Organizational Reputation. *Academy of Management Journal,* 48(6), 1033-1049.

ROBERTS, P. W. & DOWLING, G. R. 2002. Corporate Reputation and Sustained Financial Performance. *Strategic Management Journal,* 23(12), 1077-1093.

SCHWAIGER, M. 2004. Components and Parameters of Corporate Reputation - An Empirical Study. *Schmalenbach Business Review,* 56(1), 46-71.

SCHWAIGER, M., RAITHEL, S. & SCHLODERER, M. P. 2009. Recognition or Rejection - How a Company's Reputation Influences Stakeholder Behaviour. *In:* KLEWES, J. & WRESCHNIOK, R. (eds.) *Reputation Capital - Building and Maintaining Trust in the 21st century.* Heidelberg: Springer, 39-55.

SHANKAR, V. & BATRA, R. 2009. The Growing Influence of Online Marketing Communications. *Journal of Interactive Marketing,* 23(4), 285-287.

SMITH, D., MENON, S. & SIVAKUMAR, K. 2005. Online Peer and Editorial Recommendations, Trust, and Choice in Virtual Markets. *Journal of Interactive Marketing,* 19(3), 15-37.

TYMON, W. G. J., STUMPF, S. A. & DOH, J. P. 2010. Exploring Talent Management in India. *Journal of World Business,* 45(2), 109-121.

WALSH, G. & BEATTY, S. E. 2007. Measuring Customer-Based Corporate Reputation, Scale Development, Validation, and Application. *Journal of the Academy of Marketing Science,* 35(1), 127-143.

WEIGELT, K. & CAMERER, C. F. 1988. Reputation and Corporate Strategy: A Review of Recent Theory and Applications. *Strategic Management Journal,* 9(5), 443-454.

YOON, E., GUFFEY, H. J. & KIJEWSKI, V. 1993. The Effects of Information and Company Reputation on Intentions to Buy a Bussiness Service. *Journal of Business Research,* 27(3), 215-228.

Markus Kick | Martina Panico (née Littich)

I THE EFFECT OF CORPORATE REPUTATION ON HEALTH INSURANCE CHOICES IN A PUBLIC-POLICY-SHAPED ENVIRONMENT OF PREMIUM EQUALITY

Abstract

Legislation put into effect in 2009 has dramatically altered the health insurance system in Germany by introducing premium equality in order to foster new competition between the German statutory health insurance funds based on quality rather than price. The statutory health insurance (SHI) funds have reacted quickly by offering new benefits and services. However, we assume that consumers are influenced not only by product attributes but also by signals of quality, such as those delivered by corporate reputation, which can act as an information surrogate. The results of our choice-based conjoint experiment show that benefits such as elective tariffs, bonus programs, complementary insurance offers, voluntary coverage, and extended services significantly influence consumer choice of statutory health insurance. These findings argue for the success of the public policy strategy of the German government. Our findings indicate that reputation is fairly important in product choice when compared with product-based attributes. As a consequence of these findings, funds should not only adapt their offerings with regard to the benefits that insurants value the most but also place emphasis on corporate reputation management.

1   Introduction

Throughout the prior research dealing with the decision process of choosing or changing health insurance funds, price has been found to be the most distinguishing and important criterion when compared with other product attributes such as benefit details or services (BRAU and LIPPI BRUNI, 2008, MARQUIS et al., 2007, NOORDEWIER et al., 1989, THOMSON and DIXON, 2006). Within the first three years after the 1996 reform that introduced freedom of choice into the formerly non-competitive[1] German SHI system, approximately 7% of Germans insured in statutory health insurance (SHI) funds changed their sickness fund (ZOK, 1999). Research has shown that the main reason for changing the SHI fund depended on the basic question of whether equal healthcare coverage can be obtained for a better price (GREß et al., 2002, ZOK, 1999).

However, at the beginning of 2009, the most important criterion of a health insurance product — its price — was eliminated in Germany with the introduction of the *Act to Strengthen Competition (Wettbewerbsstärkungsgesetz)*. Since then, German SHI funds, which currently cover approximately 90% of the German population (GERMAN FEDERAL DEPARTMENT OF HEALTH, 2011), are forced by law to quote the same price, which is to say (in terms of the German SHI system), to quote the same percentage from insurants' gross income for their health insurance packages (GERMAN FEDERAL DEPARTMENT OF HEALTH, 2011). The basic goal of this law and the related fixed contribution rates was to create a SHI system that is highly differentiated by offered benefits as well as a new basis for competition in terms of quality rather than price (GERMAN BUNDESTAG, 2006).

Health insurance funds are allowed to charge an additional contribution in case the granted financial means do not suffice (GERMAN FEDERAL DEPARTMENT OF HEALTH, 2011). 7% of the German SHI funds currently make use of this option (HEALTH INSURANCE GERMANY, 2011). As a consequence, they have lost insurants to other funds that do not charge any additional contribution (FRIEDRICHS et al., 2009). This customer migration shifts the market focus and this paper's focus further to the major competition between SHI funds that charge equal premiums.

---

[1]   Before 1996, Germans' SHI affiliations were determined by their jobs, their employers, and their place of residence (BUSSE and RIESBERG, 2005).

Because SHI funds on this market can no longer compete via the price of their offerings, they have reacted quickly to the new market situation and to rising pressure[2] by trying to attract customers via new product attributes in the benefit sector and the service sector. On the basis of extensive desk research and an interview with an expert from the field (the head of customer services at Germany's biggest SHI fund *Barmer GEK*), we found five attributes of current health insurance packages that are increasingly used for differentiation: elective tariffs, bonus programs, complementary insurance, voluntary coverage, and customer services. Prior research from countries other than Germany has highlighted the importance of some of the abovementioned attributes for health insurance decisions. For example, some authors have found a statistically significant influence of customer service on choice decisions in the US and the Netherlands (CHAKRABORTY et al., 1994, VAN DEN BERG et al., 2008). BRAU and LIPPI BRUNI (2008) confirmed the importance of additional voluntary coverage in their study of health insurance in Italy.

We propose that, aside from these benefit details, the reputation of an SHI fund can have a major impact on its choice. Corporate reputation serves as a signal for the quality of products (FOMBRUN and SHANLEY, 1990), especially in a service industry (YOON et al., 1993) such as (health) insurance, where the offerings are difficult to evaluate before actually having to use them and, moreover, are rather complex in their nature. Corporate reputation can consequently act as an information surrogate and displace price as the most important criterion in the choice of SHI. GATES et al. (2000) included real health insurance brands as providers of insurance products in their study of the US market and found a significant influence of brand name on the choice of health insurance. However, in their study, GATES et al. (2000) have not linked this effect to the reputation of the providers nor have they excluded price from their study's set-up and concerns.

Our research sets out to determine the factors that influence the choice of SHI in an environment of premium equality, particularly in Germany. We aim to answer the following questions: Do insurants choose the best offer in terms of quality, and if so, which attributes are the main

---

[2] The rising economic pressure caused by the introduction of the *Act to Strengthen Competition* is reflected in a disappearance of 65 insurance funds in the first 36 months after the law passed the German Bundestag, which equals a decline of about 30% of all German SHI funds (THE NATIONAL ASSOCIATION OF STATUTORY HEALTH INSURANCE FUNDS, 2011).

drivers of choice? Or do they, rather, rely on a mere indicator of quality (i.e., corporate reputation) in order to make their choices?

After elaborating the theoretical framework for our study, we design and conduct a choice-based conjoint experiment to answer our research questions. From our results, we are able to draw two primary implications: On the one hand, in the current situation of premium equality, health insurance funds obtain valuable information on how to design their offerings and on the importance of their corporate reputation. On the other hand, we provide policy makers in Germany and in countries with similar healthcare systems with insight into the evaluation of recent reforms as well as the improvement in the design of future reforms.

2   Theoretical Background

2.1   Effects of Benefit Differentiation

Elective tariffs. To create a more flexible landscape of health insurance packages, elective tariffs were introduced in 2007 (SCHULZE EHRING and WEBER, 2007). As a result, insurants have the opportunity to reduce health insurance costs for themselves and for providers by designing a more customized healthcare coverage fitting their individual demands and use of health services (SCHULZE EHRING and KÖSTER, 2010). There are mandatory elective tariffs that have to be offered by each SHI fund, such as special care provision tariffs (e.g., integrated care programs) or sick payment tariffs for members who are not entitled to statutory sick pay. Aside from these mandatory elective tariffs, SHI funds are free to offer voluntary elective tariffs (PASSON et al., 2009, SCHULZE EHRING and WEBER, 2007, GERMAN FEDERAL DEPARTMENT OF HEALTH, 2010). The most common voluntary elective tariffs (accompanied by short descriptions) are displayed in Table 1.

(Voluntary) elective tariff	Description
Deductible Tariff	Bonus payments for taking over a cost deductible
Contribution Refund Tariff	Refund of contributions for not using any medical services besides preventive check-ups
Cost Reimbursement Tariff	Bonus payments for payment of health services out of own pocket and monetary reimbursement later on

Table 1: Overview of Voluntary Elective Tariffs

Although they are not a completely new feature, elective tariffs gained importance as a differentiation factor based on the *Act to Strengthen Competition* (PAQUET, 2007, SCHULZE

EHRING and WEBER, 2007). Research shows that elective tariffs are reasonable from an economic point of view. For example, deductible tariffs reduce the volume of insurance claims (MANNING et al., 1987, PÜTZ and HAGIST, 2006, VAN VLIET, 2004). Elective tariffs are, however, only effective if they are accepted by and attractive for (potential) customers, leading us to our first research question.

RQ₁: Does the offer of voluntary elective tariffs influence the choice of SHI?

Bonus programs. Bonus programs reward health-conscious behavior, such as participation in approved health-promoting activities, sports club memberships, and regular preventive check-ups. Insurants receive monetary bonus payments or payments in kind through which gifts can be selected according to the achieved number of bonus points at the end of the year (SCHULZE EHRING and KÖSTER, 2010). Shortly after legislation opened up this possibility in 2004, sickness funds rapidly introduced bonus programs (HÖPPNER et al., 2005). Since premium equality was introduced at the beginning of 2009, a great number of marketing campaigns and advertising strategies have come to use bonus programs as a differentiation factor (SCHULZE EHRING and KÖSTER, 2010, FRIEDEL and NÜRNBERGER, 2010). In addition to indicating the goal of saving costs[3], this clearly reveals the SHI funds' hope of attracting new customers (SCHULZE EHRING and KÖSTER, 2010). ZOK (2005) found in his representative survey of German SHI insurants that more than 50% appreciate the offer of bonus programs. However, to date, there is no empirical investigation of the effect of bonus programs on the choice of SHI, which leads to our second research question.

RQ₂: Does the offer of bonus programs influence the choice of SHI?

Complementary insurance. Complementary insurance offers refer to additional health insurance contracts insurants can choose: for example, for traveling abroad, for full coverage of dental care, for vision aids, or for a daily hospital allowance. With the offer of complementary insurance contracts, SHI funds provide insurants with benefits previously only available through additional contracts with private health insurers (HÖPPNER et al., 2005, ZOK, 2005). Complementary insurance is supposed to be advantageous for both the insurance companies as well as their customers: the insurers receive additional premiums (SCHULZE EHRING and

---

[3]   FRIEDRICHS et al. (2009) show that bonus programs yield an annual benefit of €129 per insurant. However, the long-term effects and effectiveness of bonus programs still remain to be examined.

WEBER, 2007), and the insurants get more than just the basic SHI package from one provider (ZOK, 2005). ZOK (2009) shows in his recent customer survey conducted after the introduction of premium equality that almost 40% of SHI customers appreciate the availability of complementary insurance packages. Moreover, DORMONT et al. (2009) and KERSSENS and GROENEWEGEN (2005) prove the importance of complementary insurance offers for customers' SHI choice decisions in the Netherlands and Switzerland, respectively. We therefore propose that the offer of complementary insurance packages is an important determinant in the decision process for or against a health insurance provider.

H₁: The offer of complementary insurance positively influences the choice of SHI.

Voluntary coverage. The German government strictly regulates which health services are covered by SHI funds. The lists of drugs, treatment methods, outpatient care, and so forth, as well as the coverage rates a SHI company has to reimburse, are predefined by law and form the so-called standard benefit catalogue (GERMAN FEDERAL DEPARTMENT OF HEALTH, 2011). Within those rigid reimbursement guidelines, approximately 98% of benefits are defined as mandatory payments that a SHI fund is required to reimburse. The remaining 2% of voluntary coverage options, also predefined by law, allow for differentiation between SHI funds. Consequently, voluntary coverage takes place in a very narrow field (HÖPPNER et al., 2005, SCHULZE EHRING and KÖSTER, 2010). However, it still provides SHI funds with the option of adjusting their benefit portfolio towards special needs (e.g., travel vaccinations, professional tooth cleaning, or direct cost transfers for constitutional courses) or special customers (e.g., women, families). Because voluntary coverage is free of charge for the customer, it is expected to enhance the attractiveness of health insurance packages (ZOK, 1999). International research proves that voluntary coverage indeed drives the choice of SHI funds (BRAU and LIPPI BRUNI, 2008, DORMONT et al., 2009, GATES et al., 2000, KERSSENS and GROENEWEGEN, 2005, MARQUIS et al., 2007). We therefore formulate our second hypothesis regarding the effect of voluntary coverage on the choice of SHI.

H₂: The offer of voluntary coverage positively influences the choice of SHI.

Customer service. A day-and-night or medical consulting service hotline or a branch network with many local subsidiaries are only a few varieties of customer service features. Prior international research on the choice of health insurance mainly supports the influence of customer service on choice behavior (CHAKRABORTY et al., 1994, VAN DEN BERG et al., 2008).

H₃: The offer of extended customer services positively influences the choice of SHI.

Although their impact was proven by CHAKRABORTY et al. (1994) as well as VAN DEN BERG et al. (2008), customer services were less important compared with other product attributes. KERSSENS and GROENEWEGEN (2005) found, for example, the service feature 'availability of a medical help-desk' to be uncorrelated with insurants' preferences. These findings indicate that the product core, that is, the benefits included in a SHI package, is more important to the customer than additional service aspects. Given the fact that the offer of complementary insurance might be important only for certain customer groups with special needs we suppose that voluntary coverage (i.e., additional coverage free of charge) is the product attribute with the greatest overall value for insurants.

H₄: The offer of voluntary coverage has the greatest effect on the choice of SHI compared with other product attributes.

2.2   Effects of Corporate Reputation

The current market situation in Germany makes it almost impossible to keep track of the various and highly differentiated offerings of SHI funds. Aside from the increasing number of different benefits, inconsistent names and labels for the same insurance offerings make it difficult to compare SHI offerings and to distinguish between mandatory and voluntary offers. Generally, the large majority of insurants lack detailed knowledge about the SHI funds' offerings (GREB et al., 2008, HAENECKE, 2001). Therefore, explaining consumers' choice behavior with facts (i.e., the offerings' characteristics) is not enough. Rather, people may be looking for a way to reduce market complexity similar to the role played by price before the introduction of premium equality. Corporate reputation is seen as just such a surrogate for this information (EBERL and SCHWAIGER, 2008, FOMBRUN and VAN RIEL, 1997, MARQUIS et al., 2007, ANDERSEN and SCHWARZE, 1998).

Corporate reputation "can be a major factor in achieving competitive advantage through differentiation" (HALL, 1992, p. 138). It impacts buying intention and attracts new customers (GOTSI and WILSON, 2001, GROENLAND, 2002, YOON et al., 1993, GARDBERG and FOMBRUN,

2002) because it serves as a signal for the quality of the corporation's offerings (NELSON, 1970, SHAPIRO, 1982, FOMBRUN and SHANLEY, 1990). This effect becomes increasingly important in service industries (YOON et al., 1993), such as the health insurance sector, in which consumers know very little about the product before actually having to use them (KOLSTAD and CHERNEW, 2009). For consumers of such experience goods, it is natural for purchase decisions to be based on a firm's reputation (ROB and FISHMAN, 2005). In their US-based study, GATES et al. (2000) found a comparably small but statistically significant influence of brand in their choice experiment. However, they do not make a connection between this influence and the respective companies' reputations. This theoretical argumentation leads us to our fifth hypothesis concerning the effect of corporate reputation:

H5: The favorable corporate reputation of a SHI fund positively influences its choice.

3   Method and Measures

3.1   Method: Choice-based Conjoint Analysis (CBCA)

In order to answer our research questions and to test our hypotheses, we rely on the approach of conjoint analysis (CA). The basic intention of CA is to evaluate the utility of product alternatives that consist of a number of different attributes and levels (RAO, 2008). The contributions of the various attributes and levels or their manifestations to the utility of a stimulus are obtained from a global rating, ranking or discrete choice task (GUSTAFSSON et al., 2007, RAO, 2008): While all attributes of a stimulus are *considered jointly* by test persons, part-worth utilities (PWUs) for the single attribute levels are estimated in a decompositional approach later on (GREEN and SRINIVASAN, 1990). Following HAAIJER and WEDEL (2007), it is commonly assumed that the overall utility of a stimulus is constructed by adding the preferences for the attribute levels. This implies a compensatory preference model, in which a low, possibly negative score of a certain attribute, which reduces the overall utility of a product, can be compensated by a high score of another attribute (HAAIJER and WEDEL, 2007).

The approach of CA is well established in the healthcare literature: by using conjoint analysis, we follow previous research on the choice of health insurance (BRAU and LIPPI BRUNI, 2008, CHAKRABORTY et al., 1994, NOORDEWIER et al., 1989, STENSRUD et al., 1997, VAN DEN BERG et al., 2008). Consistent with the studies of BRAU and LIPPI BRUNI (2008) and CHAKRABORTY et al. (1994) in particular, we applied a choice-based conjoint analysis (CBCA, also: discrete choice analysis) in order to determine the utility of individual attribute levels from global responses to a set of alternatives (PRACEJUS and OLSEN, 2004). As opposed to traditional conjoint analysis and related approaches, which rely on ranking or rating tasks to evaluate stimuli, CBCA applies the concept of choice. In a CBCA task, the test person is asked to select his or her preferred stimulus within a presented choice set (GREEN et al., 2001). The choice (or rejection) of a product as an expression of "ultimate interest" (ELROD et al., 1992, p. 368) is, as the natural behavior of consumers, supposed to be more intuitive and more realistic than the rating or ranking of single product attributes and their levels (LOUVIERE and WOODWORTH, 1983). These methodological traits have led to the general assumption of CBCA's high validity (CARSON et al., 1994, LOUVIERE and WOODWORTH, 1983, MOORE et al., 1998, RYAN et al., 1998). To avoid misleading results, the number of attributes and levels should be kept low in conjoint analysis set-ups. Within CBCA studies, an average of six to ten attributes is common (WITTINK et al., 1989, ORME, 2006). Table 2 shows a list of the (six) attributes and the corresponding levels that we included into our CBCA set-up.

#	Attribute	#	Level
1	SHI Brand	1	AOK
		2	Barmer GEK
		3	DAK
		4	TK
2	Elective Tariffs	1	Not offered
		2	Deductible tariff
		3	Contribution refund tariff
		4	Cost reimbursement tariff
3	Bonus Program	1	Not offered
		2	Nonmonetary rewards
		3	Monetary rewards
4	Complementary Insurance	1	Not offered
		2	Offered
5	Voluntary Coverage	1	Not offered
		2	Travel vaccinations
		3	Professional tooth cleaning
		4	Constitutional course
		5	Travel vaccinations and professional tooth cleaning
		6	Travel vaccinations and constitutional course
		7	Professional tooth cleaning and constitutional course
6	Service Package	1	Standard services
		2	Extended services

Table 2: CBCA Attributes and Levels

To test the effects of a SHI fund's corporate reputation, we used real SHI fund brands analogously to GATES et al. (2000). We chose four of the five biggest nationwide operating SHI funds in terms of coverage of German SHI insurants: *AOK* (34.7%), *Barmer GEK* (12.3%), *TK* (11.1%), and *DAK* (8.6%) (GERMAN FEDERAL DEPARTMENT OF HEALTH, 2011). We did not include company health insurance funds (*BKKs*) into our study set-up, although they, taken together, insure 18.6% of the German SHI insurants (GERMAN FEDERAL DEPARTMENT OF HEALTH, 2011), because company insurance funds are not represented by a common brand. Data, which was available to us, provided by the YouGovPsychonomics AG, which monitors 550 brands in 20 sectors by surveying approximately 1,000 consumers from all relevant demographic groups on a daily basis, indicated both differences in reputation and high levels of recognition among the German public for the four chosen SHI funds.

As levels for the second attribute 'elective tariffs,' we included the three voluntary elective tariff options we identified earlier (see Table 1) into the design. Despite a huge variety in the design of bonus programs, we were able to easily identify two different types on the basis of their reliance on either monetary or nonmonetary rewards. We used these two types together with a 'not offered' alternative as the levels for our third attribute. As shown in chapter 2.1, there are miscellaneous types of complementary insurances. SHI funds are usually able to offer the whole range of complementary insurances once they have set up cooperation with a private health insurance company. Consequently, the basic question is whether particular SHI funds cooperate with a private health insurer and whether they offer complementary insurance packages in general. Thus, we reduced the levels for this attribute to a simple 'yes or no' scenario. We identified travel vaccinations, professional tooth cleaning, and cost transfers for constitutional courses as the three most popular voluntary benefits. We completed our CBCA set-up with these three items, their combinations, and a 'not offered' alternative as the levels for the attribute voluntary coverage. Furthermore, we included two levels for the attribute service (standard and extended).

3.2   Empirical Design

Our questionnaire started with a screening question to exclude those people insured in private health insurance funds from the survey. After some introductory questions concerning various social demographics (e.g., sex, age, education, and occupation), the respondents had to indicate whether they knew the four selected SHI fund brands (see chapter 3.1) which we displayed in randomized order, including their respective logos. We used this question as a filter, allowing only those persons who recognized the four SHI fund brands to complete the experiment.

The part of the survey that followed consisted of the actual choice experiment. Respondents were asked to choose one from among four possible alternatives (for an exemplary choice task, see Figure 2 in the appendix) for which information on all attributes and levels could be found in hyperlinked pop-up windows. This choice task was repeated seven times. Because of the number of attribute levels in our study, not all theoretically possible stimuli[4] could be displayed to our respondents. We had to select an appropriate subset of stimuli through computer-based algorithms. The corresponding efficiency values ranged between .997 and 1.002 (see Table 6 in the appendix), indicating almost equal standard errors for our reduced design and a perfectly orthogonal main effect plan. These efficiency values easily met the standards (KUHFELD et al., 1994). Thus, our design was determined to be highly capable of collecting valid choice data.

We decided not to include a none-option, which would be the option to choose none of the offered alternatives, something that is possible in CBCA settings. This decision rested upon three deliberations: first, research shows that some respondents pick the none-option to reduce complexity (HAAIJER and WEDEL, 2007), something that could happen easily because of the complexity inherent in the choice of SHI. Second, the inclusion of a none-option produces missing data, which would have been a critical problem for our analysis, especially for the application of a Hierarchical Bayes regression to calculate pseudo-individual utilities (HAAIJER et al., 2001, JOHNSON and ORME, 2003). Third, in the German SHI environment a none-option does not exist: every German is legally obliged to pick one of the available SHI funds (GERMAN FEDERAL DEPARTMENT OF HEALTH, 2011).

After having completed the choice experiment, respondents were asked to indicate the reputation of the four SHI funds. We used the corporate reputation scale of SCHWAIGER (2004). The cognitive and emotional dimensions of this reputation construct (competence and likeability) are operationalized with three reflective items each (on seven-point Likert scales). We adjusted one item concerning the international importance of the company or the SHI fund because this international focus does not apply to German SHI funds. The values collected on

---

[4] Because each level can be present or absent for a given stimulus, a complete design comprises 2^J stimuli, with J being the number of all attributes' levels (LOUVIERE and WOODWORTH, 1983). In our case, a complete design would comprise $2^{22} = 4,194,304$ different stimuli.

a seven-point scale were standardized between the (hypothetical) values of one and 100, where higher numbers indicate a better reputation. The separate values for competence and likeability were merged into a single overall corporate reputation score following a factor analysis approach (SCHWAIGER, 2004).

Furthermore, respondents were asked for information on their current health status (e.g., general health status and existence of chronic diseases), their current SHI provider, and their intention to change their SHI fund in the near future.

The data for our study were collected via an online survey in November 2010. In total, 286 SHI insurants responded to our questionnaire, of which 36 had to be excluded, mainly because they were not familiar with all four SHI brands used in our CBCA design. Table 7 in the appendix presents a profile of the resulting 250 interviewees. Male participants were underrepresented (37.2% in the sample compared with 48.9% in Germany). The sample was (with an average age of 30.8 years) younger than the German average of 43.2 and was shifted toward higher education (GERMAN FEDERAL BUREAU OF STATISTICS, 2011). In all, 67.2% of respondents were insured within one of the four SHI funds included into the CBCA, adequately representing the proportion in the current German SHI market situation (see Figure 1). 79.2% of the respondents were insured with their respective insurer for more than three years, and satisfaction with their current SHI provider was high[5]. Consistent with this finding, participants showed limited intentions of changing their providers: 10.0% planned to change their SHI fund within the next 12 months and another 12.4% had not decided yet. These numbers are consistent with the findings of a recent representative study[6] of the German SHI market by YouGovPsychonomics AG.

---

[5]   Mean = 5.5 (n = 250) on a seven-point Likert scale from 1 = "unsatisfied" to 7 = "completely satisfied".
[6]   www.psychonomics.de/filemanager/download/2471/

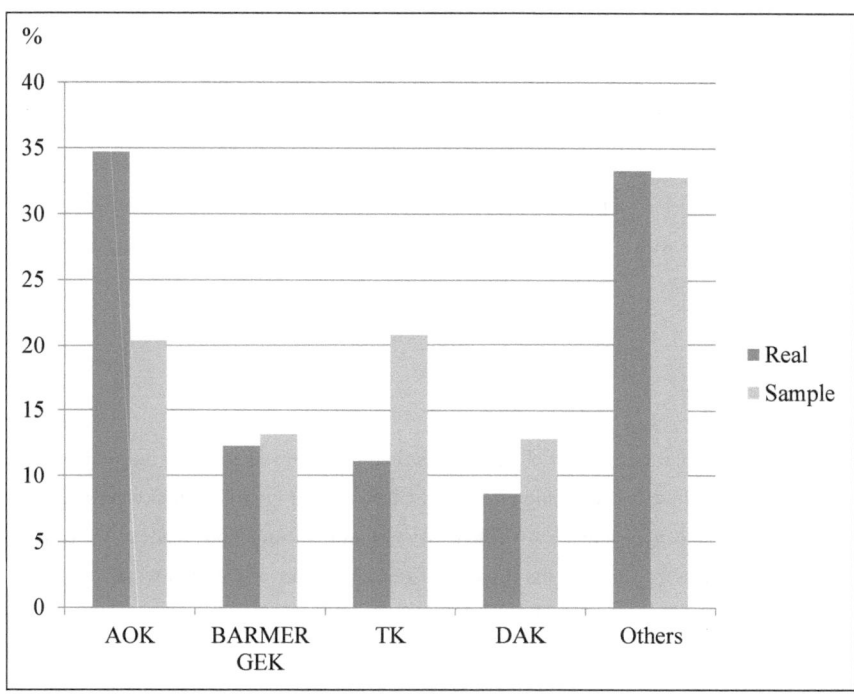

Figure 1: SHI Membership Distribution (Sample vs. Reality)

4   Analysis and Results

A Chi-Square Independency Test of the count analysis shows that the choice decision depends significantly on the levels for all of the attributes (p < .01; see Table 8 in the appendix). Therefore, the selection of attributes and levels for modeling a SHI choice decision within the conducted CBCA can be regarded as valid. For assessing the PWUs of the single attributes and levels in the aggregated dataset, we employed a multinomial logit model. As mentioned above, the basic information produced by the CBCA consists of dichotomous choice data. Following random utility theory (LOUVIERE and WOODWORTH, 1983), we considered latent utility preferences, which finally trigger the choice of alternative p out of a set of alternatives A, to consist of an explicable, deterministic utility component V_p and a non-explicable, stochastic error term e_p. U_p represents the latent true value of alternative p (KAMAKURA and RUSSELL, 1989).

$$U_p = V_p + e_p$$

Random utility theory assumes a behavior of pure utility maximization in which respondents always select the alternative with the highest perceived total utility. The deterministic, representative utility component V_{pq} can be seen as the additive result of all single PWU β_{jiq} of attribute j's level i within respondent q's mindset. The following equation shows this additive connection with s_{pjiq} as the vector of individual characteristics of person q at stimulus p (MCFADDEN, 1974).

$$V_{pq} = \sum_{j=1}^{J} \beta_{jip} s_{pjiq}$$

The multinomial logit model tests all levels regarding their relevancy within the actual choice decision and each level's contribution to the perceived total utility of a stimulus presented for the average respondent. Table 3 shows the part-worth utility estimations that can be regarded as the value a single level adds to the already existing core utility of SHI. For research question RQ_1 regarding the inclusion of elective tariffs, we see that the contribution refund tariff and the cost reimbursement tariff both increase the value of a SHI offer. The deductible tariff, which offers payments for taking over a cost deductible, and not offering an elective tariff reduce the value of a health insurance package. We also discover the effects of the inclusion of bonus programs into healthcare packages (RQ_2). Whereas monetary rewards provide insurants with additional value, nonmonetary rewards (i.e., payments in kind) do not add to the value of an insurance product. Declining to offer a bonus program at all diminishes an offer's value significantly. We confirm Hypothesis H_1 regarding the positive effects of the offer of complementary insurance. The same is true for voluntary coverage (H_2) that is free of charge for insurants. Combinations of different voluntary coverage features are highly appreciated. In other words, the more free coverage an insurance package contains, the higher is its value for insurants. Thereby, the absorption of costs for professional tooth cleaning by the insurer yields the greatest value per se which is also reflected in its combinations with the other voluntary coverage levels. Consumers also appreciate extended services packages, further confirming Hypothesis H_3.

Attribute	Level	Effect	Std. err.	t-ratio
SHI Brand	AOK	-.023	.046	-.511
	Barmer GEK	-.054	.046	-1.164
	DAK	-.091*	.047	-1.954
	TK	.169***	.044	3.873
Elective Tariff	Not offered	-.497***	.053	-9.355
	Deductible tariff	-.184***	.048	-3.812
	Contribution refund tariff	.451***	.042	10.836
	Cost reimbursement tariff	.231***	.043	5.312
Bonus Program	Not offered	-.363***	.041	-8.789
	Non-monetary rewards	.003	.039	.099
	Monetary rewards	.359***	.037	9.808
Complementary Insurance	Yes	.259***	.027	9.684
	No	-.259***	.027	-9.684
Voluntary Coverage	Not offered	-1.166***	.103	-11.319
	Only travel vaccinations (1)	-.396***	.078	-5.101
	Only professional tooth cleaning (2)	.205***	.066	3.095
	Only constitutional course (3)	-.444***	.078	-5.674
	(1) and (2)	.676***	.061	11.007
	(1) and (3)	.396***	.064	6.185
	(2) and (3)	.729***	.061	12.027
Service Package	Standard services	-.143***	.026	-5.396
	Extended services	.143***	.026	5.396

Table 3: Part-Worth Utilities (Multinomial-Logit Model)

The choice of SHI also depends significantly on the SHI brand offering the product: whereas the value of the healthcare package is enhanced when the provider is *TK*, it is reduced when *DAK* is the provider. This finding is consistent with the reputational assessments of the SHI funds in our sample. The respondents assign significantly higher values for reputation to *TK* and the lowest reputation to *DAK* (see Table 4), indicating the confirmation of Hypothesis H_4.

Means	AOK	Barmer GEK	DAK	TK
Competence	51.11[a]	55.08[a]	52.54[a]	65.29[b]
Likeability	45.29[a]	44.42[a]	42.13[a]	52.66[b]
Reputation	48.37[a]	50.06[a]	47.64[a]	59.35[b]

Note: Means on a scale from 0 to 100. Standard deviations in parentheses. Numbers with different superscripts in a given row are significantly different at the level of p < .01.

Table 4: Reputational Assessments of SHI Brands

However, to properly answer Hypothesis H_5, we had to draw inferences about the individual reputational assessments of the SHI funds that underlie the individual choices instead of analyzing data on an aggregated level. Because of the CBCA settings' limited data at the individual level, we applied a Hierarchical Bayes model, which is often used in marketing research to provide estimates of quasi individual-level parameters (ROSSI and ALLENBY, 2003), and which is supposed to perform better than alternative methods (LENK et al., 1996). Within Hierarchical Bayes models, pseudo-individual utilities are computed via an iterative process in which missing preference data for each test person are replaced by preference data of other respondents (ROSSI and ALLENBY, 2003). The resulting individual part-worth utilities for the different attribute levels of 'SHI brand' and the corresponding reputational assessments of each individual are significantly correlated (r_{AOK} = .227, $r_{BarmerGEK}$ = .247, r_{DAK} = .194, r_{TK} = .285; $p < .01$), confirming Hypothesis H_5 regarding the effect of a SHI fund's reputation on its choice[7].

We use the calculated Hierarchical Bayes part-worth utilities to quantify the relative attribute importance W_j. For each attribute j, the so-called 'spread' I_j is calculated as $\left\{ \max_i(\beta_{ji}) - \min_i(\beta_{ji}) \right\}$ divided by the sum of all considered attributes' spreads, whereby β_{ji} is the part-worth utility of level i of attribute j (ORME, 2006). Table 5 shows the resulting means for the importance of the attributes included in our study. The SHI brand, with an average importance of about 15.0%, ranks third and therefore plays a fairly important role within SHI choice decisions. It ranges behind voluntary coverage options as the most important attribute (confirming Hypothesis H_4) and the offer of elective tariffs. The brand is, however, more important than bonus programs, complementary insurances, and service packages, even though all of these are significant drivers in choice decisions (see Table 3).

We conducted additional analyses to examine whether demographic factors and the current health situation influence an individual's preferences for a specific attribute or SHI fund. These analyses show that elective tariffs are more important for male persons (mean$_{female}$ = 18.0, mean$_{male}$ = 22.2; $p < .01$) and healthier persons (mean$_{unhealthy}$ = 19.0, mean$_{healthy}$ = 21.8; $p < .05$). Complementary insurance offers are more important for women than for men (mean$_{male}$ = 7.5, mean$_{female}$ = 9.3; $p < .05$). The importance of the brand offering the insurance package is correlated with age (r = .209; $p < .01$). The brand is, moreover, more important for the less educated share of respondents (mean$_{high}$ = 14.3, mean$_{low}$ = 17.0; $p < .05$). Attribute importance

---

[7] The correlations of the individual part-worth utilities of the brands and the two components of corporate reputation, competence (r_{AOK} = .161, $r_{BarmerGEK}$ = .183, r_{DAK} = .166, r_{TK} = .199; $p < .05$), and likeability (r_{AOK} = .234, $r_{BarmerGEK}$ = .248, r_{DAK} = .163, r_{TK} = .286; $p < .05$), are also significant.

is not affected by SHI membership with two exceptions (see Table 9): the brand offering the insurance package is less important for DAK members (remember that DAK has the lowest values for corporate reputation in our sample) and voluntary coverage options are less important for TK members than for AOK/DAK members.

Attribute	Mean importance (%)	Std. dev.
Voluntary Coverage	35.89	9.21
Elective Tariff	19.55	8.54
SHI Brand	14.95	8.76
Bonus Program	13.78	7.53
Complementary Insurance	8.62	5.66
Service Package	7.20	5.00

Table 5: Importance Scores

5   Discussion

Regarding the design of health insurance packages, the most important attribute is the benefits that are offered voluntarily by the SHI fund (voluntary coverage), which is to say, health services free of charge for the insurants. The high importance of voluntary coverage, which is consistent with prior research, leads to the assumption that the former search for 'the same coverage for a better price' is replaced by the search for 'more coverage for the same price' since the introduction of premium equality into the market.

Consistent with this indirect price focus, the offer of elective tariffs, which allows saving costs, is the second most important feature in the process of choosing a SHI fund — a possibility which is more appreciated by men. Healthcare expenditures are higher for female insurants (NÖTHEN and BÖHM, 2009) for whom it is, therefore, possibly less attractive to make payments in advance as required by cost reimbursement tariffs. Moreover, men are generally more willing to take risks (WEBER et al., 2002) such as are inherent in deductible or cost reimbursement tariffs. The higher risk aversion of women is also reflected in the fact that they value the offer of complementary insurance more than men do. The finding that elective tariffs are more attractive for healthier persons is not surprising given the fact that, for example, in contribution refund tariffs, costs can only be saved if no medical services other than preventive check-ups are demanded.

Moreover, because of the obviously high price sensitivity, bonus programs are only attractive if the rewards are of a monetary nature. The offers of complementary insurance as well as an extended services package add significantly to the value of a health insurance package, although both features are relatively unimportant compared with the other attributes included in our study.

In summary, we found support for all of our research questions and confirmed all of our hypotheses concerning the effects of benefit differentiation. People value the different attributes of health insurance packages more or less and select their SHI fund accordingly. However, they are also influenced by a SHI fund's reputation. The brand offering the insurance product is the third most important criterion when choosing SHI. A comparatively low corporate reputation, such as that of *DAK*, leads to a reduction of the utility of an insurance product whereas a high reputation such as that of *TK* increases the product's perceived utility. As hypothesized, corporate reputation plays the role of an information surrogate that signals the quality of a company's (complex and immaterial) offerings to its consumers. This assumption is further backed by the fact that less educated and older people rely more on the brand than the more educated and younger consumers who can grasp the complex matter more easily.

6   Limitations and Implications

As seen above, even in times of premium equality, price still plays a major role in the selection of a SHI fund. It is indirectly included in product attributes such as voluntary coverage, where insurants aspire to obtain more coverage for the same price, and elective tariffs, which provide insurants with the possibility of getting their contributions back. Moreover, the sustained existence of price as a direct criterion cannot be neglected. Insurants can, for example, compare prices and premiums for complementary insurance offers. According to SCHULZE EHRING and KÖSTER (2010), complementary insurance can, given a scenario of premium equality, even serve as pricing substitute, a possibility that seems completely plausible that we could not account for in our empirical analysis.

Even though CBCA is generally ascribed high validity, the reality of the market for SHI is much more complex. To keep our CBCA set-up reliable, we could only include a fraction of all the existing attributes and levels of SHI products. It is, moreover, a truly difficult task to compare the SHI funds' offerings, which use various labels for the same features and often provide insufficient information to render a comprehensive comparison possible. In our conjoint analysis, in contrast, we provided participants with not only complete information on all offers but also hyperlinked descriptions in case they were unsure about the attributes' and levels' meanings. Approximately 50% of our respondents made use of these additional pieces of information. Against this background of high opacity in the SHI market, corporate reputation as an information surrogate might gain in importance in a real-life setting.

Even though the above presented importance scores (e.g., the low importance of customer service) are plausible and in line with prior research, we cannot completely rule out the possibility of a (slight) number-of-levels effect (STEENKAMP and WITTINK, 1994) according to which, in CA, respondents assign more importance to the attributes with more levels.

The proportion of those participants who intend to change their SHI fund is rather low. Even though this proportion might increase because of the collection of additional contributions by some funds, causing customer churn (see chapter 1), SHI funds still face the dilemma of wanting to attract only those customers associated with low risk, which is to say, good health because compensations from the government for high risk customers are generally considered to be too low (PIMPERTZ, 2007). Our finding that elective tariffs attract healthier people can possibly make a contribution to the easing of this conflict.

In spite of the strict regulation of what is possible within the field of voluntary coverage, SHI funds should take over the costs for at least some health-promoting activities (e.g., professional tooth cleaning). In light of the customers' high price sensitivity, it seems a promising approach to feature such measures as well as bonus programs with monetary rewards prominently in marketing communications. A SHI fund's marketing communications and public relations should also place substantial emphasis on corporate reputation management, because customers rely on the brand as a signal of quality when they choose a SHI fund. Managing and closely tracking the development of the SHI fund's reputation, therefore, is essential. However, funds have to keep in mind that, if they charge their insurants with additional contributions, this mechanism is possibly overridden — given the high price sensitivity of Germans with regards to health insurance. Further research will have to examine the new market situation if more and more companies charge additional contributions.

If necessary, costs should be cut at the expense of the offered customer services or complementary insurance. However, marketing managers in SHI funds should keep in mind that these attributes, despite being less important in the decision process, significantly influence the choice of SHI. Both features can tip the balance for or against a specific offer in a direct comparison of alternatives or act as a compensatory element of customer choice.

The German public policy strategy behind the *Act to Strengthen Competition*, which aims to encourage more quality-based competition between SHI funds, has shown its first successes. The recent reform is more effective than earlier essential modifications of the German SHI market such as the introduction of freedom of choice in 1996 that only caused insurants to look elsewhere for equal coverage for a better price. The new competition that has emerged from the *Act to Strengthen Competition* has led to changes in the benefits delivered to the insurants. Our study shows that, in the new environment of premium equality, customers indeed base their SHI choice decisions on these new features to a great extent.

Appendix

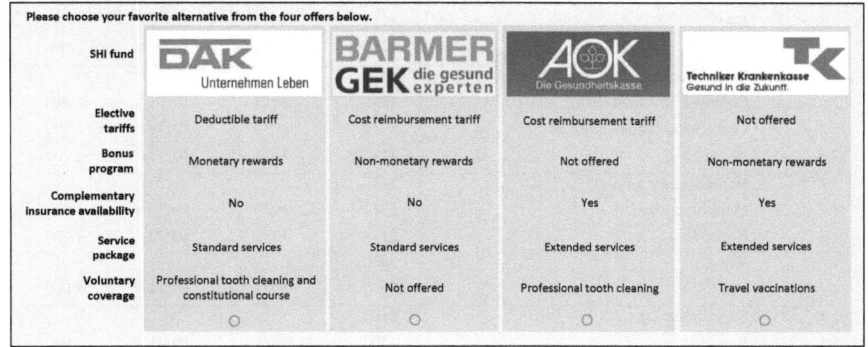

Figure 2: Exemplary Choice Task

Attr./lev.	Level	Frequency	Actual	Ideal	Efficiency
1 1	AOK	1750			
1 2	Barmer GEK	1750	0.034	0.034	1.000
1 3	DAK	1750	0.034	0.034	1.000
1 4	TK	1750	0.034	0.034	1.000
2 1	Deductible tariff	1750			
2 2	Contribution refund tariff	1750	0.034	0.034	1.000
2 3	Cost reimbursement tariff	1750	0.034	0.034	1.000
2 4	Not offered	1750	0.034	0.034	1.000
3 1	Non-monetary rewards	2333			
3 2	Monetary rewards	2333	0.030	0.030	1.000
3 3	Not offered	2334	0.030	0.030	1.000
4 1	Yes	3500			
4 2	No	3500	0.024	0.024	1.000
5 1	Standard services	3500			
5 2	Extended services	3500	0.024	0.024	1.000
6 1	Travel vaccinations	1000			
6 2	Professional tooth cleaning	1000	0.048	0.048	1.001
6 3	Constitutional course	1000	0.048	0.048	1.001
6 4	Travel vaccinations & prof. tooth cleaning	1000	0.048	0.048	1.002
6 5	Travel vaccinations & constitutional course	1000	0.048	0.048	1.001
6 6	Prof. tooth cleaning & constitutional course	1000	0.048	0.048	0.997
6 7	Not offered	1000	0.048	0.048	0.998

Note: 'Complete Enumeration task' generation method, based on 250 versions, includes 1,750 total choice tasks (7 per version). Each choice task includes four alternatives with six attributes each.

Table 6: Efficiency Calculation

Variable	Level	n	%
Sex	Male	93	37.20
	Female	157	62.80
Age	<20	5	2.00
Mean: 30.80	20-24	73	29.20
Std. dev.: 11.00	25-29	85	34.00
	30-34	27	10.80
Min: 18.00	35-39	12	4.80
Max: 79.00	40-44	10	4.00
	45-49	12	4.80
	50-54	15	6.00
	55-59	7	2.80
	60-64	2	.80
	≥65	2	.80
Family Status	Single	191	76.40
	In a relationship/married	48	19.20
	Divorced/separated/widowed	11	4.40
Education	No formal education	0	.00
	Basic secondary school	13	5.20
	Middle school	49	19.60
	High school diploma	111	44.40
	College/university	71	28.40
	Post graduate degree	6	2.40
Employment	School student	2	.80
Status	Trainee	0	.00
	Blue-collar worker	6	2.40
	Employee	105	42.00
	Public offer	3	1.20
	Entrepreneur	10	4.00
	Student (undergraduate)	115	46.00
	Retiree	2	.80
	Job seeker	1	.40
	Homemaker	3	1.20
	Others	3	1.20
Monthly net	< € 1,000	64	25.60
Household	€ 1,001 - € 1,500	26	10.40
Income (after	€ 1,501 - € 2,000	42	16.80
taxes and	€ 2,001 - € 2,500	28	11.20
social insurance)	€ 2,501 - € 3,000	22	8.80
	€ 3,001 - € 3,500	12	4.80
	€ 3,501 - € 4,000	7	2.80
	€ 4,001 - € 4,500	10	4.00
	€ 4,501 - € 5,000	4	1.60
	> € 5,000	4	1.60
	Not Specified	31	12.40
Current SHI	AOK	51	20.40
Provider	BARMER GEK	33	13.20
	DAK	32	12.80
	TK	52	20.80
	Others	82	32.80

Table 7: Selected Demographic Data (n = 250)

Attribute		Within attribute χ^2	df	Significance
SHI Brand (n = 250)		14.42	3	p < .01
AOK	.25			
Barmer GEK	.24			
DAK	.23			
TK	.29			
Elective Tariff (n = 250)		172.03	3	p < .01
Deductible tariff	.20			
Contribution refund tariff	.35			
Cost reimbursement tariff	.29			
Not offered	.15			
Bonus Program (n = 250)		96.32	2	p < .01
Non-monetary rewards	.24			
Monetary rewards	.32			
Not offered	.18			
Complementary Insurance (n = 250)		80.79	1	p < .01
Yes	.30			
No	.20			
Voluntary Coverage (n = 250)		349.50	6	p < .01
Travel vaccinations (1)	.16			
Professional tooth cleaning (2)	.26			
Constitutional course (3)	.16			
(1) and (2)	.38			
(1) and (3)	.30			
(2) and (3)	.40			
Not offered	.08			
Service Package (n = 250)		25.20	1	p < .01
Standard services	.22			
Extended services	.28			

Table 8: Count Analysis

Means	AOK	Barmer GEK	DAK	TK	Others
SHI Brand	16.13[b]	14.37[a,b]	10.77[a]	16.90[b]	14.86[b]
Elective Tariff	18.38	20.13	19.04	20.60	19.58
Bonus Program	12.93	13.23	15.71	13.44	13.99
Complementary Insurance	8.97	9.86	8.44	8.21	8.24
Voluntary Coverage	37.92[b]	34.97[a,b]	38.58[b]	33.02[a]	35.77[a,b]
Service Package	5.67	7.45	7.47	7.83	7.56

Note: Mean attribute importance. Numbers with different superscripts in a given row are significantly different at the level of $p < .05$.

Table 9: Attribute Importance per SHI Membership Group

References

ANDERSEN, H. H. & SCHWARZE, J. 1998. GKV`97: Kommt Bewegung in die Landschaft? Eine empirische Analyse der Kassenwahlentscheidungen. *Veröffentlichungsreihe des Berliner Zentrum Public Health,* 98(2), 1-34.

BRAU, R. & LIPPI BRUNI, M. 2008. Eliciting the Demand for Long-Term Care Coverage: A Discrete Choice Modelling Analysis. *Health Economics,* 17(3), 411-433.

BUSSE, R. & RIESBERG, A. 2005. *Gesundheitssysteme im Wandel: Deutschland, WHO Regionalbüro für Europa im Auftrag des Europäischen Observatoriums für Gesundheitssysteme und Gesundheitspolitik,* Kopenhagen.

CARSON, R. T., LOUVIERE, J. J., ANDERSON, D. A., PHIPPS, A., BUNCH, D. S., HENSHER, D. A., JOHNSON, R. M., KUHFELD, W. F., STEINBERG, D., SWAIT, J., TIMMERMANS, H. & WILEY, J. B. 1994. Experimental Analysis of Choice. *Marketing Letters,* 5(4), 351-368.

CHAKRABORTY, G., ETTENSON, R. & GAETH, G. 1994. How Consumers Choose Health Insurance - Analyzing Employees' Selection Process in a Multiplan Environment Identifies the Trade-Offs Consumers Make and the Benefits that Affect their Decision Making. *Journal of Health Care Marketing,* 14(1), 21-33.

DORMONT, B., GEOFFARD, P.-Y. & LAMIRAUD, K. 2009. The Influence of Supplementary Health Insurance on Switching Behaviour: Evidence from Swiss Data. *Health Economics,* 18(11), 1339-1356.

EBERL, M. & SCHWAIGER, M. 2008. Die Bedeutung der Unternehmensreputation für die Zahlungsbereitschaft von Privatkunden. *Kredit und Kapital,* 41(3), 355-394.

ELROD, T., LOUVIERE, J. J. & DAVEY, K. S. 1992. An Empirical Comparison of Ratings-Based and Choice-Based Conjoint Models. *Journal of Marketing Research,* 29(3), 368-377.

FOMBRUN, C. J. & SHANLEY, M. 1990. What's in a Name? Reputation Building and Corporate Strategy. *Academy of Management Journal,* 33(2), 233-258.

FOMBRUN, C. J. & VAN RIEL, C. 1997. The Reputational Landscape. *Corporate Reputation Review,* 1(1;2), 5-13.

FRIEDEL, H. & NÜRNBERGER, V. 2010. Bonusprogramme als Differenzierungsmerkmale im Wettbewerb der Krankenkassen. *Zeitschrift für Gesundheits- und Sozialpolitik,* 3(2010), 40-44.

FRIEDRICHS, M., FRIEDEL, H. & BÖDEKER, W. 2009. Teilnehmerstruktur und ökonomischer Nutzen präventiver Bonusprogramme in der betrieblichen Krankenversicherung. *Das Gesundheitswesen,* 71, 623-627.

GARDBERG, N. A. & FOMBRUN, C. J. 2002. The Global Reputation Quotient Project: First Steps Towards a Cross-Nationally Valid Measure of Corporate Reputation. *Corporate Reputation Review,* 4(4), 303-307.

GATES, R., MCDANIEL, C. & BRAUNSBERGER, K. 2000. Modeling Consumer Health Plan Choice Behavior To Improve Customer Value and Health Plan Market Share. *Journal of Business Research,* 48(3), 247-257.

GERMAN BUNDESTAG 2006. Entwurf eines Gesetzes zur Stärkung des Wettbewerbs in der gesetzlichen Krankenversicherung (GKV-Wettbewerbsstärkungsgesetz - GKV-WSG). *Drucksachen*, 16(3100).

GERMAN FEDERAL BUREAU OF STATISTICS. 2011. *GENESIS-Online Datenbank* [Online]. Wiesbaden: Statistisches Bundesamt Deutschland. Available: https://www-genesis.destatis.de/genesis/online [Accessed 2011-02-06].

GERMAN FEDERAL DEPARTMENT OF HEALTH. 2010. *Ratgeber zur gesetzlichen Krankenversicherung* [Online]. Available: https://www.bundesgesundheitsminis-terium.de/uploads/publications/BMG-P-07031-Ratgeber-Zur-Gesetzlichen-Kranken-versicherung_201008.pdf [Accessed 2011-01-26].

GERMAN FEDERAL DEPARTMENT OF HEALTH. 2011. *Krankenversicherung* [Online]. Available: http://www.bmg.bund.de/krankenversicherung.html [Accessed 2011-08-01].

GOTSI, M. & WILSON, A. M. 2001. Corporate Reputation: Seeking a Definition. *Corporate Communications: An International Journal,* 6(1), 24-30.

GREEN, P. E., KRIEGER, A. M. & WIND, Y. 2001. Thirty Years of Conjoint Analysis: Reflections and Prospects. *Interfaces,* 31(3), S56-S73.

GREEN, P. E. & SRINIVASAN, V. 1990. Conjoint Analysis in Marketing: New Developments with Implications for Research and Practice. *The Journal of Marketing,* 54(4), 3-19.

GREß, S., GROENEWEGEN, P., KERSSENS, J., BRAUN, B. & WASEM, J. 2002. Free Choice of Sickness Funds in Regulated Competition: Evidence from Germany and The Netherlands. *Health Policy,* 60(3), 235-254.

GREß, S., HÖPPNER, K., MARSTEDT, G., ROTHGANG, H., TAMM, M. & WASEM, J. 2008. Kassenwechsel als Mechanismus zur Durchsetzung von Versicherteninteressen. *In:* BRAUN, B., GREß, S., ROTHGANG, H. & WASEM, J. (eds.) *Einflussnehmen oder Aussteigen? Theorie und Praxis von Kassenwechsel und Selbstverwaltung in der GKV.* Berlin: edition sigma, 19-89.

GROENLAND, E. A. G. 2002. Qualitative Research to Validate the RQ - Dimensions. *Corporate Reputation Review,* 4(4), 309-315.

GUSTAFSSON, A., HERRMANN, A. & HUBER, F. 2007. Conjoint Analysis as an Instrument of Market Research Practice. *In:* GUSTAFSSON, A., HERRMANN, A. & HUBER, F. (eds.) *Conjoint Measurement.* Berlin Heidelberg: Springer, 3-30.

HAAIJER, R., KAMAKURA, W. A. & WEDEL, M. 2001. The 'No-Choice' Alternative to Conjoint Choice Experiments. *International Journal of Market Research,* 43(1), 93-106.

HAAIJER, R. & WEDEL, M. 2007. Conjoint Choice Experiments: General Characteristics and Alternative Model Specifications. *In:* GUSTAFSSON, A., HERRMANN, A. & HUBER, F. (eds.) *Conjoint Measurement.* Berlin Heidelberg: Springer, 199-229.

HAENECKE, H. 2001. Motive der Versicherten bei der Kassenwahlentscheidung - Eine qualitative empirische Analyse. *Sozialer Fortschritt,* 2001(12), 297-303.

HALL, R. 1992. The Strategic Analysis of Intangible Resources. *Strategic Management Journal,* 13(2), 135-144.

HEALTH INSURANCE GERMANY. 2011. *Zusatzbeitrag: Liste der Krankenkassen mit Zusatzbeitrag* [Online]. Available: http://www.krankenkassen.de/gesetzliche-krankenkassen/krankenkasse-beitrag/zusatzbeitrag/ [Accessed 2011-06-17].

HÖPPNER, K., GREB, S., ROTHGANG, H., WASEM, J., BRAUN, B. & BUITKAMP, M. 2005. Grenzen und Dysfunktionalitäten des Kassenwettbewerbs in der GKV: Theorie und Empirie der Risikoselektion in Deutschland. *In:* ZENTRUM FÜR SOZIALPOLITIK - UNIVERSITÄT BREMEN (ed.) *ZeS-Arbeitspapiere 4/2005.* Bremen.

JOHNSON, R. M. & ORME, B. 2003. Getting the most from CBC. *In:* SAWTOOTH SOFTWARE INC. (ed.) *Technical Paper Series.* Sequim.

KAMAKURA, W. A. & RUSSELL, G. J. 1989. A Probabilistic Choice Model for Market Segmentation and Elasticity Structure. *Journal of Marketing Research,* 26(4), 379-390.

KERSSENS, J. J. & GROENEWEGEN, P. P. 2005. Consumer Preferences in Social Health Insurance. *The European Journal of Health Economics,* 6(1), 8-15.

KOLSTAD, J. T. & CHERNEW, M. E. 2009. Quality and Consumer Decision Making in the Market for Health Insurance and Health Care Services. *Medical Care Research and Review,* 66(1 suppl.), 28-52.

KUHFELD, W. F., TOBIAS, R. D. & GARRATT, M. 1994. Efficient Experimental Design with Marketing Research Applications. *Journal of Marketing Research,* 31(4), 545-557.

LENK, P. J., DESARBO, W. S., GREEN, P. E. & YOUNG, M. R. 1996. Hierarchical Bayes Conjoint Analysis: Recovery of Partworth Heterogeneity from Reduced Experimental Design. *Marketing Science,* 15(2), 173-191.

LOUVIERE, J. J. & WOODWORTH, G. 1983. Design and Analysis of Simulated Consumer Choice or Allocation Experiments: An Approach Based on Aggregate Data. *Journal of Marketing Research,* 20(4), 350-367.

MANNING, W. G., NEWHOUSE, J. P., DUAN, N., KEELER, E. B. & LEIBOWITZ, A. 1987. Health Insurance and the Demand for Medical Care: Evidence from a Randomized Experiment. *The American Economic Review,* 77(3), 251-277.

MARQUIS, M. S., BEEUWKES BUNTIN, M., ESCARCE, J. J. & KAPUR, K. 2007. The Role of Product Design in Consumers' Choices in the Individual Insurance Market. *Health Research and Educational Trust,* 42(6), 2194-2223.

MCFADDEN, D. 1974. Conditional Logit Analysis of Qualitative Choice Behavior. *In:* ZAREMBKA, P. (ed.) *Frontiers in Econometrics.* New York, 105-142.

MOORE, W. L., GRAY-LEE, J. & LOUVIERE, J. J. 1998. A Cross-Validity Comparison of Conjoint Analysis and Choice Models at Different Levels of Aggregation. *Marketing Letters,* 9(2), 195-207.

NELSON, P. 1970. Information and Consumer Behavior. *Journal of Political Economy,* 78, 311-329.

NOORDEWIER, T. G., ROGERS, D. & BALAKRISHNAN, P. V. 1989. Evaluating Consumer Preference for Private Long-Term Care Insurance. *Journal of Health Care Marketing,* 9(4), 34-40.

NÖTHEN, M. & BÖHM, K. 2009. Krankheitskosten. *In:* ROBERT KOCH-INSTITUT (ed.) *Gesundheitsberichterstattung des Bundes.* Berlin.

ORME, B. 2006. *Getting Started with Conjoint Analysis: Strategies for Product Design and Pricing Research,* Madison.

PAQUET, R. 2007. Wahltarife als Wettbewerbsrisiko für die GKV. *Der gelbe Dienst,* 25(7), 5-6.

PASSON, A., LÜNGEN, M., GERBER, A., REDAELLI, M. & STOCK, S. 2009. Das Krankenversicherungssystem in Deutschland. *In:* LAUTERBACH, K. W., STOCK, S. & BRUNNER, H. (eds.) *Gesundheitsökonomie - Lehrbuch für Mediziner und andere Gesundheitsberufe.* Second revised edition. Bern: Huber, 209-220.

PIMPERTZ, J. 2007. Wettbewerb in der gesetzlichen Krankenversicherung - Gestaltungsoptionen unter sozialpolitischen Vorgaben. *In:* INSTITUT DER DEUTSCHEN WIRTSCHAFT (ed.) *IW-Positionen.* Köln: Deutscher Instituts Verlag.

PRACEJUS, J. W. & OLSEN, G. D. 2004. The Role of Brand/Cause Fit in the Effectiveness of Cause-Related Marketing Campaigns. *Journal of Business Research,* 57(6), 635-640.

PÜTZ, C. & HAGIST, C. 2006. Optional Deductibles in Social Health Insurance Systems. *The European Journal of Health Economics,* 7(4), 225-230.

RAO, V. R. 2008. Developments in Conjoint Analysis. *In:* WIERENGA, B. (ed.) *Handbook of Marketing Decision Models.* New York: Springer US, 23-53.

ROB, R. & FISHMAN, A. 2005. Is Bigger Better? Customer Base Expansion through Word-of-Mouth Reputation. *Journal of Political Economy,* 113(5), 1146-1162.

ROSSI, P. E. & ALLENBY, G. M. 2003. Bayesian Statistics and Marketing. *Marketing Science,* 22(3), 304-328.

RYAN, M., MCINTOSH, E. & SHACKLEY, P. 1998. Methodological Issues in the Application of Conjoint Analysis in Health Care. *Health Economics,* 7(4), 373-378.

SCHULZE EHRING, F. & KÖSTER, A.-D. 2010. Beitrags- und Leistungsdifferenzierung in der GKV? *WIP-Diskussionspapier 03/10.*

SCHULZE EHRING, F. & WEBER, C. 2007. Wahltarife in der GKV - Nutzen oder Schaden für die Versichertengemeinschaft? *WIP-Diskussionspapier 04/07.*

SCHWAIGER, M. 2004. Components and Parameters of Corporate Reputation - An Empirical Study. *Schmalenbach Business Review,* 56(1), 46-71.

SHAPIRO, C. 1982. Consumer Information, Production Quality, and Seller Reputation. *The Bell Journal of Economics,* 13(1), 20-35.

STEENKAMP, J.-B. E. M. & WITTINK, D. R. 1994. The Metric Quality of Full-Profile Judgments and the Number-of-Attribute-Levels Effect in Conjoint Analysis. *International Journal of Research in Marketing,* 11(3), 275-286.

STENSRUD, J., SYLVESTRE, E. & SIVADAS, E. 1997. Targeting Medicare Consumers - Managed Care Providers Can Make Inroads by Understanding Preference and Cost-Sensitivity Issues. *Marketing Health Services,* 17(1), 8-17.

THE NATIONAL ASSOCIATION OF STATUTORY HEALTH INSURANCE FUNDS. 2011. *Anzahl der Krankenkassen im Zeitablauf - Konzentrationsprozess durch Fusionen* [Online]. Available: http://www.gkv-spitzenverband.de/upload/Krankenkassen_Fusionen-verlauf_1970-2010_11155.pdf [Accessed 2011-01-25].

THOMSON, S. & DIXON, A. 2006. Choices in Health Care: the European Experience. *Journal of Health Services Research & Policy*, 11(3), 167-171.

VAN DEN BERG, B., VAN DOMMELEN, P., STAM, P., LASKE-ALDERSHOF, T., BUCHMUELLER, T. & SCHUT, F. T. 2008. Preferences and Choices for Care and Health Insurance. *Social Science & Medicine*, 66(12), 2448-2459.

VAN VLIET, R. C. J. A. 2004. Deductibles and Health Care Expenditures: Empirical Estimates of Price Sensitivity Based on Administrative Data. *International Journal of Health Care Finance and Economics*, 4(4), 283-305.

WEBER, E. U., BLAIS, A.-R. & BETZ, N. E. 2002. A Domain-specific Risk-attitude Scale: Measuring Risk Perceptions and Risk Behaviors. *Journal of Behavioral Decision Making*, 15(4), 263-290.

WITTINK, D. R., KRISHNAMURTHI, L. & REIBSTEIN, D. J. 1989. The Effect of Differences in the Number of Attribute Levels on Conjoint Results. *Marketing Letters*, 1, 113-123.

YOON, E., GUFFEY, H. J. & KIJEWSKI, V. 1993. The Effects of Information and Campany Reputation on Intentions to Buy a Bussiness Service. *Journal of Business Research*, 27(3), 215-228.

ZOK, K. 1999. Anforderungen an die gesetzliche Krankenversicherung. Einschätzungen und Erwartungen aus Sicht der Versicherten. *In:* WISSENSCHAFTLICHES INSTITUT DER AOK (ed.) *WIdO-Materialien Bd. 43*. Bonn.

ZOK, K. 2005. Bonusprogramme und Zusatzversicherungen in der GKV - Ergebnisse einer Repräsentativumfrage unter 3.000 GKV-Mitgliedern. *WIdo-Monitor*, 2(1), 1-8.

ZOK, K. 2009. Interesse an privaten Zusatzversicherungen - Ergebnisse aus einer Repräsentativ-Umfrage unter 3.000 GKV-Versicherten. *WIdo-Monitor*, 6(2), 1-8.

Markus Kick

II THE EFFECTS OF ADDITIONAL CONTRIBUTIONS ON STATUTORY HEALTH INSURANCE CHOICES IN GERMANY

Abstract

Germany's statutory health insurance (SHI) system has been radically changed in the year 2009 by the introduction of premium equality across all SHI funds. As of today, all funds charge the same price, which is 15.5% of each insurant's gross income. The option to charge additional contributions as a flat, monthly per head amount in case funds cannot cover their costs has only scarcely been used so far. However, research predicts that this current state of premium equality is soon to be changed (PFISTER, 2009, EIBICH et al., 2011). Based on KICK and LITTICH (2011), I conduct a choice-based conjoint experiment and include the new pricing signal of additional contributions. I find that price is not the dominating criterion on the current market, but equally important to voluntary coverage options. Corporate reputation and a provider's brand name lose importance, but are still a major quality signal within consumers' choice decisions. The brand name TK (*Technical Health Insurance Fund*), as reputational leader, provides additional value for insurants. TK is able to charge up to €1.46 additional contributions from each insurant per month without falling behind their competitors. Compared to the general contribution rate of 15.5% of each insurant's gross income, of course, €1.46 seems rather low. However, the statutory health insurance funds that already charged additional contributions from their members collected between €5 and €16 per month and head. Using this rational reveals that TK is able to charge close to 10% of the additional contribution range simply due to their reputational advantage. Thus, corporate reputation proves to enhance a fund's bargaining position towards its potential insurants, as it allows charging and justifying price premiums. A second empirical study reveals that people lack knowledge about funds' benefit and coverage portfolios and the SHI system in general. Insurants consistently overestimate funds with comparably higher corporate reputation regarding their benefit and coverage details of selected performance categories. Implications for practitioners and policy makers are discussed.

1   Motivation

The German statutory health insurance (SHI) market before the year 2009 has historically been highly price driven. Contribution rates were by far more important than any benefit, coverage, or service details. Research also confirms that the main reason for insurants to change or pick their SHI fund depended on the basic question whether equal healthcare coverage can be obtained for a better price (GREB et al., 2002, ZOK, 1999). As funds constantly tried to underprice each other, the market situation fostered a high tendency towards a positive risk selection behavior and was even labeled "manacled" or "constrained" competition (cf. BROWN and AMELUNG, 1999, p. 76, REINHARDT, 1999, p. 92). In other words, it was best for SHI companies to acquire only low risk assets, meaning healthy people that are not costly, to keep prices down (BODE, 2003, p. 439, PIMPERTZ, 2007, p. 24).

With the introduction of the *Act to Strengthen Competition* (*Wettbewerbsstärkungsgesetz*) in 2009, the German government tried to counteract the mainly price driven competition on the SHI market (MARQUIS et al., 2007, NOORDEWIER et al., 1989). By setting contribution rates equally to 15.5% of each insurant's gross income, the reform's intention was to create a SHI system that is especially differentiated by offered benefits. The reform aimed to create a new basis for competition in terms of quality rather than price on both the primary (i.e., SHI and insurants) as well as the secondary (i.e., SHI and health care providers) market (GERMAN BUNDESTAG, 2006). Since price as the major differentiation criterion broke away, SHI funds had to react promptly to counteract a potential loss of insurants. They quickly established a diverse benefit and service environment to retain their customer base.

KICK and LITTICH (2011) show that under the situation of premium equality, consumers indeed attach more importance to benefit and coverage details. The authors identified elective tariffs, bonus programs, complementary insurance, voluntary coverage, and customer services as the main drivers of consumer choice. They further state that voluntary coverage options are the most important criterion within consumers' choice decisions with about 35%. Thus, the basic message on a market of premium equality comes back to the simple question where to get the best coverage options and benefits for the same price. The brand name, and subsequently a fund's corporate reputation, ranked third with an importance score of about 15% following elective tariffs with approximately 20%. Brand and reputation can, therefore, be seen as one of the most important aspects for funds to differentiate on the current market and proved to be of higher importance than extended customer service, bonus programs and complementary insurance offers. Thus, brand name and reputation help to take over the signaling effect on a former price dominated market within a SHI landscape of premium equality and help insurants to reduce the high market complexity in the SHI system (FOMBRUN and VAN RIEL, 1997, GERLINGER et al., 2007, PASSON et al., 2009).

However, by passing the *SHI-Financial Act* (*GKV-Finanzierungsgesetz*) in 2010, the German government opened up the possibility to deviate from the premium equality of 15.5% (GERMAN BUNDESTAG, 2010). In case SHI funds are no longer able to cover their costs, they can charge an additional contribution from their insurants. This additional payment, in contrast to the regular contribution, does not depend on insurants' income, but is invoiced from every insured person within one specific SHI fund to a maximum of 1% of the earnings ceiling for mandatory SHI, which is around € 40 per month (BUCHNER and WASEM, 2009). The meaning and importance of these additional premiums can be separated into two effects. First, a strong psychological effect, which arises out of directly charging a flat, monetary amount from the insurant, second, a strong pricing signal which allows comparison of plain sums of money instead of net percentages from gross income (SCHULZE EHRING and KÖSTER, 2010). Right now, coffers of SHI funds are well-stocked and the new opportunity of additional contributions is only scarcely used on today's market[1]. The German Department of Health states that for the years 2010, 2011, and 2012 only a few (7 out of 145) SHI funds already have or will charge additional premiums (GERMAN FEDERAL DEPARTMENT OF HEALTH, 2010). However, the situation is expected to change during the next years. An economical downswing and a rise in health care expenditures are just two reasons for the prediction of experts that funds cannot avoid charging additional contributions from their members in the near future (PFISTER, 2009, EIBICH et al., 2011, BUCHNER and WASEM, 2009). Press and media also widely discussed the

---

[1]   Please note that "today" refers to the market situation in 2012. Two major reasons made it necessary to not focus on the current market situation in 2014. First, data of both empirical studies were collected in 2012 under the light of the former market situation and after insurants have had first experiences with additional contributions. Second, in the year 2014, none of the SHI funds charge additional contributions. In fact, financial resources of SHI funds currently even allow reimbursing contributions back to SHI insurants. For example, TK reimbursed €80 to each member in the year 2013 (TECHNIKER KRANKENKASSE, 2014). As research clearly predicts a prospective increase in health care expenditures and a return to a market with additional contributions (cf. PFISTER, 2009, EIBICH et al., 2011), the focus of this paper lays on the 2012 market situation where in October 2012, one out of 145 SHI funds was charging additional contributions from their members but insurants have become highly aware of this new opportunity.

new pricing signal and shaped consumers' perceptions about the imminent market with additional contributions.

The reintroduction of a new pricing signal on the German SHI market is expected to change the current SHI system and will show a major impact on health insurance choices. In this light, the study at hand wants to contribute to previous research in a fourfold way. First, I revisit the approach of KICK and LITTICH (2011) and replicate their findings on drivers of SHI choices on the German market. Second, I provide insights about the SHI choice decision under the new situation with additional contributions. I enhance the choice-based conjoint approach of KICK and LITTICH (2011) by including the attribute "additional contribution" as the new price signal and contrast the results to the market of premium equality. One main focus will be put on the interplay between price and corporate reputation, as corporate reputation was taking over the signaling role of price on a market with no price differences. Third, including a monetary amount into the choice experiment enables to extract detailed information for SHI funds about product design and pricing aspects. I derive insights about the monetary equivalents, certain coverage options or quality signals are able to compensate and shed light on the question of what the ideal SHI bundle looks like when additional contributions come into play. Fourth and last, through conducting a second empirical study, I verify the choice-based conjoint approaches of KICK and LITTICH (2011) and the study at hand. I reveal that consumers indeed lack knowledge about the SHI funds offerings (cf. e.g., HAENECKE, 2001, TSCHEULIN and DIETRICH, 2010) and face enormous market complexity (cf. e.g., DEVLIN, 2007) that argues in favor of signaling mechanisms like brand name or corporate reputation and confirms the appropriateness of the choice-based conjoint approaches.

After elaborating the theoretical framework for my study, I design and conduct a choice-based conjoint experiment to answer my hypotheses. The result section will show that the replication under premium equality has been successful, that additional contributions, indeed, change SHI choices, and that benefit, coverage, and service details as well as corporate reputation and the brand name are able to compensate additional contributions. Next, the design and results of the second empirical study are presented and discussed. The final chapter of the paper at hand presents final implications for practitioners and policy makers. Health insurance funds obtain valuable information on how to design their offerings in the predicted situation of premium inequality and on the changing importance of their corporate reputation. Furthermore, I provide policy makers in Germany and in countries with similar healthcare systems (e.g., Netherlands) with insights about the effectiveness of recent reforms as well as possible improvements in the design of future reforms.

2 Theoretical Background and Hypotheses

2.1 Effects of Benefit Differentiation

Especially after the *Act to Strengthen Competition* took effect in 2009, many small SHI funds that followed a low-price strategy felt increased pressure. Their unique differentiation criterion was taken away by premium equality. Hence, small SHI funds had and still have to expand their portfolio of benefits and services drastically to keep pace with the big SHI funds, which already have a stable and well equipped benefit and service system in place. Basically, it comes back to the concept of "bargaining power", where funds have to negotiate attractive group contracts with the actual health care service providers like hospitals, pharmaceutical industry or physicians to keep costs down. Thus, a big wave of mergers and acquisitions could be seen as a logical consequence. The *"Central Federal Association of Health Insurance Funds"* recorded a disappearance of 52 SHI funds from 221 in 2008 to 169 in spring 2010 (GKV-SPITZENVERBAND, 2012). Up to the end of 2012, they predict that the number of statutory sickness funds even declines to a total of 145. The change of thinking away from pure pricing aspects to a balanced benefit, coverage, and service system resulted in a variety of different benefit and service bundles and individualization possibilities. Press reports shortly after the introduction left the impression that SHI funds wanted to outdo each other in quickly offering more and more variable elective tariffs, bonus programs, or complementary insurances with an ubiquitous number of different names and labels (cf. e.g., SCHULZE EHRING and WEBER, 2007, SCHULZE EHRING and KÖSTER, 2010, HÖPPNER et al., 2005).

KICK and LITTICH (2011) identified five major differentiation attributes that funds use to fill the gap of a missing pricing signal[2]. In the benefit and service sector, the most important differentiation attributes that arose out of the premium equality on the German SHI market are: *Elective Tariffs, Bonus Programs, Complementary Insurance, Customer Service,* and *Voluntary Benefits/Coverage*[3].

---

[2]   Recent SHI research confirms this selection (cf. e.g., BRAU and LIPPI BRUNI, 2008, GATES et al., 2000, GREß et al., 2002, KERSSENS and GROENEWEGEN, 2005, KOLSTAD and CHERNEW, 2009, SCHULZE EHRING and KÖSTER, 2010, SCHULZE EHRING and WEBER, 2007, VAN DEN BERG et al., 2008).

[3]   For detailed information of differentiation attributes please refer to KICK and LITTICH (2011). The paper can also be found as the first document in this dissertation.

Extensive desk research confirmed that all of the upper differentiation attributes are still valid and play a crucial role in communication and marketing activities of sickness funds on today's market. Consequently, I expect the same coverage and service attributes to still show a significant influence onto insurants' SHI choice decision when additional contributions come into play. Therefore, I hypothesize:

> H_{1a-e}: *The offer of (a) elective tariffs, (b) bonus programs, (c) complementary insurance, (d)*
> *customer service aspects, and (e) voluntary benefits/coverage still positively*
> *influences the choice of SHI on a market with additional contributions.*

As the influence of these attributes was shown by KICK and LITTICH (2011) under premium equality, I expect the new pricing signal to take over a dominant role within SHI choice decisions again (cf. MARQUIS et al., 2007, NOORDEWIER et al., 1989)[4]. Consequently, I propose that benefit and service differentiation attributes will lose importance in a market with additional contributions:

> H_{1f-j}: *(f) Elective tariffs, (g) bonus programs, (h) complementary insurance, (i) customer*
> *service aspects, and (j) voluntary benefits/coverage will be less important in a market*
> *with contribution differences than in a market of premium equality.*

2.2   Quality Signals in Consumer Choice Decisions on the SHI Market

Throughout the last decades, consumers' choice decisions have been one of the key concepts in marketing research, and they are undoubtedly one of the main drivers of sales and corporate performance (MEFFERT, 2000, KELLER and LEHMANN, 2006). Being a very complex process in consumers' minds, consumers' choice was subject of extensive research throughout various industries and product categories. Research tried to shed light onto aspects that influence people's choice decisions and give advice for market participants on how to design and construct their products and services as well as their communication and marketing efforts in order to enhance the likelihood of a positive consumer choice (JACOBY et al., 1974, KROEBER-RIEL, 1992, THALER, 1985, TROMMSDORFF, 2004). When reasoning consumer behavior with the "Standard Economic model", we always deal with a rational consumer. "Homo Oeconomicus" "[…] choose[s] the best things [he] can afford" (VARIAN, 2006, p. 33). But what exactly is meant by "the best things they can afford"? From a theoretical point of view, this

---

[4]   Detailed deliberations regarding the dominating role of price can be found in the subsequent paragraph.

would mean a pure trust on obvious and rational product/service hard facts that create consumer specific value based on their individual preference functions. More precisely, the only important drivers of a rational consumer's choice decision should be observable product characteristics like price, quality or other criteria that all together form a total value that, compared to alternative options, tips the balance pro or con a certain product or service. An additional assumption is the unrestricted and immediate access to information on the product/ service market without transaction costs (VARIAN, 2006). These assumptions of rationality, of course, cannot be met in reality, because a lot of product characteristics and information are not directly observable, not accessible or simply not possible to evaluate or experience. Thus, most consumer decisions are made intuitively and are mostly derived in an elusive and inexplicable way. Almost all decisions are systematically biased by cognitive and especially emotional influences that are difficult to observe (ETZIONI, 2011, HO et al., 2006, JACOBY et al., 1974, KAHNEMANN, 2003). Consumers are exposed to a vast amount of information and marketing signals when considering the most suitable product. Due to limited processing capacity and the resulting information overload, consumers often do not have well-defined existing preferences, but construct them by using a variety of strategies and heuristics contingent on task demands (BETTMANN et al., 1998). These preferences vary from consumer to consumer, but the challenge for marketers is always the same. The key is to focus on marketing strategies which maximize the number of people willing to buy a certain product. Literature could identify experienced quality, followed by price, product attributes and marketing signals like brand names and corporate reputation as the most important drivers for consumers' choice (KIRIMANI and RAO, 2000, ZEITHAML, 1988). In case of a credence good like SHI[5], quality of a specific product/service cannot be observed beforehand. Thus, consumers' focus shifts from experienced quality to the construct of perceived quality. In order to create a high perceived quality among customers, signals are an appropriate mechanism to convey unobservable quality of a product or service (KIRIMANI and RAO, 2000). Signaling may be particularly effective in complex markets, markets for relatively new products or services, or in markets for products

---

[5] Literature provides three product categories on the basis of the ability to evaluate the quality of goods and services before and after utilization: search, experience and credence goods (DARBY and KARNI, 1973). Regarding search products, consumers are able to get full information of the quality before making their buying decision. For experience goods, the quality cannot be evaluated before but after the product was purchased and consumed. SHI plans could, thus, be seen as classical experience goods. However, the quality and features of a SHI contract cannot be observed immediately after the product was purchased. Insurance cases are needed to actually evaluate the quality of a respective health insurance plan (cf. DARBY and KARNI, 1973, EMONS, 1997). As an insurance case cannot be predicted or planned in advance, I argue that the category of credence goods fits SHI best.

about which the consumer is relatively uninformed and has no possibilities of accessing information (KIRIMANI and RAO, 2000, BETTMANN et al., 1998). They argue that as the complexity of the product/service increases, consumers are likely to resort to simpler heuristics and selective information processing, often reducing decision effectiveness (cf. also CHERNEV, 2003). Marketing literature provides important insights into quality signaling mechanisms and their related trade-offs with observable and comprehensible product attributes. Price, as the most important quality proxy, is highly important when it is the only available cue, but shows a fast decrease of importance when more quality indicators are available (RAO et al., 1999, ZEITHAML, 1988). In the consumer mindset, a higher price automatically transfers into a higher perceived quality of the offered products and services. However, on the market of SHI the situation is different. The German government (still) strictly regulates which health services are covered by SHI funds. The lists of drugs, treatment methods, outpatient care etc. as well as the respective coverage rates a SHI company has to reimburse, are predefined by law and form the so-called standard benefit catalogue (GERMAN FEDERAL DEPARTMENT OF HEALTH, 2011). Within those rigid reimbursement guidelines, approximately 98% of benefits are defined as mandatory payments that a SHI fund is required to reimburse (HÖPPNER et al., 2005, SCHULZE EHRING and KÖSTER, 2010). These strict regulations act like a safety net for insurants in a way since they do not have to worry about the major benefits and services as long as they are insured with any SHI fund. As the majority of benefits and services are independently from any price variation, I hypothesize:

H_{2a}:   *Additional contributions negatively influence the choice of a SHI fund.*

The German market for SHI has been dominated by price before premium equality of 2009 (MARQUIS et al., 2007, NOORDEWIER et al., 1989). Now that a new price signal in forms of additional contributions is returning to the market, I propose that the German SHI market will, again, react very price sensitive (cf. SCHUT et al., 2003) and hypothesize:

H_{2b}:   *Additional contributions will be the most important attribute within SHI choices.*

The marketing and quality signal corporate reputation, and a company's brand name respectively, serve as an important proxy for more detailed quality evaluations and judgments. A superior brand's claim about unobservable quality will likely be true, because a well-known brand name could not be established if the products or services did not fulfill certain quality standards. The same argument holds true for other basically intangible product attributes like warranty (ERDEM and SWAIT, 1998, KIRIMANI and RAO, 2000, TIROLE, 1988). This effect becomes increasingly important in service industries (YOON et al., 1993, KOTHA et al., 2001), such as the SHI sector, in which consumers know very little about the product and face a high market complexity (DEVLIN, 2007, HAENECKE, 2001). I consequently hypothesize:

H_{3a}:   A SHI fund's brand name, and its favorable corporate reputation respectively, significantly influences the choice of SHI on a market with additional contribution.

Following KICK and LITTICH (2011), corporate reputation and a company's brand name took over the most important signaling role on the market of premium equality. I expect additional contributions to reverse this effect — away from "more coverage for the same price" to a pre-2009 situation of "where to get the same coverage for a better price". Therefore, I hypothesize that the brand name and corporate reputation of a SHI fund also lose importance within SHI choice decisions when additional contributions come into play:

H_{3b}:   A SHI fund's brand name and its favorable corporate reputation respectively, will lose importance on a market with additional contributions compared to the situation of premium equality.

3   Study I: Additional Contributions and Consumer Choice

3.1   Design

To model consumers' choice decisions in a realistic way (cf. CHAKRABORTY et al., 1994), I use conjoint analysis to investigate consumers' choice decisions on the SHI market. In particular, a choice-based conjoint analysis (CBCA, also: discrete choice analysis) is applied, similar to related research in the health care sector (cf. e.g., STENSRUD et al., 1997, VAN DEN BERG et al., 2008, BRAU and LIPPI BRUNI, 2008). Following KICK and LITTICH (2011), I replicate the approach and feed all six attributes (i.e., *SHI brand, elective tariff, bonus program, complementary insurance, voluntary coverage, service package*) with their respective levels into the CBCA. All attributes and levels were again confirmed by extensive desk research to assure a proper modeling of the current SHI choice decision. Given the fact that respondents might lack knowledge about the different options of SHI funds, information screens were presented in the CBCA choice task. A detailed description of the single attributes and their respective levels were included via hyperlinks into the choice screens. Thus, participants always had the possibility to gather additional information. Similar to KICK and LITTICH (2011), close to 50% of participants used these options to clarify attributes and levels when making choice decisions[6].

SHI Brand. As corporate reputation scores cannot be directly implemented into the CBCA screen, SHI brand names are used. For replication purposes I also decided to use real SHI brands analogously to GATES et al. (2000). Brand names of the four biggest nationwide SHI funds in terms of coverage of German SHI insurants were included: *AOK* (27.1%), *Barmer GEK* (12.3%), *TK* (11.5%), and *DAK* (9.5%) (cf. AOK BUNDESVERBAND, 2012, BARMER GEK, 2012, DAK GESUNDHEIT, 2012, TECHNIKER KRANKENKASSE, 2012).

Elective Tariffs. Analogous to KICK and LITTICH (2011), I included the three major voluntary elective tariff options into the CBCA design. The deductible tariff offers bonus payments for taking over a cost deductible; the contribution refund tariff pays back up to one month's premium (i.e., 15.5% of an insurant's gross income) in case no medical services are used besides routine check-ups; the cost reimbursement tariff grants bonus payments in case medical services are paid in advance out of each insurant's own pocket which are partly reimbursed by the SHI fund later.

Bonus Program. Bonus programs basically reward health-conscious behavior like fitness club memberships, regular check-ups, or courses on nutrition or mental health. Insurants collect points similar to loyalty programs that can be exchanged in monetary or non-monetary rewards.

Complementary Insurance. In cooperation with private health insurers in the background, SHI funds can act as a broker for complementary insurance offers. As the variety of different possible complementary insurances is huge, I follow KICK and LITTICH (2011) and include binary Yes/No levels in case SHI funds have or have not set up cooperation models to offer complementary insurances.

Voluntary Coverage. As the German government strictly regulates about 98% of all health care services a SHI fund is bound to reimburse, only the remaining 2% allow for individual differentiation among funds. Even though there is also a catalogue defining what is possible within the 2%, it is up to each fund to pick certain options of that scope and enhance their

---

[6] The numbers were generated based on the click-rates on the info-screen links divided by all participants. 250 respondents participated in the CBCA-online survey and the individual click-rate of each screen, on average, was 108.

offerings. The most important and popular voluntary coverage options are: travel vaccinations, professional tooth cleaning, and cost transfer for constitutional health courses. All three are included into the CBCA as well as their respective combinations. Literature provides no evidence that including combinations of levels within a single attribute harms the CBCA results. Moreover, it seems to be accepted among scholars (cf. e.g., D'SOUZA and RAO, 1995).

Service package. Again, different service options across all SHI funds show a huge variety that cannot be included into the CBCA at hand to keep the designs complexity low. Rather, I included the two levels standard and extended service package.

Additional Contribution. First, the new attribute that is fed into the CBCA approach at hand had to be in line with the overall design. In other words, the number of levels had to be similar to the other attributes. Therefore, four levels representing the additional monetary component seemed sufficient. Second, research provides evidence about realistic levels of additional contribution. A representative study among SHI insurants featuring different SHI fund characteristics revealed that funds that already have charged additional contributions from their members, on average, collected €8 per month and head (ZOK, 2011). The maximum amount that was charged on the market stems from the SHI fund *"BKK Publik"* with €16 per month and head in the year 2010 (EURO-INFORMATIONEN GBR, n.d.). For this reason, I decided to include four different levels of the attribute additional contribution all invoiced per head[7] and month: €0 representing no additional contribution charged, €5, €10, and €15 as the representative level close to the maximum that has been on the market so far. Due to the additive utility construction underlying the CBCA approach, levels of additional contribution were chosen equidistantly. Table 1 provides an overview of the attributes and levels included into the CBCA.

---

[7]   The term "per head" refers to SHI members of a fund excluding co-insured people (e.g., children or homemakers) of a dependents' SHI contract.

#	Attribute	#	Level
1	SHI Brand	1	AOK
		2	Barmer GEK
		3	DAK
		4	TK
2	Elective Tariffs	1	Not offered
		2	Deductible tariff
		3	Contribution refund tariff
		4	Cost reimbursement tariff
3	Bonus Program	1	Not offered
		2	Nonmonetary rewards
		3	Monetary rewards
4	Complementary Insurance	1	Yes
		2	No
5	Voluntary Coverage	1	Not offered
		2	Travel vaccinations
		3	Professional tooth cleaning
		4	Constitutional course
		5	Travel vaccinations and professional tooth cleaning
		6	Travel vaccinations and constitutional course
		7	Professional tooth cleaning and constitutional course
6	Service Package	1	Standard services
		2	Extended services
7	Additional Contributions	1	€0 / month
		2	€5 / month
		3	€10 / month
		4	€15 / month

Table 1: CBCA Attributes and Levels

The actual choice experiment formed the middle part of an online survey collected in September 2012. The questionnaire started with a screener question to assure respondents were insured at a SHI fund and not part of the private health insurance sector. In addition, respondents had to be aware of the four included SHI brands. After some introductory demographic questions, participants had to run through seven choice tasks with four alternatives each. A none-option was not included due to the inherent choice complexity and comparability issues. Figure 1 provides an exemplary choice task. Efficiency scores of the underlying CBCA design range between 0.997 und 1.002 and, therefore, show the design's capability of collecting valid choice data[8].

---

[8]   Table 11 in the appendix shows the detailed efficiency calculations.

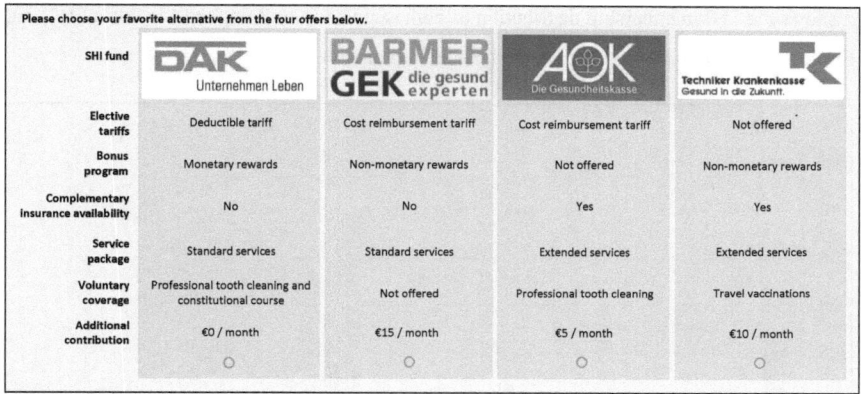

	SHI fund	DAK Unternehmen Leben	BARMER GEK die gesund experten	AOK Die Gesundheitskasse	TK Techniker Krankenkasse Gesund in die Zukunft.
Elective tariffs		Deductible tariff	Cost reimbursement tariff	Cost reimbursement tariff	Not offered
Bonus program		Monetary rewards	Non-monetary rewards	Not offered	Non-monetary rewards
Complementary insurance availability		No	No	Yes	Yes
Service package		Standard services	Standard services	Extended services	Extended services
Voluntary coverage		Professional tooth cleaning and constitutional course	Not offered	Professional tooth cleaning	Travel vaccinations
Additional contribution		€0 / month	€15 / month	€5 / month	€10 / month
		○	○	○	○

Please choose your favorite alternative from the four offers below.

Figure 1: Exemplary Choice Task

After the CBCA part, respondents had to indicate the corporate reputation of the four SHI funds. I used the corporate reputation scale of SCHWAIGER (2004). The scores of the six reflective items were collected on seven-point Likert scales and standardized between zero and 100. In the last section of the online survey, respondents were asked for information on their current health status and their current SHI provider. In total, 250 SHI insurants responded to our questionnaire. Looking at the demographic data reveals that the current sample is comparable to the sample of KICK and LITTICH (2011). Respondents are mainly female (58.8%), highly educated (around 80% at least have a high school diploma), and mostly undergraduate students (46.4%). The average age of participants with 31.86 is still younger than the German average (GERMAN FEDERAL BUREAU OF STATISTICS, 2011) but comparable to the average age of 30.8 in the study of KICK and LITTICH (2011)[9]. Insurants show a high satisfaction with their SHI funds (M = 5.34 on a seven point scale from 1 = "not at all" to 7 = "fully satisfied") and a low intention to change their SHI provider (7.2% indicate that they want to change within the next 12 month and another 11.6% are still undecided). In line with the sample's younger age, their perceived health situation was fairly good (M = 5.56 from 1 = "very bad" to 7 = "very good"). The membership distribution across different SHI funds showed that 8.4% of participants were members of DAK, 11.6% of Barmer GEK, another 22.0% of AOK, and an additional 26.4% of TK. The remaining 31.6% were insured at other SHI funds not included into the CBCA. Figure

---

[9] A detailed overview of the collected socio-demographic data can be found in Table 9 in the appendix.

2 shows the SHI membership distribution of both samples from KICK and LITTICH (2011) and the current study contrasted to the real membership distribution.

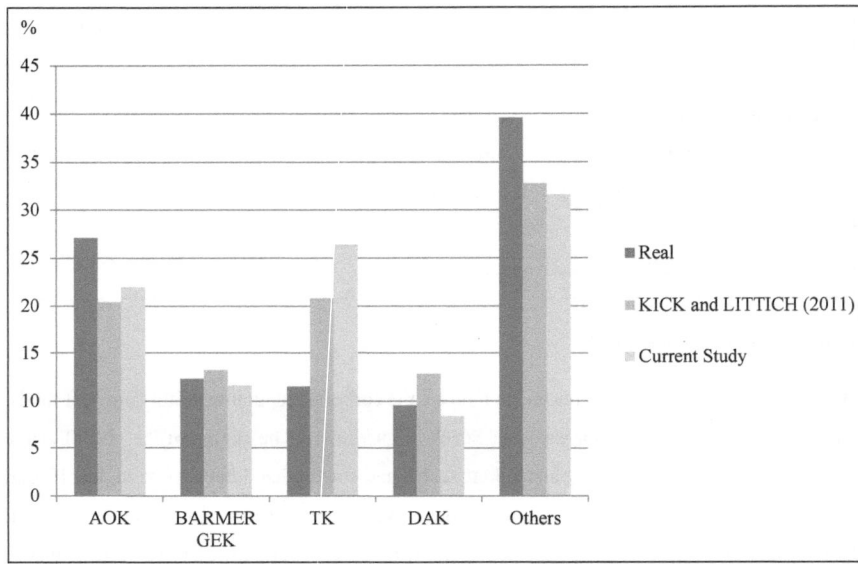

Figure 2: SHI Membership Distribution

3.2   Analysis and Results

Count Analysis

To answer the question if benefit differentiation aspects still show a significant effect on people's choice behavior (cf. Hypotheses $H_{1a\text{-}e}$), count analysis with its underlying χ^2-test is applied. Table 10 in the appendix shows the complete output of the conducted count analysis. Results reveal that the choices of participants depend on the presented benefit and service attributes and level. Elective tariffs ($\chi^2 = 58.21$, df $= 3$), bonus programs ($\chi^2 = 18.60$, df $= 2$), complementary insurance offers ($\chi^2 = 46.09$, df $= 1$), service offers ($\chi^2 = 15.75$, df $= 1$), and voluntary coverage options ($\chi^2 = 204.74$, df $= 6$) all exceed the theoretical χ^2 value for an α-level of 1%. It can be concluded that the attributes and levels chosen by KICK and LITTICH (2011) are still valid in 2012 under the new market situation of additional contributions, which supports Hypotheses $H_{1a\text{-}e}$.

Count analysis further helps to answer the question if a SHI brand name still has a significant influence on SHI choices of participants as raised in Hypothesis H_{3a}. Results indicate that with df = 3, the respective within attribute $\chi^2 = 7.53 > \chi^2_{theoretical\ (df = 3;\ p = 0.1)} = 6.25$. Therefore, the attribute brand shows a significant influence on SHI choice decisions only on a 10% level. Looking at the detailed results of the count analysis reveals that DAK, Barmer GEK, and AOK were chosen in 24% of all choice tasks. TK was picked in 28% of all decisions. This not only reflects participants' preferences, but also the already existing market share of TK in the sample at hand (cf. Figure 2). However, if choice decisions are biased by the SHI membership of the sample at hand, the calculated importance scores would also be skewed. Additional calculations revealed that participants' actual SHI memberships have no effect on the reported importance scores (cf. Table 12 in the appendix). For this reason, the sample is capable of providing information about the consumer preferences where the Technical Health Insurance Fund (i.e., TK) seems to attract people more than the remaining brands. However, the difference was not large enough to turn the whole attribute brand highly significant. Therefore, I find weak evidence for the influence of the overall attribute "*SHI brand*" on the respective choice behavior. To properly comment on H_{3a}, the link between the CBCA attribute brand name and a SHI fund's corporate reputation has to be established. Hypothesis H_{3a} will be finally discussed after individual part-worth utilities have been created and connected to a fund's corporate reputation scores.

Reputational Assessments

Under the situation of premium equality, the SHI fund TK was found to be far ahead in terms of corporate reputation (KICK and LITTICH, 2011). Those findings are also confirmed by the study at hand and, thus, support the results of the count analysis above. Table 2 presents the reputational assessments of the included SHI brands. Overall, TK, again, proves to be significantly ahead of the remaining SHI providers, which argues in favor of their superior quality signals. The other SHI funds cannot be separated from each other regarding their corporate reputation.

Means	AOK	Barmer GEK	DAK	TK
Competence	56.20[a]	58.17[a]	55.57[a]	68.39[b]
	(27.84)	(23.39)	(22.01)	(26.01)
Likeability	39.14[a]	35.98[a]	36.75[a]	50.48[b]
	(33.29)	(28.66)	(27.01)	(32.77)
Reputation	48.17[a]	47.73[a]	46.71[a]	59.96[b]
	(25.35)	(21.15)	(19.51)	(24.13)

Note: Means on a scale from 0 to 100. Standard deviations in parentheses. Numbers with different superscripts in a given row are significantly different at the level of $p < .01$.

Table 2: Reputational Assessments of SHI brands

The comparison of reputational assessments of KICK and LITTICH (2011) and the current study can be found in Figure 4 in the appendix. It reveals that all SHI funds gained competence, but clearly lost on the likeability dimension. However, overall reputational assessments calculated by means of a factor analytical approach out of both dimensions (i.e., likeability and competence) almost remain constant. A contradictory movement of likeability and competence, of course, might be reasoned within sample compositions of both studies. However, chapter 3.1 could already rule out obvious sample biases as this study's sample is comparable to the composition of KICK and LITTICH (2011). Nevertheless, there could be unobserved variables in the background that might have biased reputational perceptions. On the contrary, there are also two reasons that argue in favor of the observed competence and likeability movement. First, between 2010 and 2012 insurants have become highly aware of the possibility for SHI funds to charge additional contributions. As only a small minority of funds was charging additional contributions through that time, this positively fed into the competence dimension. However, the mere possibility to charge additional contributions even though the general contribution rate was adjusted to 15.5% in 2009 might have led to a drop in the likeability dimension. Second, during that time, the majority of funds reported tremendously good financial statements. The coffers of SHI funds were well stocked and they generated high profits which positively influenced competence perceptions. However, the SHI system is strictly non-profit. Not reimbursing and distributing profits but still being highly regulative with their benefit and service coverage might seem unappealing to the majority of insurants which can explain the drop in likeability.

Multinomial-Logit Model

After analyzing count data and looking at the reputational assessment of SHI funds, a multinomial logit model to assess the part-worth utility (PWU) for the single levels of each attribute is employed[10]. If positive, the PWU-estimates add to the already existing core utility of SHI. If negative, they decrease to overall utility and diminish the attractiveness of a certain bundle or option. They form the average "effect" of each level onto the average participant's perceived utility. Table 3 shows all included attributes and levels with their respective PWU estimations (i.e., effect scores).

Within elective tariffs, the contribution refund option, where insurants can get up to one month premium back if not using any medical services besides preventive checkups options, enhances the perceived value within consumers' choice decision significantly (+.338). In contrast, offering a deductible tariff option (-.224) turns out to be even worse than not offering any voluntary elective tariffs at all (-.169). To take over medical treatment costs up to a certain deductible out of their own pocket seems to contradict participants' preferences.

A monetary bonus program, in which insurants can enroll and basically earn rewards for health-conscious behavior like participation in approved health-promoting activities and regular preventive checkups, positively adds to a fund's offer. Further, complementary insurances as well as an extended service package show a significant positive influence onto insurants' health plan choices.

The voluntary coverage option of travel vaccinations in combination with professional tooth cleaning creates a high positive contribution for SHI offers. With an effect score of .701 it is the most considerable level throughout all benefit and service details on the current market.

---

[10] A detailed description of the CBCA rationale and approach can be found in KICK and LITTICH (2011).

Attribute	Level	Effect	Std. err.	t-ratio
SHI Brand	AOK	-.056	.046	-1.220
	Barmer GEK	-.032	.046	-0.689
	DAK	-.056	.046	-1.229
	TK	.145***	.044	3.289
Elective Tariff	Not offered	-.169***	.047	-3.566
	Deductible tariff	-.224***	.048	-4.641
	Contribution refund tariff	.338***	.042	7.942
	Cost reimbursement tariff	.054	.045	1.212
Bonus Program	Not offered	-.159***	.039	-4.004
	Non-monetary rewards	.013	.038	0.332
	Monetary rewards	.146***	.038	3.892
Complementary Insurance	Yes	.200***	.026	7.497
	No	-.200***	.026	-7.497
Voluntary Coverage	Not offered	-.665***	.083	-8.005
	[Only] travel vaccinations (1)	-.032	.070	-0.453
	[Only] professional tooth cleaning (2)	-.082	.070	-1.172
	[Only] constitutional course (3)	-.568***	.080	-7.057
	(1) and (2)	.701***	.061	11.464
	(1) and (3)	.332***	.064	5.1435
	(2) and (3)	.314***	.064	4.878
Service Package	Standard services	-.115***	.026	-4.355
	Extended services	.115***	.026	4.355
Additional Contributions	€0 / month	.785***	.040	19.603
	€5 / month	.201***	.040	4.509
	€10 / month	-.277***	.051	-5.452
	€15 / month	-.709***	.058	-12.098

Table 3: Part-worth Utilities (Multinomial-logit Model)

Deliberations above, together with the results of count analysis and its underlying χ^2-independency test, proved that respondents' choices depend on the presented benefit and service attributes and levels. This is in line with our Hypotheses H_{1a-e}, which finds additional support through the multinomial-logit model.

Looking at the attribute SHI brand name, PWUs show that only the *Technical Health Insurance Fund* is able to create positive value for the respondent. All other brands do hardly differentiate from a consumer perspective and do not enhance the underlying utility of an SHI contract. This is confirmed by the respective reputational assessments and count analysis and also argues in line with Hypothesis H_{3a}. SHI brand, indeed, can trigger the balance pro or con a certain offer. H_{3a} again receives support.

Additional contributions, as the new price signal, were included with the realistic levels of €0 (status quo), €5, €10, and €15 per head and month. Figure 3 shows the plot of part-worth utilities for the respective additional contribution levels. A higher amount of additional contributions goes in hand with a lower PWU. Not charging additional contributions enhances the total SHI utility by +.785, whereas the highest level of €15 / month reduces respondents' perceived utility by -.709. PWUs decrease in a linear way in line with the increasing additional contribution amount. However, it has to be noted that the positive PWU of €5 in additional contributions, on first sight, seems counterintuitive. As each choice situation presented a SHI option with no additional contribution, I would have expected that additional contributions of €5 already create a negative PWU and, thus, diminish the value of a SHI offering. There might be technical or statistical reasons in the background for the positive PWU of the €5 level that could not be controlled beforehand. However, two functional reasons argue in favor of €5 adding positive value to a SHI plan. First, through extensive media coverage and a lively discussion about the SHI system, people are aware of additional contributions and the possible range they can take. Second, funds that already charged additional contributions between 2010 and 2012, on average, collected €8 per month and head (ZOK, 2011). This might lead to the consumer perception that €5 is still better than the average and, thus, creates a positive PWU. Looking at Figure 3 also reveals that the neutral-utility point on the x-axis almost reflects the average additional contribution amount of €8.

Summarizing, charging additional contributions decreases the overall value of SHI. H_{2a} is consequently supported.

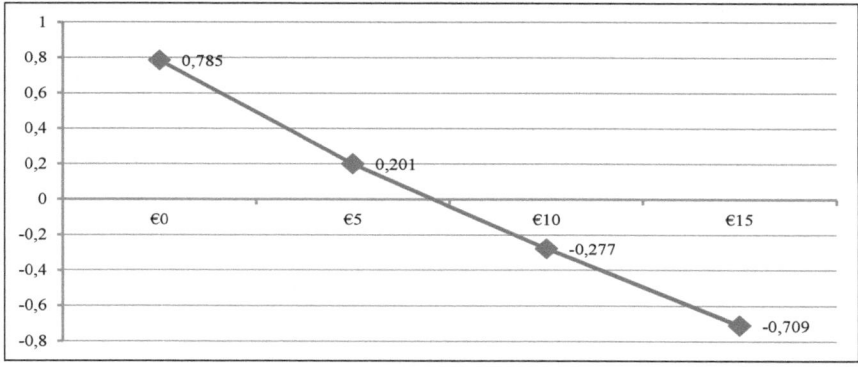

Figure 3: Part-Worth Utilities for Additional Contribution Levels

Hierarchical Bayes Estimation

To calculate importance scores, I applied a Hierarchical Bayes model, which is often used in marketing research to provide estimates of quasi individual-level parameters (ROSSI and ALLENBY, 2003). I used the concept of 'spread' to calculate the respective importance scores (cf. ORME, 2006). Table 4 shows the resulting means for each attribute's importance in contrast to the results of KICK and LITTICH (2011).

Attribute	KICK and LITTICH (2011)		Current Paper			
	Mean importance (%)	SD	Mean importance (%)	SD	Δ Importance in percentage points	t - ratio
Voluntary Coverage	35.89	9.21	28.26	7.80	-7.63***	-9.995
Elective Tariff	19.55	8.54	13.10	5.93	-6.45***	-9.809
SHI Brand	14.95	8.76	11.02	7.67	-3.93***	-5.337
Bonus Program	13.78	7.53	7.42	4.32	-6.36***	-11.584
Complementary Insurance	8.62	5.66	7.11	5.54	-1.51***	-3.015
Service Package	7.20	5.00	4.63	4.10	-2.57***	-6.284
Additional Contributions	------	------	28.46	14.83	------	------

Table 4: Importance Scores

As proposed within Hypothesis H_{2b}, additional contributions as the new pricing signal show the highest importance score of 28.46%. But voluntary coverage options follow closely and are almost on eye level (i.e., 28.26%). Testing both values for significant differences confirms that the evidence at hand is much too weak to speak of a dominating price criterion on the current market[11]. Therefore, Hypothesis H_{2b} has to be rejected and it can be concluded that the new price signal is not the single most important attribute within consumers' SHI choice.

However, additional contributions take over a meaningful role in SHI choice decisions. Looking at Table 4 reveals that the importance score for additional contribution with about 30% stems from all the other attributes of the CBCA. Following Hypotheses H_{1f-j}, it can be concluded that all benefit and service differentiation attributes (i.e., elective tariffs, voluntary coverage, bonus programs, service package, and complementary insurances) loose importance due to the introduction of additional contributions. Hypotheses H_{1f-j} are supported.

---

[11] T-ratio = -.189, p-value: 0.850, n. sig.

In addition, the quality signal brand name also loses importance (-3.93 percentage points). This confirms the expectations made in Hypothesis H_{3b}. However, a funds brand name still ranks as the forth most important attribute of SHI choice decision with explaining more than 11% of consumers' choices. The quality signal brand name is not eliminated by the new price signal. It rather stays fairly important and is still superior to service packages, complementary insurances, and bonus programs. Taken together, price and brand name are responsible for almost 40% of a SHI choice decision, which emphasizes the high importance of signaling mechanisms on the complex market for SHI. To fully investigate and confirm the hypotheses on SHI brand and corporate reputation (i.e., H_{3a} and H_{3b}), pseudo individual Hierarchical Bayes PWUs of the different brand names have to be in line with the respective reputational assessments to also prove the influence of corporate reputation within the choice decisions at hand. For this reason I correlated the reputational assessments (aggregated over all brands) with the brand name PWUs. The significant correlation of $r = .231$, $p < 0.001$ confirms that brand name and corporate reputation are closely related[12]. Conclusively, Hypotheses H_{3a} and H_{3b} can be confirmed.

Similar to the findings of KICK and LITTICH (2011), I found that a SHI brand name is more important for older participants. Age and the importance score of the brand name show a significant correlation ($r = .197$, $p < 0.01$). Further, brand is more important for the less educated share of respondents (mean$_{high}$ = 10.40%, mean$_{low}$ = 13.95%; $p < .01$). Analyzing the importance scores split by each respondent's actual SHI membership revealed no significant differences. Attribute importance, thus, is independent from SHI membership in the sample at hand (cf. Table 12 in the appendix).

3.3 Pricing and Product Design

By using the additive preference function underlying the choice-based conjoint approach, important deliberations for the design and adjustment of bundles and offers can be derived. The compensatory preference model for the total utility calculation states that a "low" score (i.e., PWU) on a certain attribute or level can be compensated by a "high" score on another (HAAIJER and WEDEL, 2007). Hence, there are promising trade-off situations that help product managers to adjust their product portfolio without harming the overall perceived utility for consumers.

---

[12] The PWUs of brand names are also significantly correlated ($p < 0.001$) with the single dimensions of competence ($r = .156$) and likeability ($r = .224$).

Referencing the PWU values of Table 3, the ideal health insurance plan is offered by TK (+.145), with a contribution refund tariff (+.338), a bonus program with monetary rewards (+.146), complementary insurance offers (+.200), travel vaccinations and tooth cleaning as voluntary coverage options (+.701), an extended service package (+.115), and no additional contributions (+.785). The linear relationship of additional contribution's PWUs (cf. Figure 3) enables to transfer the underlying PWU onto other, non-monetary attributes and levels[13]. The spread of PWUs (i.e., +.785 to -.709 = 1.494) equals a total amount of €15 per month and head. Hence, each Euro of additional contribution equals a PWU value of 0.0996. Table 5 shows the respective monetary equivalents for all levels of the CBCA. Of course, calculated monetary equivalents are only valid for the sample at hand under the assumption that the actual choice decision is only influenced by the presented attributes and levels. Just by their brand name and the underlying corporate reputation, TK delivers additional value to insurants which is worth €1.46 of additional contribution. In other words, TK could charge €1.46 from each paying insurant (again, excluding co-insured members like children or homemakers) without falling behind their competitors. As the general contribution rate of 15.5% of each insurant's gross income has to be paid by each insurant independently of their respective SHI fund, the €1.46 have to be interpreted only within the additional contribution attribute. As the range of already collected additional contributions between 2010 and 2012 was between €0 and €16 per month and head, TK is able to charge close to 10% of the additional contribution range simply due to their reputational advantage without competitive disadvantage. Taking into account that TK has about 6.2 million paying insurants, the additional contribution equivalent would imply roughly nine million Euros of potential revenues per month. However, the economic activities of SHI funds in Germany have to be nonprofit. Funds cannot realize those revenues immediately. It rather has to be kept in mind that in case an introduction of additional contributions becomes necessary, a high corporate reputation acts as a safety net. Hence, a comparably high corporate reputation proves to enhance a fund's bargaining position towards its potential customers, as it allows realizing and charging price premiums (FOMBRUN, 1996). Further, insurants' perceived utility of a SHI package would also stay constant, if a fund would voluntarily cover travel vaccination together with professional tooth cleaning but charges €7 additional contribution.

Table 5 also provides results from the market share calculator. Results, again, only hold within my sample and under the assumption that the SHI choice decision is only influenced by the

---

[13]   Please consider the limitations made in chapter 3.2 regarding the positive PWU of the €5 level.

presented attributes and levels. Moreover, the provided market shares only refer to within attribute variance, meaning all other attributes are kept constant. For example, if all funds would offer identical benefit and coverage levels, the brand name as the only difference would transfer in a market share for TK of 29.03% compared to 23.52% of the AOK sickness fund. It can, thus, outperform the hypothetical 25% if all brand names would be perceived equally. Further, if the only differentiation criterion on the market would be voluntary coverage and each option is equally offered, a fund that decides to offer not only travel vaccinations but also the additional tooth cleaning could enhance its market share by 26.11% - 12.60% = 13.51 percentage points. It could exceed the hypothetical value of 14.28% if all voluntary coverage options would be perceived equally (i.e. 100% divided by seven levels of the attribute voluntary coverage options).

Attribute	Level	Monetary equivalents	Market Share Calculation
SHI Brand	AOK	- € 0.56	23.52%
	Barmer GEK	- € 0.32	23.87%
	DAK	- € 0.56	23.57%
	TK	+ € 1.46	29.03%
Elective Tariff	Not offered	- € 1.60	20.66%
	Deductible	- € 2.25	19.58%
	Contribution refund	+ € 3.39	33.99%
	Cost reimbursement	+ € 0.54	25.77%
Bonus Program	Not offered	- € 1.60	28.42%
	Non-monetary rewards	+ € 0.13	33.53%
	Monetary rewards	+ € 1.46	38.05%
Complementary Insurance	Yes	+ € 2.01	59.99%
	No	- € 2.01	40.01%
Voluntary Coverage	Not offered	- € 6.68	6.60%
	Travel vaccinations (1)	- € 0.32	12.60%
	Professional tooth cleaning (2)	- € 0.82	11.76%
	Constitutional course (3)	- € 5.71	7.27%
	(1) and (2)	+ € 7.03	26.11%
	(1) and (3)	+ € 3.33	17.88%
	(2) and (3)	+ € 3.15	17.78%
Service Package	Standard services	- € 1.15	44.19%
	Extended services	+ € 1.15	55.81%

Table 5: Monetary Equivalents and Market Shares

The hypothetical take rates have to be treated with caution as they are highly restricted to the sample characteristics and only valid within the set of attributes and levels included into the CBCA. However, as my sample consists of mainly younger people and students that still face their first independent SHI choice decision when graduating, it is able to give important advice for the future developments of the SHI landscape. TK has the possibility to exploit their strategic advantage. A market situation where TK also offers favorable voluntary coverage options (with all other attributes equal across funds) than the remaining three competitors could result in a market share for TK of about 50%. The remaining three funds AOK, Barmer GEK, and DAK would share the rest almost equally. The remaining funds have to develop and manage their corporate reputation as well as they have to offer attractive bundles within important attributes to counteract the strategic advantage that TK has already gained on today's market.

4   Study II: Consumer Choice and Market Complexity

Taking one step back and looking at the overall results, one could argue that the generated outcomes of the conjoint analysis do not hold in reality. Health care, indeed, "[…] is a complex decision encompassing a plethora of attributes" (CHAKRABORTY et al., 1994, p. 23). The CBCA approach in the paper at hand had to make major decisions of how to reduce complexity of the SHI decision reality to be able to use conjoint analytical techniques to generate valid choice data. As the brand name and corporate reputation of funds were also included, it could be argued that, in reality, when choice decisions are much more complex, the importance of signaling mechanisms like brand name or corporate reputation even increases. The actual affect of quality signals on the market would, therefore, be underestimated. However, it might be the other way round. Having left out or simply missed important drivers of SHI choice from a consumer perspective might bias the results. If people are aware of certain advantages, benefit details or coverage options of a single SHI fund that were simply not presented within the choice tasks of the CBCA, participants would directly project this effect onto a fund's brand name. Due to omitted attributes or levels, the brand name and corporate reputation effect might be overestimated and biased. Even though research confirms that insurants are highly uniformed about SHI offers (cf. e.g., HAENECKE, 2001, TSCHEULIN and DIETRICH, 2010) and have problems to deal with the high market complexity (cf. e.g., DEVLIN, 2007), study II wants to rule out the bias of omitted attributes and levels and validate the generated results. It wants to verify, if insurants are aware of service attributes and levels that have not been included into the CBCA and if insurants are aware of the actual performance spectrum across different SHI funds. In addition, the decision why insurants chose a certain fund is investigated in more detail.

4.1   Design

The questionnaire consists of two parts. After a screener question excluding those participants that were not insured in the statutory system, the first part deals with the choice decision for their current fund. I ask participants about their current SHI provider and to indicate the reasons why they chose their current SHI provider. Answers in the open text field where compressed by content analysis and will be presented in the upcoming results chapter. The unaided question is followed up by a closed question for the main reason why they picked the fund. Respondents could choose from seven preselected answering options. The second part of the survey contains questions regarding the benefit and coverage portfolio of the four SHI funds from the CBCA (i.e., DAK, TK, AOK, and Barmer GEK). Especially participants' perceptions regarding the benefit and service landscape of different SHI funds were of main interest. To identify the status quo of benefit and service portfolios of the four SHI funds, I conducted extensive desk research on the website of the funds and screened reports of professional and independent quality tests about the coverage rates of different SHI providers (i.e., HINTERBERGER, 2012, SCHERFF, 2012, GESELLENSETTER, 2010). Test reports mostly examine the offers of different sickness funds and assign percentage rates to quantify the service offers in the respective category. For example, to assess the performance category "*Naturopathic Treatments*", HINTERBERGER (2012) evaluates 18 different subdimensions[14] and assigns one credit if the special treatment is covered. He reports the overall percentage score for each fund in the respective category. In case of TK, 15 out of 18 subdimensions are reimbursed and, consequently, a score of 83.33% reported. For the performane category "*Overall Travelling Abroad Coverage*", the subdimensions travel vaccinations, travel insurance (two credits assigned if included, one credit if additional premium necessary), 24/7 emergency call abroad, and extended coverage abroad are used. A maximum of five credits can be achieved in this category. TK scored 4 out of 5 and, thus, 80% are reported. GESELLENSETTER (2010) uses the same system to assess SHI funds with minor differences in the evaluated subdimensions. SCHERFF (2012) does not report detailed information on the subdimensions but rates SHI funds in the same way. The assesment criteria for the performance category "*Skin-Cancer Prevention*" included subdimensions like the

---

[14]   i.e. alternative cancer treatments, anthroposophical medicine, respiratory therapy, Ayurveda, chelation therapy, autohemotherapy, urinary therapy, electrotherapeutics, heliotherapy, homeopathic treatments, hydrotherapy, iridodiagnostics, cryotherapy, osteopathy, phototherapy, phytotherapy, reflexology, and shiatsu.

number of check-ups paid per year, the threshold of age after which skin-cancer screenings are reimbursed, or the range of different alternative treatments an insurant can choose from

I selected performance categories for the questionnaire regarding three deliberations: first, they had to be assessed by all three quality tests. Second, the websites of the SHI funds had to provide clear information about the details of the respective category. And third, I purposely included performance categories so that each depicts a different fund (or group of funds) as the best in class of the respective category. Table 6 presents the scores of each test report and the mean values across all three test reviews for the selected performance categories.

Test Report	Performance category	AOK	Barmer GEK	DAK	TK
Hinterberger (2012)	Skin-Cancer Preventions	68.58%	74.55%	74.17%	75.98%
	Naturopathic Treatments	61.11%	83.33%	83.33%	83.33%
	Overall Vaccinations	100.00%	100.00%	100.00%	100.00%
	Overall Travelling Abroad Coverage	80.00%	80.00%	80.00%	80.00%
Gsellenstetter (2010)	Skin-Cancer Preventions	75.00%	100.00%	75.00%	100.00%
	Naturopathic Treatments	46.15%	84.62%	84.62%	84.62%
	Overall Vaccinations	100.00%	100.00%	100.00%	100.00%
	Overall Travelling Abroad Coverage	100.00%	100.00%	100.00%	100.00%
Scherff (2012)	Skin-Cancer Preventions	30.00%	82.00%	78.00%	92.00%
	Naturopathic Treatments	70.00%	87.00%	87.00%	87.00%
	Overall Vaccinations	74.00%	82.00%	100.00%	90.00%
	Overall Travelling Abroad Coverage	34.00%	34.00%	34.00%	34.00%
Σ **Mean Values**	Skin-Cancer Preventions	57.86%	85.52%	75.72%	89.33%[†]
	Naturopathic Treatments	59.09%	84.98%[†]	84.98%[†]	84.98%[†]
	Overall Vaccinations	91.33%	94.00%	100.00%[†]	96.67%
	Overall Travelling Abroad Coverage	71.33%[†]	71.33%[†]	71.33%[†]	71.33%[†]
Additional Category	Treatments by Natural Health Practitioners	No fund is legally allowed to reimburse any costs			

Note: %-value assessments of test reports represent the coverage rates of different SHI funds for selected performance categories. Superscript (†) in the last rows indicate the fund(s) with the best coverage in the respective category calculated as mean value across all three test reports.

Table 6: Desk Research Assessment of Benefit and Service Offers

One question was included into the survey for every performance category. Respondents were asked: "*How do you perceive the service offer of the following four SHI funds with regard to the [performance category]?*" on a seven-point scale from 1 = "very bad service offer" to 7 = "very good service offer". Further, to not only assess if respondents are aware of the benefit and service details of a specific fund but also the SHI system in general, I decided to also include the performance category *"Treatments by natural health practitioners"*. Within their social security statues (i.e., *Sozialgesetzbuch - SGB*), the German government strictly regulates that natural health practitioners do not belong to the group of healthcare professionals that are eligible to cooperate with the SHI system (cf. § 124(4), SGB). The survey concluded with questions regarding respondents' health status, their satisfaction with their SHI fund, and one question regarding their age and their gender.

In sum, 266 participants answered the questionnaire that was fielded in October 2012. 32.7% were male and 67.3% female. The average age was at 28.86 years. 30.1% are members of TK, 19.2% of AOK, 16.9 of Barmer GEK, and 6% of DAK. People have mostly been insured at the respective fund for more than three years (83.8% of the sample). On average, they are, again, rather satisfied with their SHI fund (M = 5.42, seven-point Likert scale). Consequently, only 6.8% plan to change SHI provider in the upcoming year.

4.2   Results

Reasons for choosing a sickness fund

In an open text field, respondents indicated their main reasons for picking a certain SHI fund. Content analysis resulted in 433 evaluable statements (multiple answers/statements possible). About 35% of the statements referred to the fact that insurants have "always been at a SHI fund", meaning that they mostly have been insured within a family insurance plan and after opting out simply did not change the provider. Price/value perception and certain benefits and services are mentioned by only 13% of respondents. The remaining answers split up across the categories of good service (6%), local branch (3.5%), word-of-mouth (8%), and a historically low price premium before 2009 (12%). Ten respondents (2%) explicitly state that changing the SHI provider is too effortful to conduct. The remaining 20.5% of the statements could not be assessed to any category and were labeled with "others". When presented with the aided question[15] what they perceive as the main driver of their choice, over 60% of the 266 respondents indicated that the family insurance contract and recommendations of family members play the most important role. About 11% indicate a word-of-mouth effect from others

---

[15] Answering options were: Family insurance contract and family recommendation, word-of-mouth of others, special benefits/coverage, recommendation by employer, local subsidiary, personally addressed by fund sales/marketing unit, and others.

and only 6% mention performance attributes like benefits or coverage rates. Of those 6% only half could name the specific service or benefit detail like vaccinations, naturopathic treatments, or health courses.

Evaluation of Funds' Performance Categories

The assessment of the performance categories across SHI funds revealed that the reputation leader TK is consistently perceived as having the best benefit and coverage portfolio among the presented brands. This effect could also be confirmed for performance categories in which TK is clearly not ahead (i.e., naturopathic treatments, overall vaccinations, and overall travelling abroad coverage – cf. also Table 6). Results further indicate that the remaining funds AOK, Barmer GEK, and DAK do not significantly differ from each other. In the category *treatments by natural health practitioners* I would have expected to not see any significant advantage for the Technical Health Insurance fund as the SHI laws clearly prohibit a cost transfer for alternative medicine practitioners for all funds. Even though scores for the perceived performance regarding natural health practitioners apparently drop compared to the other categories, TK is, again, clearly ahead. Mean scores between $M_{AOK} = 3.03$ and $M_{TK} = 3.73$ show that insurants are, nevertheless, not fully aware of the statutory regulations in the background. AOK is consistently perceived as the fund offering the fewest benefits and services of all funds regarding the presented categories. Table 7 provides an overview of the respective results.

Performance category (n = 266)	AOK	Barmer GEK	DAK	TK
Skin-Cancer Preventions	4.18[a]	4.30[a]	4.30[a]	4.62[b]
Naturopathic Treatments	3.11[a]	3.26[a]	3.29[a]	3.79[b]
Overall Vaccinations	4.84[a]	4.89[a]	4.84[a]	5.30[b]
Overall Travelling Abroad Coverage	4.15[a]	4.23[a]	4.26[a]	4.67[b]
Treatments by Natural Health Practitioners	3.03[a]	3.18[a]	3.25[a]	3.73[b]
All Categories Together (n = 1,330)	3.86[a]	3.97[a]	3.99[a]	4.42[b]

Note: Mean perceived performance. Superscripts in a given row indicate that there are significant differences at the level of $p < .01$.

Table 7: Assessment of Benefit and Service Offers

As mentioned above, the sample at hand consists of 30% TK, 19.2% of AOK, 16.9% of Barmer GEK, and 6% of DAK members. To check the robustness of the generated results, I recalculated the analyses of Table 7 by excluding each single membership group. I treated all performance categories equally and, again, conducted subsequent analyses of variance with additional post-hoc tests. The results are displayed in Table 8.

All performance categories	AOK	Barmer GEK	DAK	TK
Without AOK Insurants (n = 1,075)	3.85[a]	4.00[b]	4.01[b]	4.49[c]
Without Barmer GEK Insurants (n = 1,105)	3.85[a]	3.96[a]	3.99[a]	4.43[b]
Without DAK Insurants (n = 1,250)	3.87[a]	3.98[a]	4.00[a]	4.45[b]
Without TK Insurants (n = 930)	3.81[a]	3.88[a]	3.89[a]	4.18[b]
Only Insurants from other SHI Funds (n = 370)	3.72[a]	3.84[a]	3.86[a]	4.14[b]
Only Insurants from Funds Included (n = 960)	3.92[a]	4.02[a]	4.03[a]	4.53[b]

Note: Mean perceived performance across all performance categories. Superscripts in a given row indicate that there are significant differences at the level of p < .01.

Table 8: Assessment of Benefit and Service Offers Controlled for Membership

Excluding members of a specific SHI fund reveals no difference in the results compared to the overall sample. Leaving out insurants of TK, as the biggest subgroup in the sample at hand, shows that the non-TK respondents still perceive the Technical Health Insurance fund to be the performance-leader across all categories ($M_{TK} = 4.18$). Further, the external performance image of AOK is significantly worse compared to the other sickness funds. When AOK customers were excluded, evaluations of the AOK revealed that it shows a significantly lower performance perception among respondents and, thus, significantly deviates from Barmer GEK and DAK. Looking at the evaluations of SHI members from none of the included funds confirms that TK is seen as the SHI fund with the highest performance overall.

The results of study II argue in line with the results of reputational assessments and PWU estimations. People indeed show a high lack of knowledge about SHI offerings and benefit and service details. The SHI system with its complex set of laws and regulations leads insurants to use quality signals like corporate reputation, brand names, and price differences to diminish offerings (cf. chapter 3.2). They rely more on perceptions than actual facts. Hence, quality signals play a major role on the current SHI market.

5   Discussion, Implications, and Limitations

By applying two empirical studies, the paper at hand delivers important insight on SHI choice decisions under the new situation of additional contributions. As KICK and LITTICH (2011) investigated SHI choice decisions under a situation of premium equality, this study uses the introduction of additional contributions and the resulting natural experimental constellation to examine how choices are influenced when a new pricing signal is introduced on the market. By means of a CBCA approach and additional investigations about insurants perceptions on the current market, I derive important insights for policy makers as well as for managers of SHI funds.

Additional contributions indeed alter the German SHI system. The new pricing signal takes over a significant role within people's choice decisions for or against a specific sickness fund. Benefit and service details loose importance within the SHI market. Even though the attribute SHI brand name also loses importance, it remains a noticeable driver of choice decisions with about 11%. As reputation took over one of the most important signaling functions on the premium equality market (KICK and LITTICH, 2011), I would have expected a higher drop in the importance score of the SHI brand attribute when price comes into play again (MARQUIS et al., 2007, NOORDEWIER et al., 1989). Even though price still is the most important quality proxy, it loses importance when another quality indicator like brand name and corporate reputation is present (RAO et al., 1999, ZEITHAML, 1988). Thus, the period of premium equality has slightly shifted consumers' perceptions over to other signals than pure pricing aspects. People might have started to put focus on brand names and voluntary coverage options when they were the most obvious differentiation attribute available in the abstinence of price. As experts predict the extensive introduction of additional contributions in the upcoming years (cf. PFISTER, 2009, EIBICH et al., 2011), it can be expected that the German SHI market will not exhibit the same price sensitivity like before 2009's premium equality (cf. SCHUT et al., 2003).

As intended by the GERMAN BUNDESTAG (2006), the present market has more shifted toward benefit and service details after the recent reforms. However, it has to be kept in mind that nearly one third of people's SHI choice decisions can still be traced back to a pure pricing effect. The tight regulations on the German SHI market, with about 98% of benefits and coverage details being mandatory, act like a safety net and increase insurants sensitivity to any kind of pricing signal. To further follow a policy of SHI competition based on quality rather than price, the German government should introduce more opportunities for funds to differentiate from each other. Opening up the range of voluntary coverage options seems to be appreciated by SHI customers as additional health care benefits free of charge show a high importance in SHI choice decisions (i.e., 28.26%).

From a consumer perspective, the SHI system turns out to be highly complex and confusing. People are not aware of different performance levels across funds and the underlying governmental regulations in the background. Within their choice decisions, they rely on their perceptions, which automatically strengthen the importance of superior quality signals. TK, as the fund with the highest corporate reputation, is perceived to be performance leader in all questioned categories even if the obvious statues clearly show the opposite. Further, this study confirms that strong brand names as well as a favorable corporate reputation allow charging price premiums from insurants. The brand name of TK (*Technical Health Insurance Fund*) provides additional value for insurants and is able to compensate the drawbacks from charging additional contributions up to about €1.50 per month and head. Funds should emphasize corporate reputation in their corporate communication to be able to successfully exploit reputational advantages. However, without opportunities to significantly differentiate from each other through benefits and coverage details, it will be a difficult goal for funds to achieve. For SHI brand managers it is a key factor to focus on the most important differentiators. That means they should put weight on the communication of low/no additional contributions and key voluntary coverage options (i.e., travel vaccinations and professional tooth cleaning) before designing campaigns based on customer service aspects or bonus programs. A campaign of simplifying the complexity also seems promising. In other words, there is evidence in this study that a marketing campaign which communicates certain selected benefits and coverage options in an easy to understand and non-confusing way is worth considering. Reducing complexity in consumers' heads to enable customers to differentiate has to be on the agenda of SHI fund's marketing managers.

To grasp all facets of the SHI market within a CBCA is truly challenging. To keep the choice set reliable, I had to carefully select a subset of attributes (i.e., the most important) for the creation of the stimuli. Study II confirms, the CBCA approach at hand does not suffer under an omitted attribute or level bias. People are not aware of benefit and service differences among funds. The choice screens in the CBCA provided detailed information about the attributes and levels included. Thus, the choice situation in the CBCA can be seen as an aided choice decision, where complexity was reduced because a) only a subset of relevant attributes and levels was presented and b) necessary information was given on the respective screen via hyperlinks. However, choice decisions in reality are not supported in the same way. People have to collect information themselves, face a confusingly large number of attributes and levels that result in a choice situation which is much more complex than in the study at hand. For this reason, I argue that signaling mechanisms like corporate reputation, a SHI fund's brand name, and additional contributions are underestimated in the study at hand. Reducing the inherent complexity through quality indicators will gain importance in a real-life setting.

Even though this study was conducted thoroughly, some limitations have to be mentioned and addressed. First, I only included the four major SHI brands into the approach at hand. Future research should take this study's approach as starting point and investigate the interplay of well known SHI funds and smaller SHI insurances to find out if the effects are generalizable across funds of different size. Second, the generated insights on pricing and product design for marketing managers have to be treated with caution as they suffer from a strong sample bias. The calculated monetary equivalents as well as the market shares can only be taken as an indication of an estimated movement. Market shares and price equivalents are calculated out of choice data from the sample at hand and cannot be transferred onto actual market scenarios. Third, Study II revealed that people do not choose their SHI provider like products on other, non-regulated markets. Over 60% of respondents indicated that they stick to the fund that their family has always been insured with or that the preferences of their families actually play a dominating role. In combination with the high lock-in power of a SHI insurance contract mentioned by ten respondents in Study II, choices pro or against a certain fund might be, at least partly, independent from SHI funds' offerings. Insurants do not have to worry about the basic coverage defined by law of about 98% of benefits. The remaining 2% might simply be too little to differentiate. Future studies could pick up this thought and investigate the question how to properly create the need for a new SHI provider and trigger changing intentions. Forth, the paper at hand confirms that corporate reputation indeed matters. But how to positively influence a fund's corporate reputation can only vaguely be answered. Only the performance dimension of a fund's offerings was analyzed in detail. Further research should take my results as a starting point and develop a comprehensive driver model to identify resources of corporate reputation development on the regulated market of SHI.

Appendix

Variable	Level	n	%
Sex	Male	103	41.20
	Female	147	58.80
Age	<20	0	0.00
Mean: 31.86	20-24	94	37.60
Std. dev.: 12.33	25-29	67	26.80
	30-34	21	8.40
Min: 20.00	35-39	8	3.20
Max: 67.00	40-44	11	4.40
	45-49	13	5.20
	50-54	13	5.20
	55-59	12	4.80
	60-64	9	3.60
	≥65	2	.80
Family Status	Single	81	32.40
	In a relationship/married	159	63.60
	Divorced/separated/widowed	10	4.00
Education	No formal education	1	.40
	Basic secondary school	9	3.60
	Middle school	34	13.60
	High school diploma	119	47.60
	College/university	79	31.60
	Post graduate degree	8	3.20
Employment	School student	1	.40
Status	Trainee	4	1.60
	Blue-collar worker	5	2.00
	Employee	83	33.20
	Public offer	7	2.80
	Entrepreneur	15	6.00
	Student (undergraduate)	116	46.40
	Retiree	4	1.60
	Job seeker	1	.40
	Homemaker	8	3.20
	Others	6	2.40
Monthly net	< €1,000	67	26.80
Household	€1,001 - €1,500	27	10.80
Income (after	€1,501 - €2,000	35	14.00
taxes and	€2,001 - €2,500	25	10.00
social insurance)	€2,501 - €3,000	18	7.20
	€3,001 - €3,500	8	3.20
	€3,501 - €4,000	6	2.40
	€4,001 - €4,500	7	2.80
	€4,501 - €5,000	10	4.00
	> €5,000	18	7.20
	Not Specified	29	11.60
Current SHI	AOK	55	22.00
Provider	BARMER GEK	29	11.60
	DAK	21	8.40
	TK	66	26.40
	Others	79	31.60

Table 9: Selected Demographic Data (n = 250)

Attribute		Within attribute χ^2	Df	Significance
SHI Brand (n = 250)		7.53	3	p < .10
AOK	.24			
Barmer GEK	.24			
DAK	.24			
TK	.28			
Elective Tariff (n = 250)		58.21	3	p < .01
Deductible tariff	.20			
Contribution refund tariff	.32			
Cost reimbursement tariff	.26			
Not offered	.22			
Bonus Program (n = 250)		18.60	2	p < .01
Non-monetary rewards	.25			
Monetary rewards	.28			
Not offered	.22			
Complementary Insurance (n = 250)		46.09	1	p < .01
Yes	.29			
No	.21			
Voluntary Coverage (n = 250)		204.74	6	p < .01
Travel vaccinations (1)	.23			
Professional tooth cleaning (2)	.23			
Constitutional course (3)	.15			
(1) and (2)	.40			
(1) and (3)	.30			
(2) and (3)	.31			
Not offered	.14			
Service Package (n = 250)		15.75	1	p < .01
Standard services	.23			
Extended services	.27			
Additional Contributions (n = 250)		437.60	3	p < .01
€0 / month	.45			
€5 / month	.27			
€10 / month	.17			
€15 / month	.12			

Table 10: Count Analysis

Attr./lev.	Level	Frequency	Actual	Ideal	Efficiency
1 1	AOK	1750			
1 2	Barmer GEK	1750	0.034	0.034	1.000
1 3	DAK	1750	0.034	0.034	1.000
1 4	TK	1750	0.034	0.034	1.000
2 1	Deductible tariff	1750			
2 2	Contribution refund tariff	1750	0.034	0.034	1.000
2 3	Cost reimbursement tariff	1750	0.034	0.034	1.000
2 4	Not offered	1750	0.034	0.034	1.000
3 1	Non-monetary rewards	2333			
3 2	Monetary rewards	2333	0.030	0.030	1.000
3 3	Not offered	2334	0.030	0.030	1.000
4 1	Yes	3500			
4 2	No	3500	0.024	0.024	1.000
5 1	Standard services	3500			
5 2	Extended services	3500	0.024	0.024	1.000
6 1	Travel vaccinations	1000			
6 2	Professional tooth cleaning	1000	0.048	0.048	0.999
6 3	Constitutional course	1000	0.048	0.048	0.997
6 4	Travel vaccinations & prof. tooth cleaning	1000	0.048	0.048	1.001
6 5	Travel vaccinations & constitutional course	1000	0.048	0.048	0.998
6 6	Prof. tooth cleaning & constitutional course	1000	0.048	0.048	0.999
6 7	Not offered	1000	0.048	0.048	1.002
7 1	€0 / month	1750			
7 2	€5 / month	1750	0.034	0.034	0.999
7 3	€10 / month	1750	0.034	0.034	0.999
7 4	€15 / month	1750	0.034	0.034	0.999

Note: 'Complete Enumeration task' generation method, based on 250 versions, includes 1,750 total choice tasks
(7 per version). Each choice task includes four alternatives with six attributes each.

Table 11: Efficiency Scores

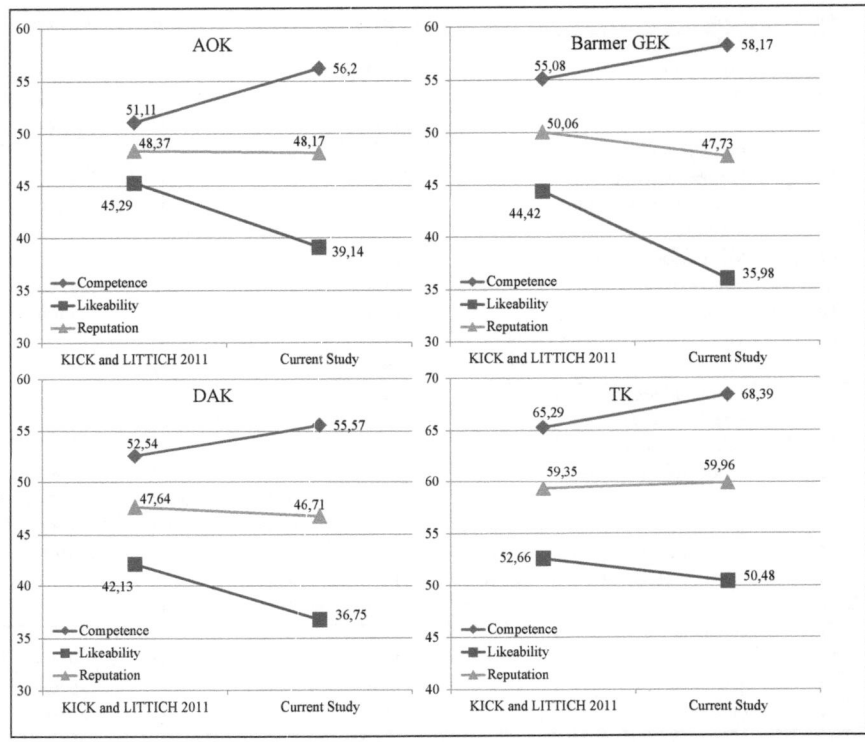

Figure 4: Development of Reputational Assessments over Time

Means	AOK	Barmer GEK	DAK	TK	Others
SHI Brand	10.28[a]	10.52[a]	10.40[a]	12.89[a]	10.33[a]
Elective Tariff	13.64[a]	11.34[a]	13.54[a]	13.23[a]	13.15[a]
Bonus Program	8.19[a]	7.32[a]	8.61[a]	7.24[a]	6.75[a]
Complementary Insurance	7.00[a]	6.38[a]	7.83[a]	6.94[a]	7.40[a]
Service Package	5.01[a]	3.92[a]	5.14[a]	4.88[a]	4.29[a]
Voluntary Coverage	28.62[a]	28.75[a]	27.45[a]	28.09[a]	28.17[a]
Additional Contributions	27.26[a]	31.76[a]	27.02[a]	26.72[a]	29.91[a]

Note: *Mean attribute importance. Superscripts in a given row indicate that there are no significant differences at the level of p < .10*

Table 12: Attribute Importance per SHI Membership Group

References

AOK BUNDESVERBAND. 2012. *Marktanteile der Krankenkassen* [Online]. Available: http://www.aok-bv.de/zahlen/aok/index.html [Accessed 2012-09-29].

BARMER GEK. 2012. *Kerndaten der Barmer GEK* [Online]. Available: https://www.barmer-gek.de/barmer/web/Portale/Presseportal/Subportal/Infothek/Daten-und-Fakten/Kernda ten-der-BARMER-GEK/Daten-und-Fakten.html?w-cm=CenterColumn_t358706 [Accessed 2012-09-29].

BETTMANN, J. R., LUCE, M. F. & PAYNE, J. W. 1998. Constructive Consumer Choice Processes. *Journal of Consumer Research*, 25(3), 187-217.

BODE, I. 2003. Multireferenzialität und Marktorientierung? Krankenkassen als hybride Organisationen im Wandel. *Zeitschrift für Soziologie*, 32(5), 435-453.

BRAU, R. & LIPPI BRUNI, M. 2008. Eliciting the Demand for Long-Term Care Coverage: A Discrete Choice Modelling Analysis. *Health Economics*, 17(3), 411-433.

BROWN, L. D. & AMELUNG, V. E. 1999. 'Manacled Competition': Market Reforms in German Health Care - Is Managed Competition Really a New Paradigm or Simply a Stalemated Strategy? Recent German Experience Helps to Answer this Question. *Health Affairs*, 18(3), 76-91.

BUCHNER, F. & WASEM, J. 2009. *Die Einführung des Gesundheitsfonds im deutschen Gesundheitssystem: Mehr freier Wettbewerb oder mehr zentrale Regulierung?* [Online]. Available: http://www.hauptverband.at/mediaDB/623146_Buchner-Wasem_ Gesundheitsfonds.pdf [Accessed 10-25].

CHAKRABORTY, G., ETTENSON, R. & GAETH, G. 1994. How Consumers Choose Health Insurance. *Journal of Health Care Marketing*, 14(1), 21-33.

CHERNEV, A. 2003. When More Is Less and Less Is More: The Role of Ideal Point Availability and Assortment in Consumer Choice. *Journal of Consumer Research*, 30(2), 170-183.

D'SOUZA, G. & RAO, R. C. 1995. Can Repeating an Advertisement More Frequently Than the Competition Affect Brand Preference in a Mature Market? *Journal of Marketing*, 59(2), 32-42.

DAK GESUNDHEIT. 2012. *Zahlen und Fakten* [Online]. Available: http://www.presse.dak.de/ ps.nsf/0ccdf85185bb3992c12568c0006f1e0f/bc8097b296a1e62cc12575dd0029e019? OpenDocument [Accessed 2012-09-29].

DARBY, M. & KARNI E. 1973. Free Competition and the Optimal Amount of Fraud. *Journal of Law and Economics*, 16(1), 67-88.

DEVLIN, J. F. 2007. Complex Services and Choice Criteria: An Example from the Life Insurance Market. *Journal of Marketing Management*, 23(7-8), 631-650.

EIBICH, P., SCHMITZ, H. & ZIEBARTH, N. R. 2011. Zusatzbeiträge erhöhen die Preistransparenz: mehr Versicherte wechseln die Krankenkasse. *Wochenbericht*, 78(51/52), 3-12.

EMONS, W. 1997. Credence Goods and Fraudelent Experts. *RAND Journal of Economics*, 28(1), 107-119.

ERDEM, T. & SWAIT, J. 1998. Brand Equity as a Signaling Phenomenon. *Journal of Consumer Psychology*, 7(2), 131-157.

ETZIONI, A. 2011. Behavioural Economics: Next Steps. *Journal of Consumer Policy*, 34(3), 277-287.

EURO-INFORMATIONEN GBR. n.d. *Krankenkassen mit Zusatzbeitrag* [Online]. Available: http://www.der-zusatzbeitrag.de/krankenkassen/krankenkasse-mit-zusatzbeitrag.html [Accessed 2011-09-29].

FOMBRUN, C. J. 1996. *Reputation: Realizing Value from the Corporate Image*, Boston: Harvard Business School Press.

FOMBRUN, C. J. & VAN RIEL, C. 1997. The Reputational Landscape. *Corporate Reputation Review*, 1(1;2), 5-13.

GATES, R., MCDANIEL, C. & BRAUNSBERGER, K. 2000. Modeling Consumer Health Plan Choice Behavior to Improve Customer Value and Health Plan Market Share. *Journal of Business Research*, 48(3), 247-257.

GERLINGER, T., MOSEBACH, K. & SCHMUCKER, R. 2007. Wettbewerbssteuerung in der Gesundheitspolitik - Die Auswirkungen des GKV-WSG auf das Akteurshandeln im Gesundheitswesen. *Diskussionspapier am Institut für medizinische Soziologie in Frankfurt am Main*. Frankfurt am Main: Diskussionspapier 2007-1. Institut für medizinische Soziologie - Fachbereich Humanmedizin der Wolfgang Goethe-Universität in Frankfurt am Main.

GERMAN BUNDESTAG 2006. Entwurf eines Gesetzes zur Stärkung des Wettbewerbs in der gesetzlichen Krankenversicherung (GKV-Wettbewerbsstärkungsgesetz - GKV-WSG). *Drucksachen*, 16(3100).

GERMAN BUNDESTAG 2010. Entwurf eines Gesetzes zur nachhaltigen und sozial ausgewogenen Finanzierung der Gesetzlichen Krankenversicherung (GKV-Finanzierungsgesetz - GKV-FinG). *Drucksachen*, 17(3360).

GERMAN FEDERAL BUREAU OF STATISTICS. 2011. *GENESIS-Online Datenbank* [Online]. Wiesbaden: Statistisches Bundesamt Deutschland. Available: https://www-genesis.de statis.de/genesis/online [Accessed 2012-06-15].

GERMAN FEDERAL DEPARTMENT OF HEALTH. 2010. *Finanzierungsgrundlagen der gesetzlichen Krankenversicherung (GKV)* [Online]. Available: http://www.bmg.bund. de/krankenversicherung/finanzierung/finanzierungsgrundlagen-der-gkv.html [Accessed 2011-01-25].

GERMAN FEDERAL DEPARTMENT OF HEALTH. 2011. *Krankenversicherung* [Online]. Available: http://www.bmg.bund.de/krankenversicherung.html [Accessed 2011-08-01].

GESELLENSETTER, C. 2010. *Krankenversicherung - Der große Kassenvergleich* [Online]. Focus Money Online. Available: http://www.focus.de/finanzen/versicherungen/

krankenversicherung/krankenkassen/krankenkassen_aid_10579.html [Accessed 2012-09-29].

GKV-SPITZENVERBAND. 2012. *Grundprinzipien - Die gesetzliche Krankenversicherung* [Online]. Available: http://www.gkv-spitzenverband.de/krankenversicherung/kranken versicherung_grundprinzipien/ alle_gesetzlichen_krankenkassen/alle_gesetzlichen_kra nkenkassen.jsp [Accessed 2012-10-31].

GREß, S., GROENEWEGEN, P., KERSSENS, J., BRAUN, B. & WASEM, J. 2002. Free Choice of Sickness Funds in Regulated Competition: Evidence from Germany and The Netherlands. *Health Policy*, 60(3), 235-254.

HAAIJER, R. & WEDEL, M. 2007. Conjoint Choice Experiments: General Characteristics and Alternative Model Specifications. *In:* GUSTAFSSON, A., HERRMANN, A. & HUBER, F. (eds.) *Conjoint Measurement.* Berlin Heidelberg: Springer, 199-229.

HAENECKE, H. 2001. Motive der Versicherten bei der Kassenwahlentscheidung - Eine qualitative empirische Analyse. *Sozialer Fortschritt*, 2001(12), 297-303.

HINTERBERGER, M. 2012. Klasse Kasse - Die gesetzlichen Krankenkassen schwimmen im Geld. Was nicht immer zu besseren Leistungen führt. Die Anbieter im Euro-Leistungscheck. *Euro - finanzen.net*, 4(2012), 94-97.

HO, T. H., LIM, N. & CAMERER, C. F. 2006. Modeling the Psychology of Consumer and Firm Behavior with Behavioral Economics. *Journal of Marketing Research*, 43(3), 307-331.

HÖPPNER, K., GREß, S., ROTHGANG, H., WASEM, J., BRAUN, B. & BUITKAMP, M. 2005. Grenzen und Dysfunktionalitäten des Kassenwettbewerbs in der GKV: Theorie und Empirie der Risikoselektion in Deutschland. *In:* ZENTRUM FÜR SOZIALPOLITIK - UNIVERSITÄT BREMEN (ed.) *ZeS-Arbeitspapiere 4/2005.* Bremen.

JACOBY, J., SPELLER, D. E. & KOHN, C. A. 1974. Brand Choice Behavior as a Function of Information Load. *Journal of Marketing Research*, 11(1), 63-69.

KAHNEMANN, D. 2003. Maps of Bounded Rationality: Psychology for Behavioral Economics. *American Economic Review*, 93(2), 1449-1475.

KELLER, K. L. & LEHMANN, D. R. 2006. Brands and Branding: Research Findings and Future Priorities. *Marketing Science*, 25(6), 740-759.

KERSSENS, J. J. & GROENEWEGEN, P. P. 2005. Consumer Preferences in Social Health Insurance. *The European Journal of Health Economics*, 6(1), 8-15.

KICK, M. & LITTICH, M. 2011. The Effect of Corporate Reputation on Health Insurance Choices in a Public-Policy-Shaped Environment of Premium Equality *In:* LITTICH, M. (ed.) *Understanding the Impact of Communication on Firm Performance* München: Inaugural-Dissertation, Ludwig-Maximilians-Universität, 87-115.

KIRMANI, A. & RAO, A. R. 2000. No Pain, No Gain: A Critical Review of the Literature on Signaling Unobservable Product Quality. *Journal of Marketing*, 64(2), 66-79.

KOLSTAD, J. T. & CHERNEW, M. E. 2009. Quality and Consumer Decision Making in the Market for Health Insurance and Health Care Services. *Medical Care Research and Review,* 66(1 (suppl.)), 28-52.

KOTHA, S., RAJGOPAL, S. & RINDOVA, V. 2001. Reputation Building and Performance: An Empirical Analysis of the Top-50 Pure Internet Firms. *European Management Journal,* 19(6), 571-586.

KROEBER-RIEL, W. 1992. *Konsumentenverhalten,* München: Vahlen.

MARQUIS, M. S., BEEUWKES BUNTIN, M., ESCARCE, J. J. & KAPUR, K. 2007. The Role of Product Design in Consumers' Choices in the Individual Insurance Market. *Health Research and Educational Trust,* 42(6), 2194-2223.

MEFFERT, H. 2000. *Marketing - Grundlagen marktorientierter Unternehmensführung - Konzepte - Instrumente - Praxisbeispiele,* Wiesbaden.

NOORDEWIER, T. G., ROGERS, D. & BALAKRISHNAN, P. V. 1989. Evaluating Consumer Preference for Private Long-Term Care Insurance. *Journal of Health Care Marketing,* 9(4), 34-40.

ORME, B. 2006. *Getting Started with Conjoint Analysis: Strategies for Product Design and Pricing Research,* Madison.

PASSON, A., LÜNGEN, M., GERBER, A., REDAELLI, M. & STOCK, S. 2009. Das Krankenversicherungssystem in Deutschland. *In:* LAUTERBACH, K. W., STOCK, S. & BRUNNER, H. (eds.) *Gesundheitsökonomie - Lehrbuch für Mediziner und andere Gesundheitsberufe.* Second revised edition. Bern: Huber, 209-220.

PFISTER, F. 2009. Der Gesundheitsfonds: Eine Analyse. *Orientierungen zur Wirtschafts- und Gesellschaftspolitik,* 120(120), 39-44.

PIMPERTZ, J. 2007. Wettbewerb in der gesetzlichen Krankenversicherung - Gestaltungsoptionen unter sozialpolitischen Vorgaben. *In:* INSTITUT DER DEUTSCHEN WIRTSCHAFT (ed.) *IW-Positionen.* Köln: Deutscher Instituts Vlg.

RAO, A. R., QU, L. & RUEKERT, R. W. 1999. Signaling Unobservable Product Quality through a Brand Ally. *Journal of Marketing Research,* 36(2), 258-268.

REINHARDT, U. E. 1999. 'Mangled Competition' And 'Managed Whatever'. *Health Affairs,* 18(3), 92-94.

ROSSI, P. E. & ALLENBY, G. M. 2003. Bayesian Statistics and Marketing. *Marketing Science,* 22(3), 304-328.

SCHERFF, D. 2012. *Krankenkassen - Das sind die besten* [Online]. Frankfurter Allgemeine Zeitung. Available: http://www.faz.net/dynamic/download/krankenkassenvergleich-2012.pdf [Accessed 2012-09-29].

SCHULZE EHRING, F. & KÖSTER, A.-D. 2010. Beitrags- und Leistungsdifferenzierung in der GKV? *WIP-Diskussionspapier 03/10.*

SCHULZE EHRING, F. & WEBER, C. 2007. Wahltarife in der GKV - Nutzen oder Schaden für die Versichertengemeinschaft? *WIP-Diskussionspapier 04/07.*

SCHUT, F. T., GREß, S. & WASEM, J. 2003. Consumer Price Sensitivity and Social Health Insurer Choice in Germany and the Netherlands. *International Journal of Health Care Finance and Economics,* 3(2), 117-138.

SCHWAIGER, M. 2004. Components and Parameters of Corporate Reputation - An Empirical Study. *Schmalenbach Business Review,* 56(1), 46-71.

STENSRUD, J., SYLVESTRE, E. & SIVADAS, E. 1997. Targeting Medicare Consumers - Managed Care Providers Can Make Inroads by Understanding Preference and Cost-Sensitivity Issues. *Marketing Health Services,* 17(1), 8-17.

TECHNIKER KRANKENKASSE. 2012. *Die TK auf einen Blick* [Online]. Available: http://www. tk.de/tk/unternehmen-und-karriere/ueber-die-tk/die-tk-auf-einen-blick/8168 [Accessed 2012-09-29].

TECHNIKER KRANKENKASSE. 2014. *TK-Dividende* [Online]. Available: http://www.tk.de/tk/ aktionen/dividende/tk-dividende/480510 [Accessed 2014-04-26].

THALER, R. 1985. Mental Accounting and Consumer Choice. *Marketing Science,* 4(3), 199-214.

TIROLE, J. 1988. *The Theory of Industrial Organization,* Cambridge: MIT Press.

TROMMSDORFF, V. 2004. Konsumentenverhalten. 6th ed. Stuttgart: Kohlhammer.

TSCHEULIN, D. K. & DIETRICH, M. 2010. Das Management von Kundenbeziehungen im Gesundheitswesen. *In:* GEORGI, D. & HADWICH, K. (eds.) *Management von Kundenbeziehungen - Perspektiven - Analysen - Strategien - Instrumente.* First edition. Wiesbaden: Gabler, 251-276.

VAN DEN BERG, B., VAN DOMMELEN, P., STAM, P., LASKE-ALDERSHOF, T., BUCHMUELLER, T. & SCHUT, F. T. 2008. Preferences and Choices for Care and Health Insurance. *Social Science & Medicine,* 66(12), 2448-2459.

VARIAN, H. R. 2006. *Intermediate Microeconomics - A Modern Approach,* New York: Norton.

YOON, E., GUFFEY, H. J. & KIJEWSKI, V. 1993. The Effects of Information and Campany Reputation on Intentions to Buy a Bussiness Service. *Journal of Business Research,* 27(3), 215-228.

ZEITHAML, V. A. 1988. Consumer Perceptions of Price, Quality, and Value: A Means-End Model and Synthesis of Evidence. *Journal of Marketing,* 52(3), 2-22.

ZOK, K. 1999. Anforderungen an die gesetzliche Krankenversicherung. Einschätzungen und Erwartungen aus Sicht der Versicherten. *In:* WISSENSCHAFTLICHES INSTITUT DER AOK (ed.) *WIdO-Materialien Bd. 43.* Bonn.

ZOK, K. 2011. Reaktionen auf Zusatzbeiträge in der GKV - Ergebnisse einer representativen Umfrage. *WIdo-Monitor,* 1(2011), 1-8.

Markus Kick

III SOCIAL MEDIA EFFECTS ALONG THE VALUE CHAIN - A NARRATIVE REVIEW

Abstract

Even though the technological developments of web 2.0 and social media opened up a multitude of possibilities for companies to communicate with their customers, marketers, to a certain extent, lost direct control of their brands. Users are able to exchange opinions about companies, products, services, or brands independent of corporate influences at high speed and almost no cost. Marketing research has quickly picked up the new technological developments, generating enormous numbers of studies. However, the findings are highly diverse and confusing at the same time. This paper provides a systematic overview of top-tier social media research. A main emphasis is put on empirical studies that investigate the effects of user-generated content on measurable corporate performance indicators. A total of 102 articles are used as input for the conducted qualitative meta-analysis. Findings are sorted along the proposed framework of the *"social media value chain"*. The analysis encompasses effects of electronic word-of-mouth on corporate consumer mindset metrics, product and market performance indicators, and financial performance measures. The analysis extracts the inherent moderators of electronic word-of-mouth-effects and provides a suitable framework for discussion. In addition, the dual role of companies as moderators of ongoing social media communication and content creators within viral marketing campaigns is also dissected. Social media conversations are a powerful force that shows effect along the whole value chain. Pure volume measures show the strongest effect. Even though valence measures contain a high degree of information, inconsistent results can be observed depending on valence operationalization and empirical methods used. Research needs to develop a better and deeper understanding of valence measures. Further, experimental field studies provide a good starting point for future empirical work. The multitude of moderator effects reveals that the impact of electronic word-of-mouth is not generalizable across industries, product categories, and social media platforms. However, social media conversations contain rich information that has to be utilized by the marketing profession.

1 Motivation

Within the last 15 years, the term "Social Media" has undergone a significant change from a simple buzzword to a widely accepted marketing and communication tool (e.g., EYRICH et al., 2008, p. 412, WILSON et al., 2011, p. 25). Emerging from the technological evolutions of Web 2.0, it is now on top of the agenda of business executives (KAPLAN and HAENLEIN, 2010, p. 59). With about 1.5 billion users worldwide, social media forms an essential part of today's online environment and, therefore, plays a key role for marketing managers (CHUI et al., 2012, p. 1). An immeasurable number of social networks and websites like Facebook, YouTube, Twitter, and a vast amount of discussion forums and blogs have opened up tremendous new possibilities for marketers across all industries to immediately and directly engage with their customer base (JAHN and KUNZ, 2011, pp. 96-97). More and more, companies try to exploit these new opportunities and jump on the social media bandwagon. The opportunities for businesses are quite obvious. Companies can extract precious information directly from their (potential) customers by monitoring forums or discussion boards (HENNIG-THURAU and WALSH, 2004, p. 66). They can use social media channels for viral marketing activities (DE BRUYN and LILIEN, 2008, p. 151, HO and DEMPSEY, 2010, p. 1000) and implement crowdsourcing competitions or platforms for customers and brand evangelists to bond them to the brand they admire (PATTERSON, 2012, p. 527). Moreover, firms can implement social media as interactive and individual communication tool in service environments to foster relationship marketing (THORBJØRNSEN et al., 2002, p. 17). Marketing managers face the challenge to integrate social media into their existing strategies to remain competitive in today's market. Consequently, marketing budgets are shifted more and more towards the social media sector. The "CMO Survey" from Duke University and the American Marketing Association shows a peak in social media marketing expenses in 2014 with 7.4% of total marketing budgets. A predicted increase in spending of up to 18.1% within the next five years confirms the ongoing change of mind (CMOSURVEY, 2014, p. 25).

Social Media has drastically changed the marketing game. Rather than pushing a brand's message at its consumers, brands have to involve consumers into an ongoing dialogue (HENNIG-THURAU et al., 2010, p. 313). Social media allows consumers to directly and immediately engage in the process by producing, distributing, and consuming information in real time. Social media-based conversations occurring between consumers are outside managers' direct control

(MANGOLD and FAULDS, 2009, p. 357) and the flow of information about brands, products, services, and companies has become multidirectional, interconnected, and difficult to predict (HENNIG-THURAU et al., 2010, p. 313). This new balance of power allows less influential stakeholder groups to share their positions, needs, or thoughts in a public, almost real-time, and highly visible way. Consequently, marketers in those peer-to-peer environments have become an intruder, more talked-about than actually talking (DEIGHTON and KORNFELD, 2009, p. 4). Consumer product reviews, product ratings, recommendations, status updates, blog posts, or discussion board conversations are just some examples that all play into the multifaceted and complex term of social media (LEE et al., 2008, p. 341). They are all pre-purchase information sources that are available 24/7, show influence on people's buying behavior, and, therefore, a firm's sales (GU et al., 2011, p. 182). Even though social media is omnipresent and its importance unquestioned, many executives are still hesitant and uncertain about this new form of media, because they do not completely understand the various forms it can take, the different consequences it may have, and how to engage with it and learn (KIETZMANN et al., 2011, p. 241).

Not surprisingly, social media has attracted scholarly attention from diverse disciplines within the last decade. The internet's accessibility, reach, and transparency, as well as the almost unlimited access to archived consumer interactions have provided research with valuable data resources (KOZINETS et al., 2010). Especially marketing scholars provided a multitude of studies that investigate different effects of the new social media phenomenon. Reasoned within the works about traditional word-of-mouth, effects of online consumer interactions could be shown on consumer mindset metrics (e.g., NAMBISAN and WATT, 2011), market performance indicators (e.g., CHEVALIER and MAYZLIN, 2006), and even stock market movements (e.g., ANTWEILER and FRANK, 2004). However, literature states that published studies on the effectiveness of electronic word-of-mouth and social media are fragmented, use a multitude of different research approaches, and lack a conclusive overall picture of the current state-of-the-art (CHEUNG and THADANI, 2012). Research calls for integrative works that provide a more generalizable picture (LABRECQUE et al., 2013) and systematically identifies the current challenges (GENSLER et al., 2013).

It is necessary to step back, synthesize research outcomes, and identify flaws within the current research landscape. The background of loosing direct control of brands and the constellation of nearly unfiltered information transfer within a web 2.0 environment, exhibits the necessity for companies to understand the underlying processes of how social media might impact one's business. Companies strive to know how to appropriately counteract negative developments and how to take advantage of social media communications. Therefore, the need for an overall picture, rather than compartmentalized partial aspects, becomes obvious. To the best of my knowledge, there is no study that offers an aggregation of high quality research within social media with a focus on the effects on measurable corporate performance indicators. The objective of this paper is twofold. First, I summarize and aggregate research outcomes along the social media value chain inspired by the framework of KELLER and LEHMANN (2003, p. 29). Second, I derive implications for research by identifying research gaps for further investigation and give advice for practitioners how to beneficially use social media.

In the following, I derive an operational definition of social media for the paper at hand and shed light onto the complex phenomenon. In addition, I lay stress on the necessity for consolidation within the research stream, the contribution of my work, and introduce the social media value chain as an efficient framework for this study's purposes. After the introduction to the methodology, I present the results of the analysis. I subsequently conclude this paper with an evaluation of results, derive final implications for practitioners, and identify promising avenues for further research.

2   Conceptual Framework

2.1   Word-of-Mouth in an Interactive Environment

The information exchange on social media platforms about companies and their products and services has been given different names like *"user generated content"* (UGC)[1], *"voice of the consumer"*, *"chatter"*, or simply *"buzz"* (GODES and MAYZLIN, 2004, CABLE et al., 2000, LIBAI et al., 2009, TIRUNILLAI and TELLIS, 2012). But what exactly is meant by those terms on the different channels like blogs, Facebook, Twitter, or discussion boards? The bottom line of all information exchange on social media platforms comes back to a *"[...] person-to-person communication between a perceived non-commercial communicator and a receiver concerning a brand, a product, or a service offered for sale"* (ARNDT, 1967, p. 190), the basic definition of word-of-mouth (WOM). As a key factor, WOM communication is independent from any commercial influences and mostly takes place after a certain purchase, service, or product experience. WOM, as commercially unbiased, shows a high credibility and is even more effective than traditional marketing tools (BICKART and SCHINDLER, 2001, p. 36, ENGEL et al., 1969, p. 4, KATZ and LAZARFELD, 1955, p. 44). Whereas ARNDT (1967, p. 190) was defining WOM as an oral person-to-person communication process between two individuals, the definition was further shaped and adapted to new situations. Research expanded the view to a group phenomenon (BONE, 1992, p. 579) and scholars also included other communication types than face-to-face into the definition (BROWN et al., 2005, p. 125). After the developments of Web 2.0, "electronic Word-of-Mouth" (eWOM), as *"[...] any positive or negative statement made by potential, actual, or former customers about a product or company, which is made available to a multitude of people and institutions via the Internet"* (HENNIG-THURAU et al., 2004a, p. 39), became ubiquitous and an even more powerful tool than traditional WOM of today's society (e.g., CLEMONS, 2009a, p. 15, GODES and MAYZLIN, 2004, p. 545).

A fundamental aspect of both WOM and eWOM is that they mostly result of a previous product or service experience. It is typically not biased by the desire for a sale which, at the same time, does not imply a disregard of a sender's motivations behind the WOM messages for recipients

---

[1]   Please note that UGC is a broad term for social online communication. Videos on YouTube, knowledge contributions to Wikipedia, or pictures on Flickr are examples for UGC that does not necessarily have to be about products, services, or brands. As this paper strives to investigate effects of social media along the value chain, I understand the term UGC as online information exchange on social media platforms that talks about companies, their products, services, or brands.

(GODES et al., 2005, p. 418). Research developed different views on the antecedents of WOM activities. In their meta-analysis, MATOS and ROSSI (2008, pp. 579-582) sum up the diverse landscape and identify the most investigated antecedents. They discover a high satisfaction with products and services, a high loyalty with a company or brand, a high quality of products and services, a high commitment, a high level of trust, and an elevated level of perceived value as the main drivers for positive word-of-mouth (pWOM) creation and vice versa for negative word-of-mouth (nWOM). SUNDARAM et al. (1983, p. 530) find that satisfying employee-consumer contact experiences are one of the main drivers of pWOM and BROWN et al. (2005) add that consumers' identification with a company or brand also enhances WOM contributions. From a more psychological angle, BERGER and SCHWARTZ (2011, p. 870) state the importance of motivations (e.g., self-presentation) for WOM contributions, because consumers do not only communicate product related information, but also partly reveal their personalities. The antecedents mentioned above are mostly derived from traditional WOM settings but can also be seen as valid frameworks for eWOM communications (GRUEN et al., 2006, p. 450). For this reason, the next paragraphs will show general similarities and key differences between the two notions.

The majority of scholars see WOM and eWOM communications as quite similar and closely related concepts. HENNIG-THURAU et al. (2004a, p. 40) showed that contributors within eWOM communications exhibit a similar set of motivations as traditional WOM participants. Prior research also showed that nWOM has a higher persuasiveness than pWOM in offline (e.g., AHLUWALIA, 2002, p. 271) and online settings (e.g., SEN and LERMAN, 2007, p. 90). The high influence on people's purchase intention could also be shown in both situations (e.g., PARK et al., 2007, p. 136, EAST et al., 2008, p. 215). Even though the face-to-face aspect of traditional WOM was partially lost, eWOM still shows higher credibility and higher influence on people's choice behavior than traditional marketing and advertising measures (GODES and MAYZLIN, 2004, p. 545, TRUSOV et al., 2009, p. 90, SENECAL and NANTEL, 2004, p. 167), even though the majority of WOM communications with 76% still occur face-to-face (KELLER and LIBAI, 2009, p. 5).

While WOM and eWOM communications have much in common, there are also key differences. Internet users now have global access to archived consumer articulations and are able to reach far beyond the local community (CHEN and XIE, 2008, p. 479). At almost no cost, internet users can post reviews in real time (DELLAROCAS, 2003, p. 1407). Consumers receive and are influenced by information and evaluations about products, services, and also companies not only from people they personally know, but from a myriad of totally unrelated participants (HENNIG-THURAU and WALSH, 2004, p. 51). Within the traditional WOM setting, people interact with strong and weak ties (BROWN and REINGEN, 1987, p. 350). In contrast, the online environment leads to mostly anonymous communications based on weak tie relationships (SMITH et al., 2005, p. 20). However, eWOM still can be seen as a trustworthy and commercially unbiased source of information that helps consumers to manage product variety, handle market complexity, and reduce inherent uncertainty in the complex online environment (PATHAK et al., 2010, p. 166, PARK and LEE, 2009, p. 62). Taking into account that 60% of all online purchases are directly influenced by eWOM and UGC[2], justifies the high attention given by practitioners and academics (FREEDMAN, 2011, p. 9, WINER, 2009, pp. 110-111).

As data access for traditional WOM research has always been limited to an offline setting, the developments of web 2.0 not only strengthened the role of the consumer, but also opened up possibilities for academics and practitioners to access a tremendous amount of data by simply reading the internet (GODES and MAYZLIN, 2004, p. 558). They now can learn from conversations on the internet and even use the unbiased UGC information as inexpensive market research tool to measure the current temperature of their products and brands (KOZINETS et al., 2010, p. 71, DROGE et al., 2010, p. 79). Scholars now bring the insights from traditional WOM back to life in an online environment of large-scale data access (OINAS-KUKKONEN et al., 2010, p. 62). Thus, a boost in (e)WOM literature from 829 articles before the year 2000 to 3,877 after the introduction of web 2.0 can be recorded[3].

Scholars approach the eWOM phenomenon from many different angles. Literature mentions two important research streams (AGARWAL et al., 2008, p. 244, IRIBERRI and LEROY, 2009, p. 6, OINAS-KUKKONEN et al., 2010, pp. 62-63). First, the field of computer sciences and information systems research focuses on the technical backgrounds behind the social media environment. Scholars try to answer questions of how to program, design, and implement social media platforms or other social media tools in a way that enhances utility for customers and corporations and investigate consumer interactions with these tools (e.g., WANG and BENBASAT, 2008, KANE and ALAVI, 2008, MA and AGARWAL, 2007). Second, researchers from

---

[2]   Due to the restrictions made to the term UGC, eWOM and UGC shall be used as synonyms.
[3]   To generate these numbers, a keyword search was carried out in the EBSCO databases with the general search term "(electronic) word-of-mouth", its abbreviations and spellings.

social and organizational sciences emphasize the social dynamics and individual personality traits and attitudes in the social media world to explain participation and behavior in these interactive environments (e.g., CHEN et al., 2010, WEISS et al., 2008, YUN et al., 2008, SCHAU and GILLY, 2003).

Even though both research streams form a major area of the scientific landscape, this paper wants to change perspective and shift the focus onto studies that take eWOM as an exogenous basis and investigate its influence on corporate performance indicators and preceding marketing metrics. Works with this focus can be categorized in market-level and individual-level analyses (LEE and LEE, 2009, p. 302). Whereas market-level studies mostly rely on large scale datasets extracted from the internet or social media platforms, individual-level studies see eWOM as a process of personal influence, in which communications between two individuals can change the receiver's attitude towards a brand or influence the purchasing decision (CHEUNG and THADANI, 2012, p. 461). Market-level studies try to find effects of eWOM on dependent variables aggregated on company or industry level, whereas individual-level studies focus on how eWOM exposure influences each individual. They both investigate effects of eWOM on corporate performance measures and contribute to the discussion raised in this paper.

To this date, only a few systematic reviews of eWOM research have been published. To the best of my knowledge, there are only three major contributions to the field. First, HENNIG-THURAU et al. (2010) introduce a pinball framework for the illustration of the highly complex social media landscape. In their review, they focus on the impact of new media on customer relationships and, furthermore, also include IT technologies like search and shopping bots, or automated recommendation systems into their analysis. A pinball-like framework with over ten bilateral and dynamic interconnections makes it less suitable for a practical implementation. Unfortunately, the authors do not provide any evidence about how papers have been selected for their study. Thus, it remains questionable how this necessary work has been done in advance of the framework development. Second, GENSLER et al. (2013) take over a brand management perspective. They emphasize the active part of companies in the social media environment through moderating and creating brand stories that can shape consumer' perceptions. However, they do not entirely discuss brand and company related outcomes of online consumer interactions. Further, GENSLER et al. (2013, p. 252) explicitly state that further research should focus on the "[i]mpact of consumer-generated brand stories on brand performance" which argues in favor of the work at hand. Third, CHEUNG and THADANI (2012) apply a classical transmitter-receiver model from social communication literature and add the concepts of stimulus and response. Within their framework, they include effects of eWOM as exogenous and endogenous concepts. This leads to an inconclusive overview of today's research. Furthermore, they see the stimulus (i.e., the communicated message content) as independent from the communicator, which remains doubtful. Moreover, their framework ends at the response level of purchase intention which falls short when aggregating results especially from market-level studies.

The need for a systematic overview of eWOM research is evident based on the high complexity of interrelationships and potential moderators. A lack of comprehensive review work fuels this opaque landscape and practitioner's hesitation to engage in social media. This paper wants to close this gap and provides a systematic, comprehensive, and qualitative review of main effects of eWOM on corporate performance variables. To provide this narrative review with a solid framework, the concept of the "*brand value chain*" shall be utilized and modified to systematize the large quantity of empirical and theoretical evidence.

2.2   The Social Media Value Chain

With the introduction of the brand value chain, KELLER and LEHMANN offered a holistic and integrated approach to understand the value created by brands. As one of the most valuable company assets, it is important to create, develop, and manage a brand to maximize its "brand equity" to the firm (KELLER and LEHMANN, 2003, p. 27). In addition, the marketing profession is constantly challenged to assess and to declare the value created by their actions on shareholder value (SRINIVASAN and HANSSENS, 2009, p. 293). For branding and marketing research it is essential to develop a comprehensive view of how marketing activities lead to brand equity, how it operates, and what causal effect chains can be observed (KELLER and LEHMANN, 2006, p. 753). The brand value chain in the offline environment of marketing assumes that companies are solely in charge of their marketing communication activities. They induce *marketing actions* to influence *perceptual measures* of consumers. These consumer mindset metrics should act as precursor to observable, *behavioral outcomes* that lead to a superior product and market performance and a superior *financial performance* respectively. Thus, the concept of the brand value chain shows how marketing activities create value (GUPTA and ZEITHAML, 2006, pp. 718-719, AMBLER et al., 2002, pp. 14-15). KELLER and LEHMANN (2006, pp. 753-754) further state that it can be seen as a journey from *what companies do* to *what customers think and feel.* The consumer mindset metrics consist of the "Five As" (i.e., awareness, associations, attitude, attachment, and activity) and should trigger sales as the outcome of *what customers do* (i.e., product and market performance). In the last step, these consumer actions are reflected in financial performance measures and show *how the financial markets react.* The value chain can be seen as fairly simple (i.e., it has only four main components). However, feedback effects on previous stages quickly increase the models complexity (KELLER and LEHMANN, 2006, p. 754). In this paper, I focus on the main effects along the value chain and disregard the inherent problem of endogeneity of the different stages.

SRINIVASAN et al. (2010, p. 674) and KELLER and LEHMANN (2006, p. 754) start the brand value chain journey from *"what marketers do"* by considering the typical marketing mix elements for their framework. However, within the web 2.0 environment it is a new ballgame. Naturally, eWOM does not refer to what marketers or companies do anymore. It rather refers to the question of *what customers do and how they talk about the brand, product, or service.* Even though eWOM takes place next to traditional advertising and marketing actions, it demands a new framework. In Figure 1 I suggest a social media value chain that reflects the structure of chapter 4.

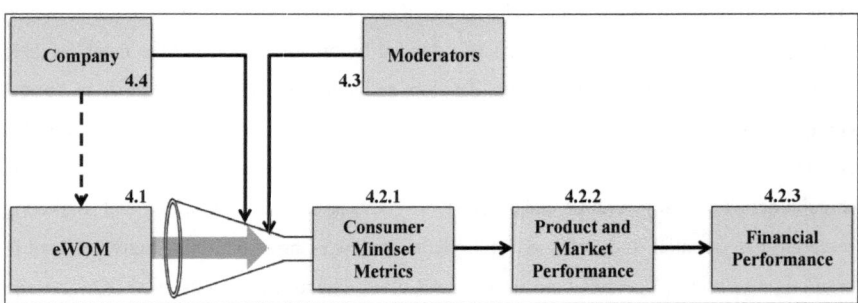

Figure 1: Social Media Value Chain

The operationalization of eWOM with its different measures and variables is discussed in chapter 4.1 and tackles the question of how to measure *"what customers do"* in the social web. In chapter 4.2, the main effects along the value chain are presented before I focus on the moderator effects of those relationships in chapter 4.3. GODES et al. (2005, p. 416) state that companies are moderator, mediator, observer, and participant in the eWOM environment. Thus, there is a constant level of independent buzz about a firm and its products and services that is outside a company's direct reach. For this reason, I propose a dual role of corporations. First, firms can partly stimulate eWOM discussions by targeted viral marketing campaigns (cf. dashed line in Figure 1). Second, they act as a moderator of the constant noise about their brand and products by moderating ongoing discussions through an active participation in social media conversations. These roles of a company are discussed in chapter 4.4.

3   Literature Review

Literature Research

To compile and systematize the relevant literature in the broad field of social media, procedures suggested by WEBSTER and WATSON (2002), ROSENTHAL (1995), and FARLEY et al. (2004) are closely followed. To identify the relevant works in the area of business studies, a general keyword search was carried out within the three databases of EBSCO, JSTOR, and ELSEVIER. Even though this paper looks at the emerging research stream of social media from a brand and marketing perspective, eWOM and UGC are still multifaceted concepts that can be looked at from many perspectives that are relevant for this study's purpose. Therefore, the database search focused on all journals that are ranked within VHB JOURQUAL 2.1[4] with a "B" or better to assure quality standards of publications (HENNIG-THURAU et al., 2004b, p. 521). This resulted in 258 target journals for the review at hand from all relevant areas of the business and economic sector. Publications up to the year 2013 have been considered. Subsequently, issue-by-issue research was conducted within the major journals to assure that no important contributions have been missed (FARLEY et al., 2004, p. 148). After the most important contributions have been identified, I went iteratively through their citations to identify relevant prior work. As a last step, conference proceedings and current working papers were identified that can be seen as reflections of the status quo and a real time picture of current research attempts (ROSENTHAL, 1995, p. 184) and partly solve the problem of an inherent "publication bias" (FARLEY et al., 2004, p. 148). Because these unpublished works did not go through journal-peer-review processes, I only included working papers and conference proceedings from well known authors that already published social media research in high quality journals. The existing literature formed the baseline for creating a list of keywords. Important notions were extracted from highly-cited major contributions to the field of social media. To solve the

---

[4] The complete list of all journals ranked within VHB JOURQUAL 2.1 can be found on http://vhbonline.org/uploads/media/Ranking_Gesamt_2.1.pdf .

problem that many authors apply different notions for key concepts within social media, I extended the keyword list to abbreviation, spellings, and synonyms for the key concepts (cf. FRANKE, 2001, p. 194). The list was dynamically updated after important contributions with new keywords were identified.

Keywords	social(-)media, social(-)network(s), online, (online) communities, (e)WOM, electronic word-of-mouth, online word-of-mouth, word(-)of(-)mouth, (online) recommendations, blog(s), YouTube, Facebook, Twitter, net promoter, chatter, buzz, noise, user generated content, UGC, web 2.0, forum(s), discussion board(s)

Table 1: Keywords of Literature Search

The issue by issue research was conducted within the journals with the most hits after the keyword search to ensure that no relevant articles of important periodicals have been missed.

A+	Journal of Marketing, Journal of Marketing Research, Marketing Science
A	International Journal of Research in Marketing, Journal of Management Information Systems, MIS Quarterly
B	Journal of Business Research, Journal of Interactive Marketing, International Journal of Electronic Commerce

Table 2: Journals of Issue-by-Issue Search

A total of 374 articles could be identified after all literature-gathering stages. 88 papers in journals ranked as "A+", 92 in "A" journals, 184 in "B" journals, four conference papers, and six working papers.

Methodological deliberations

Within the literature on meta-analyses, two major types of meta-analysis techniques can be identified. Quantitative studies try to statistically investigate a general effect through an aggregation of empirical results from a relevant set of publications (cf. e.g., HALL and ROSENTHAL, 1995, p. 395, BIJMOLT and PIETERS, 2001, pp. 157-158). This, however, is only possible, when a substantial amount of publications show similar characteristics regarding their empirical methods, study designs, or sampling methods (LIPSEY and WILSON, 2001, pp. 16-23). As outlined in the previous chapters, there is a high methodological and empirical diversity in the current social media research landscape making a quantitative approach inapplicable. Rather, a qualitative meta-analysis in form of a narrative review shall be conducted to compare and combine research results within the eWOM and UGC sector and generate a common framework of understanding (HALL and ROSENTHAL, 1995, p. 396).

Systematization

By screening the abstract and result section of each of the 374 papers identified through the literature compilation stage, I assigned tags to all articles with regard to their topics and variables of interest. After a list of more than 300 tags was created, the catalog was compressed via content-analysis. The so created research clusters were examined regarding their suitability for this study's purpose to identify works that treat eWOM as an exogenous factor and discuss the influences on corporate performance indicators along the introduced social media value chain. A total of 272 articles were sorted because they did not show a direct link to the eWOM or corporate outcome perspective along the brand value chain (e.g., focus on traditional WOM, editorial articles, etc.). The resulting 102 articles were aligned in consonance with the value chain regarding their dependent variable (cf. Figure 1)[5]. 30 articles were found to investigate effects on consumer mindset metrics, 29 were assigned to product and market performance, and 15 papers focused on eWOM effects on financial performance measures. The role of the company was discussed in 28 articles.

4   Analysis and Results

4.1   Operationalization and Measures of eWOM

When investigating the phenomenon of eWOM, one of the first thoughts goes to the obvious question of how many conversations about a company, brand, product, or service can be found online. The concept of *"volume"* is used in the vast majority of the studies as a starting point for their investigations. *Volume* shows a positive influence across all dependent variables along the value chain. PARK et al. (2007) show that a higher eWOM *volume* has a positive effect on recipients' consumer mindset. Within their experimental setup, they use artificially created consumer reviews as treatment to verify the positive influence on purchasing intentions of a multimedia player. The segment of studies focusing on eWOM effects on product and market performance indicators note a positive link between eWOM *volume* and subsequent online and offline sales, higher early sales, or box office revenues (e.g., DELLAROCAS et al., 2007, GODES

---

[5]   Additional material (i.e. detailed excerpts of the identified literature along the social media value chain) can be found on the product page of the book at hand on www.springer.com.

and MAYZLIN, 2004, LIU, 2006). *Volume* also forms one of the key measures regarding the effects of eWOM on financial performance metrics. ANTWEILER and FRANK (2004), MCALISTER et al. (2011), or TIRUNILLAI and TELLIS (2012) are just exemplary works that use the *volume* of eWOM about stocks and general eWOM *volume* to predict subsequent trading volume, stock volatility, and stock return. However, the ways in which *volume* numbers are extracted from the different sources on the internet are diverse. The question of how much eWOM can be found on the internet is tackled by extracting eWOM messages with computer based web scrapers, crawlers or scripts with predefined keywords (e.g., SHIN et al., 2011, BERGER and MILKMAN, 2012). Other studies try to gather UGC *volume* by simply looking at the pure numbers of e.g., consumer reviews on Amazon or similar platforms (e.g., CHEVALIER and MAYZLIN, 2006, GODES and MAYZLIN, 2004). Although the methods of accessing *volume* data differ across the identified literature, eWOM *volume* remains one of the strongest and most significant predictors of brand value outcomes (TIRUNILLAI and TELLIS, 2012, p. 198, DUAN et al., 2008b, p. 235). The information inherent in *volume* measures basically answers the question of how much eWOM is out there. The more conversations can be found, the more people will become informed about a specific company, brand, product, or service (GODES and MAYZLIN, 2004, p. 548). But without assessing what consumers actually talk about, the use of a *volume* variable is restricted for practitioners and academics. Consequently, SONNIER et al. (2011, p. 713) state that measuring pure *volume* masks the real effects of eWOM on dependent variables like e.g., sales. The need for a more differentiated measure with a higher degree of information to comprehensibly assess the construct of eWOM and its effects became obvious.

Research quickly drew from traditional theories about WOM and transferred the existing concept of *valence on* the social media landscape. In contrast to volume as a simple "count" approach, posts are now assigned with meaning based on the words, language, or tonality used. Within the literature at hand, many different approaches are assigned with the label *valence*. Mostly divided into positive, neutral, and negative postings, it has gained high attention in the research sector due to putting weight on the mostly undifferentiated effects of pure volume measures. Along the social media value chain, there are contrary results about the multifaceted construct of eWOM *valence*. Especially within large scale empirical datasets, studies report inconsistent results. Table 3 provides an overview of the different *valence* measures applied in social media research.

Valence Measure	Description	Exemplary Studies	Main Results
Ratings	Consumer generated categorical product ratings (e.g., Amazon 5-star rating scale) are extracted and used as proxy of eWOM valence	CHINTAGUNTA et al. (2010); TIRUNILLAI and TELLIS (2012); DUAN et al. (2008a); ETZION and AWAD (2007); ANDERSON and MAGRUDER (2012)	Positive effect on sales No effect on stock returns No effect on sales Positive effect on online and offline sales
Hand-Coded	Consumer generated posts like product reviews or postings, manually coded regarding their tonality (positive/negative/neutral)	GODES and MAYZLIN (2004); ADJEI et al. (2009); LIU (2006)	No effect on sales Positive effect on purchase behavior No effect on offline sales
IT- Coded[6]	Consumer generated posts like product reviews or message board postings, automatically valence-coded by means of e.g., language processing algorithms	MCALISTER et al. (2011); SHIN et al. (2011); SONNIER et al. (2011)	No effect on stock return Positive effect on market prices Positive effect on sales
Ratios	Based on the valence measures above, the ratio of pWOM/nWOM is calculated	COOK and LU (2009); OH and LIU SHENG (2011)	Positive effect on stock return Positive effect on stock return
Dispersion /Variance	The diversity or dispersion of consumer ratings (e.g., Amazon 5-star scale) is calculated and transferred into measures of disagreement or variance of eWOM	ANTWEILER and FRANK (2004); DAS and CHEN (2007); ZHU and ZHANG (2010); JIMÉNEZ and MENDOZA (2013); SUN (2012)	Negative effect on trading volume No effect on stock variables Negative effect on sales Negative effect on purchase intention

Table 3: Overview of Different Valence Measures

The versatile and partly contradictory effects reported along the social media value chain make it hard to extract a common best practice for the operationalization of *valence*. Research ascribes the stark differences within and across the results of the single *valence* measures mostly to miscellaneous methods applied, industries investigated, or product types looked at (cf. ZHU and ZHANG, 2010, p. 145, DUAN et al., 2008a, p. 1008). However, to the best of my knowledge, no single study investigates the relationships between the different *valence* measures. Whereas the relation and similarity of the hand- and IT-coded *valence* can be calculated statistically, this evidence and knowledge does not exist for the other measures. As ratings are the most applied proxy of eWOM in large scale empirical datasets and are easy to access at almost no cost, it is key for research to investigate questions like: How do star ratings relate to other *valence* measures like written consumer reviews? What makes a positive review a four- or five-star

---

[6] DAS and CHEN (2007, p. 1377) provide a detailed overview of different "valence classifiers" for sentiment extraction of eWOM data collected by web-scraper programs (i.e., naive-, adjective-, vector distance-, Bayesian-, and discriminant classifier).

review? Is a three-star review perceived as neutral? What customer articulations lead to one or two star ratings? Answering these questions would help to achieve a better understanding of the underlying interrelationships and would help to see the overall picture of *valence* measures. Taking a closer look at studies that demonstrate significant influences, it has to be noted that even though the results presented in Table 3 are jagged, there are methodologically accurate studies throughout all stages that show significant effects of eWOM *valence* (e.g., DELLAROCAS et al., 2007, CHAKRAVARTY et al., 2010, OH and LIU SHENG, 2011). Consistent with traditional WOM, the magnitude of nWOM effects is larger than the magnitude of pWOM effects[7] along the whole social media value chain (e.g., CHEN et al., 2011b, SONNIER et al., 2011, TIRUNILLAI and TELLIS, 2012). Although literature is ambiguous regarding the effects of *valence*, the reasons for its importance is pretty straight forward. PWOM enhances consumers' expectations about product quality, while nWOM reduces it. *Valence* can, thus, be seen as the persuasiveness-factor of eWOM on consumers' attitude (LIU, 2006, p. 76) and its variance as a measure of agreement/disagreement among reviewers or users generating content (JIMÉNEZ and MENDOZA, 2013).

Next to valence and volume, there are also other variables that are applied to investigate eWOM effects along the value chain. The *length* of consumer reviews is regressed by ADJEI et al. (2009) on customers' purchasing behavior. CHEVALIER and MAYZLIN (2006) also examine the effects of the number of words to explain effects on online sales ranks. Both studies do not report any significant influence onto their dependent variables. Another important variable to operationalize eWOM is the concept of *visibility* defined as: "[…] the extent to which product-related conversations are taking place across a broad range of communities" (GODES and MAYZLIN, 2004, p. 546)[8]. In line with the work of HU et al. (2011), they find that visibility has a high influence on people's product judgments and a firm's value respectively. The *visibility* of eWOM is even seen as a stronger predictor than pure volume measures (GODES and MAYZLIN, 2004, p. 559). However, empirical results are too scarce to speak of an overall and generalizable effect.

---

[7]   In the following, the higher magnitude of nWOM effects compared to pWOM effects will be referred to as the "negativity bias" (e.g., AHLUWALIA, 2002, p. 270). NWOM information, therefore, is more persuasive than comparable positive product ratings, reviews, or evaluations (e.g., ZHANG et al., 2010, p. 1336).

[8]   Note that GODES and MAYZLIN (2004, p. 546) introduce the concept of visibility under the term "dispersion". As dispersion, is referring to a variance in judgments (cf. LUO et al., 2013a, p. 399), I use the term *visibility* for the eWOM distribution across different social media channels.

4.2   Main Effects along the Value Chain

4.2.1 EWOM and the Consumer Mindset

Research on effects of eWOM on consumer mindset metrics fits into the tradition of brand equity literature. Mindset metrics act as an early warning system that indicates not only the effect of specific advertising campaigns, but also that of the entire marketing mix and strategy. Furthermore, mindset metrics are also the building blocks of the hierarchy-of-effects model of advertising. They mostly assume that any marketing stimuli moves the consumer through a hierarchical sequence of events that include cognitions, affection, and result in behavior (SRINIVASAN et al., 2010, p. 673). Even though the marketing profession is always struggling with the fact that marketing actions may not translate into numerable results immediately, the measurement of mindset-metrics on a regular basis can evaluate if marketing is moving customers into the intended direction (KELLER and LEHMANN, 2006, p. 740). As KELLER and LEHMANN (2006, p. 754) add, mindset metrics are not only influenced by a company's actions, but also by personal experience and experiences made by others. Therefore, consumer mindset metrics form an ideal base for the investigation of eWOM effects. Throughout the literature, many hierarchical models have been developed to arrange mindset metrics in an appropriate way to easily follow the process from consumers' first marketing touch-point to the actual purchasing act (VAKRATSAS and AMBLER, 1999, p. 27). Many of them are referred to as "*brand funnel*" or "*purchase funnel*". These causal effect chains in the consumer mindset mostly start with *awareness* measures that subsequently trigger a change in people's *familiarity* with the brand and foster their *attitude* towards the brand. Following, people start to put a brand on their shortlist and *consider* the specific products or services in a pre-purchase stage. This manifests in the actual *purchase decision* and, if repeated, in *loyal* customer behavior (BRIGGS et al., 2005, p. 85). The articles identified in this section are presented in Table 4 and sorted regarding their dependent variable. I follow the logic of KELLER and LEHMANN (2006, p. 745) to sort the articles in a hierarchical order from simple *awareness* aspects as the lowest level within consumer mindset metrics, to *loyalty and satisfaction* as the highest level of post-purchase measures[9].

---

[9]   Please note that not all studies are in line with treating purchase decision, satisfaction, or loyalty as consumer mindset metric. For example MUNOZ and KUMAR (2004, p. 383) argue that purchase decision, satisfaction, and loyalty already reflect how customers act and, therefore, belong to the category of performance measures.

Brand Funnel Construct	Illustrative Endogenous Variables	Illustrative Studies	Empirical Findings
Awareness	Product awareness, Interest in products	BICKART and SCHINDLER (2001); DE BRUYN and LILIEN (2008)	EWOM volume and valence foster product awareness and interest.
Attitude	Attitude towards product/brand	NAMBISAN and WATT (2011); PAN and CHIOU (2011); WANG et al. (2012); SEN and LERMAN (2007)	EWOM volume and valence strengthen attitude towards the product/brand. Negativity bias for utilitarian products.
Trust	Brand trust, retailer trust, online trust	ALJUKHADAR.et al. (2010); BART et al. (2005); BRODIE et al. (2011)	EWOM exchange fosters community, product, and brand trust. By increasing perceived social presence, firms can enhance this effect.
Value	Perceived value, product evaluation	CHAKRAVARTY et al. (2010); GRUEN et al. (2006)	EWOM increases product evaluations and perceived value. EWOM is more persistent than professional reviews.
Purchase	Purchase intention, consumer preferences, need recognition	ADJEI et al. (2009); DE VALCK et al. (2009); AGGARWAL and SINGH (2013); DECKER and TRUSOV (2010); PARK et al. (2007); PARK and LEE (2009); JIMÉNEZ and MENDOZA (2013); BENLIAN et al. (2012); PARRY et al. (2012)	The eWOM effect of volume and valence is valid in all decision making phases. This effect is higher for earlier decision stages. Quality and reliability issues show the highest impact on purchase intention. EWOM shows high effect on purchase intention. EWOM and traditional WOM both able to trigger purchase intent.
Adoption/ Choice	Product adoption, Product choice, choice optimality, choice behavior	DE BRUYN and LILIEN (2008); THOMPSON and SINHA (2008); GUPTA and HARRIS (2010); NARAYAN et al. (2011); SENECAL and NANTEL (2004); SMITH et al. (2005); DEWAN and RAMAPRASAD (2012)	EWOM volume and valence foster product adoption and act as information surrogate that reduces inherent choice insecurity. It decreases the time to adopt and the likelihood that customers switch to competitors.
Satisfaction/ Commitment	Satisfaction/ Commitment	BRODIE et al. (2011)	EWOM volume and valence positively influence satisfaction and commitment
Loyalty	Behavioral loyalty	GARNEFELD et al. (2010); GRUEN et al. (2006); JANG et al. (2008); SCARPI (2010)	EWOM volume and valence increase behavioral loyalty dimensions including WOM behavior and repurchase rates.

Table 4: Effects of eWOM on Consumer Mindset Metrics

Research on the effects of eWOM on consumer mindset metrics is closely related to the variables discussed in the chapter above. EWOM valence is primarily used since the research stream is dominated by experimental setups. However, other variables like social presence of websites (e.g., AHLUWALIA, 2002) or consumer engagement with communities (e.g., BRODIE et al., 2011, THOMPSON and SINHA, 2008) are also applied.

Awareness. By means of an online experiment over a 12 week period, BICKART and SCHINDLER (2001), as one of the oldest studies in the sample at hand, show that the interest in a product category (i.e., cycling, exercise, nutrition, photography, and stereo equipment) can be fostered when people are interacting with discussion forums. Interacting with a corporate website showed significantly smaller effects. Product interest and awareness can further be enhanced by eWOM from friends and acquaintances independent from any platform. DE BRUYN and LILIEN (2008) showed in their experimental setup that viral e-mail chains, induced by 634 student initiators, are able to create higher product awareness and even create an above average interest in the topic, offer, product, or service recommended.

Attitude. Further down the brand funnel, NAMBISAN and WATT (2011) show with data from 206 users of the forums of Intel, IBM, Microsoft and Adobe that the higher a consumer's exposure with product, brand, or service-related eWOM exchange, the better his attitude towards the brand and products. Even though their study only examines the IT sector, the authors add that it has to be kept in mind that eWOM exchange platforms are increasingly becoming a "lounge" area for customers to hang out and talk to one another. Therefore, online communities can play a crucial role in shaping customers' perceptions regarding the product, service, or brand discussed. An influence of eWOM valence on attitudinal measures was observed in the experimental studies of PAN and CHIOU (2011), and SEN and LERMAN (2007). Both studies confirm the influence of valence onto people's attitude towards a product or brand. The negativity bias could be shown for utilitarian products (i.e., PDAs) in the lab setting (SEN and LERMAN, 2007, p. 76). By means of an online questionnaire sampling within Chinese social media users, WANG et al. (2012) further confirm that positive discussions on social media platforms are able to increase respondents' attitude toward the product. The reported eWOM effect appears to be stronger for consumers who scored low in their need for uniqueness.

Trust. By means of their netnographic analysis of 427 posts from an internet platform of a whole body vibration device between the years 2006 and 2008, BRODIE et al. (2011) showed that trust measures could be increased when consumers showed a higher engagement in virtual brand communities. Sharing knowledge and content through eWOM, learning from others by consuming eWOM, as well as simple socializing factors foster higher levels of trust towards the community, the brand, and its product. ALJUKHADAR et al. (2010) and BART et al. (2005) add that companies have the opportunity to elevate trust measures through website design aspects. By means of experimental setups and SEM, they both argue that the perceived social presence of sections like privacy disclosure, navigation, and order fulfillment enhance trust measures towards the website, brands and products presented.

Value. Pre-release product evaluations, as an indicator of perceived product or service value, are also significantly increased after the exposure to eWOM messages. CHAKRAVARTY et al. (2010) reported within their experimental setup that movie evaluations from other consumers are even more persistent than professional critic reviews. In their study, infrequent moviegoers are more influenced by eWOM than frequent moviegoers. Whereas all studies hypothesize that WOM is highly capable to influence the receivers' way of thinking about a product or brand, GRUEN et al. (2006) explicitly provide evidence for a change in perceived value of a firm's offerings. Their questionnaire within participants of a company-independent internet forum of a software product for video editing revealed that consumer-to-consumer interactions positively affect the perceived value of a firm's offerings. Therefore, eWOM can be seen as a strong source of information for internet users that can even tip the balance pro or con an actual purchase decision.

Purchase. Through regression and conjoint analysis, DECKER and TRUSOV (2010) provide evidence for eWOM's capability to form overall consumer preferences. They show a connection between topics discussed in eWOM communications and the resulting overall consumer preferences, operationalized as the sum of rating measures available. Reliability topics and quality issues in consumer reviews show the highest influence on consumer preferences. By using a dataset of disclosed deal flow data of venture capitalists, AGGARWAL and SINGH (2013) could also show that the volume of blog coverage increases the probability with which an entity passes the screening stage of a venture capitalist. The authors conclude that the decision making process of a venture capitalist is also influenced by eWOM discussions. When it comes to the purchase decision, literature also provides evidence of a considerable eWOM effect. All decision making phases from need recognition to post-purchase evaluation are influenced by the frequency of interaction with an online community. This was shown by DE VALCK et al. (2009) by means of a large scale questionnaire within about 1,000 participants of a recipe exchange community. The more interaction with the community, the more positive influence could be observed. The positive effect of eWOM volume, valence, and review quality on a receiver's purchase intention was also confirmed by other experimental contributions (PARK et al., 2007, PARK and LEE, 2009, ADJEI et al., 2009). In addition, JIMÉNEZ and MENDOZA (2013) add that the level of detail in eWOM messages actually increases the eWOM effect. The experimental setup with a fictitious shopping task of BENLIAN et al. (2012) revealed that the eWOM effect is considerably strong in influencing the preceding constructs of trust and affective beliefs before positively influencing purchase intent. PARRY et al. (2012) used an online questionnaire to investigate the eWOM effect of over 1,200 Japanese customers of consumer electronics. They show that both traditional and electronic WOM are able to positively influence purchase intention. In addition, eWOM is more persistent in the case of high social or symbolic consumption (i.e., smart phone).

Adoption/Choice. As many studies confirmed the positive effect of eWOM on measures like purchase intention, it is not a long stretch to assume a similar positive effect on product adoption. THOMPSON and SINHA (2008) could show by a large scale regression with close to 100,000 eWOM messages extracted from four major IT brand communities (i.e., Intel, AMD, ATI, NVIDIA) that the adoption of new products is enhanced by eWOM and community engagement. It takes less time for people to adopt and additionally decreases the likelihood that participants will switch to a new product from a competing brand. DE BRUYN and LILIEN (2008) confirm these findings and report that consumer-to-consumer recommendations not only in communities but also via email foster recipients' product adoption. NARAYAN et al. (2011) investigate the effects on people's product choices. Within their choice-based conjoint experiment they come to the conclusion that consumers' weight on their own preferences diminishes with an increasing number of peer influencers. They find evidence for an attribution within consumers' uncertainty about the importance of certain product attributes when facing a specific choice decision. EWOM acts as an information surrogate to fill this gap. In line with this argumentation, GUPTA and HARRIS (2010) argue that with an increasing number of eWOM messages the time spent to consider the eWOM messages and the total time spent on the decision task also increases. Moderated by the construct of "need for cognition", the presence of eWOM messages can, under certain circumstances (i.e., low need for cognition), significantly reduce choice optimality. Even though GUPTA and HARRIS (2010) only use pWOM as a treatment and only rely on one product (i.e., laptop), the results indicate that outside of laboratory setting where a multitude of distracting information is present, the effect of eWOM on consumer preferences or choice can be different and even guide consumers into a suboptimal decision. In general, people perceive eWOM messages from other consumers as more convincing and trustworthy when compared with IT-based recommendation systems or human expert referrals (SENECAL and NANTEL, 2004). UGC also shows higher influence onto consumers' actual choice behavior (SMITH et al., 2005). However, SENECAL and NANTEL (2004) report that with regard to the actual purchase consequences, algorithm-based recommendation systems show a higher influence on people's choice behavior than advice from other consumers or human experts. DEWAN and RAMAPRASAD (2012) investigated the effect in a music setting. They combined data of music sampling frequency as proxy for consumer preferences with data from 281 blogs posting between 07/2006 – 08/2006, Amazon reviews, and sales rank data. Blog popularity was found to have a stronger association with music sampling in the case of niche compared with mainstream music. The more popular or visible a music blog becomes, the higher its effect on music sampling.

Satisfaction/Commitment/Loyalty. According to OLIVER (1999, p. 34), loyalty, satisfaction, and commitment are closely related concepts that form one of the most beneficial corporate goals: to enhance repurchase rates and to lower defection rates to increase net present value. Within their netnographic study, BRODIE et al. (2011) find that consumer engagement in brand communities leads to a higher customer satisfaction, commitment, and higher loyalty to the brand. The engagement in an online community as well as the participation within eWOM discussions increases behavioral loyalty dimensions (GARNEFELD et al., 2010, JANG et al., 2008, SCARPI, 2010). GRUEN et al. (2006) confirmed the eWOM effect on the loyalty dimensions of repurchase and WOM behavior using data from a forum for video editing.

Even though the research section looking at the effects on the consumer mindset broadly accepts the existing link between volume and the consumer mindset (e.g., CHAKRAVARTY et al., 2010, p. 185), emphasis is clearly put on valence measures. Through the application of mainly laboratory experimental setups, studies concentrate on the investigation of theoretical effects with high internal but low external validity. Distracting information comparable to a real life setting in the web 2.0 environment is often neglected. Besides these methodological deliberations it is noticeable that no single study investigates the effects of eWOM on brand image measures. Even though brand image is typically not included in market response models, partly because they are difficult to measure reliably and in a consistent way across different product categories (SRINIVASAN et al., 2010, p. 681), it still has great significance in consumer behavior research and enormous predictive potential to indicate ramifications of eWOM (DOBNI and ZINKHAN, 1990, p. 118). The purely positive results in this chapter might of course be a result of a publication bias. But the reported outcomes also show similarities to effects that have already been reported within traditional WOM and advertising literature (cf. e.g.,

AHLUWALIA, 2002, p. 278, WESTBROOK, 1987, p. 268). This poses the question if the proven effects along the brand funnel can be taken as granted and generalizable. If and how these relationships sustain within a real life setting outside of artificial situations has to be looked at by means of subsequent field experiments.

4.2.2 EWOM and Product and Market Performance

Drawing from signaling theory, ERDEM and SWAIT (1998, p. 131) show that brand related communication activities, such as eWOM, pay into a change of each individual's mindset and behavior. The sum of those changes, therefore, triggers measurable performance indicators on product and brand level such as sales, market shares, or price premiums (GUPTA and ZEITHAML, 2006, pp. 722-724). Following KELLER and LEHMANN (2006, p. 754), product and market performance measures are the observable result of *"what customers do"*. The articles in this section all treat eWOM as an exogenous variable and try to explain observable market performance outcomes on an aggregated product, company or brand level. Table 5 presents the identified studies sorted by their product performance measure used as dependent variable.

The majority of studies operationalize product and market performance mostly by means of online and/or offline sales data or use accessible online sales ranks from big online retailers. As the studies deal with the aggregated consumer preferences and their manifestation on the market, large scale panel regression is the dominating method. Datasets often consist of more than 100,000 observations (e.g., FORMAN et al., 2008, LI and HITT, 2008). Thus, valence coding by hand is mostly not conducted. Valence operationalization is dominated by ratings taken from online retailers (e.g., GU et al., 2011), movie review sites (e.g., DELLAROCAS et al., 2007), or blogs (e.g., DHAR and CHANG, 2009).

Product Performance Measure	Illustrative Dependent Variables	Illustrative Studies	Empirical Findings
Online Sales Ranks	Amazon sales rank, online album charts	AMBLEE and BUI (2008)	Positive effect of volume
		LI and HITT (2008)	Positive self-selection bias found
		CHEN et al. (2004)	No effect of valence (ratings)
		DHAR and CHANG (2009)	Valence effect (ratings) < volume
		CHEVALIER and MAYZLIN (2006)	Mixed effect of volume, positive effect of valence (ratings), nWOM> pWOM, no effect of length
		CHEN et al. (2011b)	NWOM has negative effect, pWOM only vague evidence (ratings)
		FORMAN et al. (2008)	Positive effect of valence (ratings)
		PATHAK et al. (2010)	Positive effect volume and valence (ratings)
		GU et al. (2011)	Positive effect of internal and external volume and valence (ratings)
		GU et al. (2013)	Valence (ratings) positive effect, positivity effect for popular products
		HO-DAC et al. (2013)	Valence (ratings) positive effect for weak brand equity (vice versa)
		SUN (2012)	Volume and valence positive effect, variance positive when valence is low
Online Sales	Online sales data from retailers	ETZION and AWAD (2007)	Positive effect of valence (ratings), volume only when valence does not differentiate
		MOE and TRUSOV (2011)	Positive short term effect of valence (ratings) and indirect effect (+) dispersion
Offline Sales	TV-viewership rating, box office ticket sales or revenues, election results	DUAN et al. (2008a)	Positive effect volume, no valence (ratings)
		DUAN et al. (2008b); LIU (2006)	Positive effect of volume; no effect of valence (hand-coded)
		GODES and MAYZLIN (2004)	Positive effect of volume in later periods, no effect of valence (hand coded), dispersion positive effect
		DELLAROCAS et al. (2007)	Positive effect volume and valence (ratings)
		TUMASJAN et al. (2011)	Positive effect of volume (tweets) on election results, valence (IT-coded) reflects political discussions
		ANDERSON and MAGRUDER (2012); CHINTAGUNTA et al. (2010)	Positive effect of valence (ratings); Positive effect of valence (ratings) and no effect of volume and dispersion,
Total Sales	Sales figures from firms	SONNIER et al. (2011)	Positive effect of valence (IT-coded)
		ZHU and ZHANG (2010)	Positive effect of volume, valence (ratings) and dispersion only show effect on less popular products
		STEPHEN and GALAK (2012)	EWOM volume and valence (ratings) are able to predict total sales
Market Prices	Prices on Amazon, average prices	PATHAK et al. (2010)	Positive effect of valence (ratings)
		SHIN et al. (2011)	Negative effect of nWOM (IT-coded), nWOM and pWOM both lead to price increases for low priced products

Table 5: Effects of eWOM on Product and Market Performance Measures

Online Sales Ranks. AMBLEE and BUI (2008) extracted consumer reviews from Amazon.com of nearly 400 e-books sold in 2006. By means of a logistic and a time series regression, they find a positive connection between eWOM volume and online sales rank. The positive effect of pure volume measures[10] is also in line with the findings of LI and HITT (2008), who report that the number of reviews posted since product release influences sales rank data. They add that especially early consumer reviews tend to be positive which implies a positive self-selection bias people do not fully correct when they consider these early reviews in a later period. CHEN et al. (2004) also confirm these findings by an application within online book reviews from Amazon. They show a strong effect for volume, but clearly report no effect for the included consumer ratings. DHAR and CHANG (2009) pick up these thoughts within their research predicting online music album sales ranks by means of blog chatter from "Technorati". Their main focus is to investigate differences in effect of volume, valence, and social network connectivity of an artist and contrast results to traditional reviews about new music albums. They report that eWOM volume has predictive power for online album sales ranks one and two weeks ahead, whereas eWOM valence is only able to predict sales in week t+1. Traditional critics' reviews still have the strongest impact up to three weeks. In contrast to the findings above, CHEVALIER and MAYZLIN (2006) do not find a clear overall effect of eWOM volume. In their study on book reviews from Barnesandnoble.com and Amazon.com, they only report the effect of volume on Amazon.com. Valence measures (i.e., average star ratings) prove to be a small but significant predictor of future sales independent of the respective platform. The length of each review did not turn out to be a significant predictor. The authors, furthermore, provide evidence for the negativity bias. CHEN et al. (2011b) support these findings in their natural experiment using Amazon.com camera review and sales rank data from 2005 to 2007. With regards to eWOM volume they find that the impact of volume declines over time. The valence effect clearly dominates the reported effect for eWOM volume. FORMAN et al. (2008) also report a more stable influence of eWOM valence compared to volume measures. Clear evidence for a strong positive effect of both volume and valence is provided by the works of PATHAK et al. (2010) and GU et al. (2011). The latter even provide additional proof that product ratings and reviews from one retail website show effect on sales ranks of another platform. By

---

[10] Note that volume measures, of course, are highly influenced by previously posted consumer reviews. The inherent endogeneity forms one of the major challenges for academics and is more and more addressed in publications (e.g., SONNIER et al., 2011, pp. 703-704, TRUSOV et al., 2009, pp. 91-92, CHINTAGUNTA et al., 2010, pp. 945-946). For clarity purposes, endogeneity of eWOM communication shall not be a major focus of the paper at hand.

means of a large scale panel dataset, GU et al. (2013) showed that consumers are more receptive to pWOM in case of popular products, whereas nWOM has a stronger negative effect on the online sales rank of unpopular products. The research group of HO-DAC et al. (2013) partly contradicts those findings by saying that pWOM (nWOM) messages show a significant positive (negative) effect on online sales rank for brands with weaker brand equity. The variance of eWOM valence ratings was found to positively influence book sales rank data on Amazon and Barnes & Noble in the difference-in-difference approach of SUN (2012) only if the average star rating was comparably low. The author adds that the variance of eWOM messages shows a significant interaction with the average valence rating. Researchers should, therefore, incorporate the interaction term of valence and variance in their methodological approaches.

In summary, evidence at hand points towards a stronger link of eWOM volume and online sales rank data. Whereas no single study neglects the influence of eWOM volume, I found plenty of works raising serious doubts concerning the effect of eWOM valence (i.e., GU et al., 2011, PATHAK et al., 2010, FORMAN et al., 2008, CHEN et al., 2004, CHEN et al., 2011b). No single study in this first subsection uses other valence measures than average ratings, which even enhances the need for an in-depth investigation of valence by content analysis. As it can be assumed that strong brand equity correlates with higher product popularity, the contradictory results of HO-DAC et al. (2013) and GU et al. (2013) are worth mentioning. They both work with panel data. For this reason, a methodological bias can at least partly be ruled out. Further research should pick up these contradictions and clarify the effect of product popularity and brand equity. The identification of a significant interaction term of eWOM valence and variance is noticable and has to be picked up and validated by future research following SUN (2012).

Online Sales. Due to data availability reasons, there are only two studies that apply real online sales data from cooperating firms, i.e., online retailer of bath, fragrance, and beauty products (MOE and TRUSOV, 2011) as well as a large online retailer (ETZION and AWAD, 2007). Both studies confirm the positive effect of volume and also find evidence for a positive valence influence. By means of hazard models, MOE and TRUSOV (2011) investigate the impact of social dynamics in the ratings environment on subsequent rating behavior and look at the effects on product sales. They find that eWOM valence directly influences sales. However, the effect is relatively short-lived when indirect effects (i.e., eWOM volume and eWOM valence also being influenced by previously posted eWOM[11]) are also taken into account. EWOM volume is found to have an impact on the respective sales measures. The authors also showed an indirect influence of eWOM dispersion. ETZION and AWAD (2007), in contrast, demonstrate within their time series regressions that volume is only associated with higher sales when the average product ratings are above a certain anchor point. If valence already provides enough differentiation possibilities, consumers do not take pure volume metrics into account. Thus, valence is clearly related to an increase in sales and superior to pure volume measures.

Offline Sales. Another major part of research uses offline sales data as dependent variable. Papers in this section try to show the transferability from eWOM information into the offline purchase behavior. The movie and TV industry are prevalent within the studies at hand due to vivid pre-release discussions online and relatively short product life cycles with many new products coming on the market every year. Again, time series models are the common method to analyze eWOM effects. Volume measures are, again, the strongest and most persistent predictor across all studies that use offline sales data. The volume measures of movie reviews taken from "Yahoo! Movies" are found to positively influence box office performance (DUAN et al., 2008a, DUAN et al., 2008b, LIU, 2006). The studies also reveal that the valence of reviews did not significantly influence sales and box office performance. These findings are in line with the reported effect of GODES and MAYZLIN (2004). Volume and dispersion measures of eWOM conversations in 20 "Usenet" discussion groups about new TV-shows significantly influence the TV-show's offline sales in term of TV-ratings. Dispersion even shows a higher influence than pure volume metrics which only turn significant in the later periods of a TV-show's lifecycle. On the contrary, the authors note that eWOM valence has no significant effect on subsequent ratings. Furthermore, the positive volume effect is also confirmed by the study of DELLAROCAS et al. (2007). They apply pre-release eWOM data from different movie review platforms (i.e., Yahoo! Movies, BoxOfficeMojo, and Hollywood Reporter) to predict box office revenues during the opening week. Valence is only found to be driving subsequent eWOM volume and merely predicts a movie's publicity in general. TUMASJAN et al. (2011), as the only study within this paper's sample, uses Twitter posts (i.e., tweets)[12] to forecast offline sales in terms of elections results of the 2009 federal election in Germany. They come to the conclusion

---

[11] Note that even though this dynamic is not the major focus within the paper at hand, MOE and TRUSOV (2011) seem to be the first who model the whole eWOM creation process as a dynamic construct of previous and current posts and do control for endogeneity in every stage.

[12] JANSEN et al. (2009, p. 2186) confirm that tweets form eWOM limited to 140 characters at a time.

that the volume of tweets predicts election results even better than traditional voting polls. The valence of tweets is able to provide a textual manifestation of the election campaigns. Besides the solely positive volume effects reported by studies above, CHINTAGUNTA et al. (2010) demonstrate that eWOM volume and dispersion taken from the Yahoo! Movies platform is not related to box office ticket sales. Moreover, eWOM valence turns out to be strong, significant predictor of subsequent opening earnings and box office performance. EWOM valence, operationalized as star ratings from the restaurant review platform Yelp, also shows a strong impact in the study of ANDERSON and MAGRUDER (2012). The regression discontinuity design revealed that an extra half-star rating means that restaurants sell out 49% more frequently. The effect was found to be especially strong if alternative resources of information about the restaurant were scarce.

In summary, volume once more turns out to be the most important measure that influences offline sales. Only two studies could show a small effect of valence (i.e., DELLAROCAS et al., 2007, TUMASJAN et al., 2011) and two studies speaks of a high influence of eWOM valence metrics (i.e., CHINTAGUNTA et al., 2010, ANDERSON and MAGRUDER, 2012). Interestingly, GODES and MAYZLIN (2004) and LIU (2006), as the only two studies within this paragraph that apply a valence classification by hand-coding, clearly show no effect of valence onto the respective offline sales measures. There seems to be evidence that consumers do not process the whole information inherent in a specific review when rating measures are available to reduce information processing costs or simply save time.

Total Sales. Three studies focus on eWOM effects on total firm sales. SONNIER et al. (2011) analyzes the effects of chatter about one technical firm on their total sales volume. They report that chatter valence shows a significant effect on sales. The authors find a "positivity bias" so that pWOM has a higher effect size than nWOM. They argue that these results are in line with behavioral research that confirms the higher persuasiveness of pWOM in case of a familiar brand (cf. AHLUWALIA, 2002, p. 278). However, the majority of studies that search for differences in pWOM and nWOM effect strengths conclusively report a negativity bias (e.g., CHEN et al., 2011b, SEN and LERMAN, 2007). SONNIER et al. (2011) further state that the aggregation of eWOM messages across valence masks the real effects on sales. They suggest that, although obtaining the sentiment analysis data is costly relative to publicly available data on the total volume of comments, it improves predictive power of their proposed eWOM model. ZHU and ZHANG (2010) try to predict total sales of Xbox and Playstation 3 game sales by posts on gamespot.com. Volume has a positive influence on sales of all games that demand an online connection of the player. Surprisingly, no effect was found on sales of games that can also be played offline. In addition, eWOM valence and dispersion only drive sales for less popular games. A positive effect was found for valence and a negative effect for dispersion. The authors suggest that datasets with different product types, even for the same product category, could lead to different conclusions. STEPHEN and GALAK (2012) applied a large scale panel regression with data from an online marketplace for microloans. Using the eWOM data from blogs and discussion forums, they could show that valence ratings indeed affect sales. They state that even though both traditional media and eWOM show a positive effect on sales, eWOM's sales elasticity is significantly greater due to the higher frequency of eWOM discussions.

Market Prices. EWOM valence can have a positive effect on market prices (PATHAK et al., 2010). PWOM allows retailers to charge higher prices whereas nWOM, naturally, leads to a decrease. SHIN et al. (2011) analyze the interplay between online chatter about MP3 players, the inherent quality perceptions, and the respective market price. They confirm the negative effect of nWOM and the positive effect of pWOM. The authors also add that the effect of pWOM (nWOM) is higher for low (high) priced products. The market leader's market prices decline stronger by negative chatter, whereas the following brands benefit more than the market leader from positive statements on the internet.

The diverse results in this chapter unveil that across all studies the inherent problem of endogeneity seems to be the greatest challenges. As eWOM proved efficacy to drive sales, the resulting sales, again, increase subsequent eWOM volume. Studies more and more model eWOM as a dynamic process in order to tackle this inherent problem (MOE and TRUSOV, 2011, p. 447). Reported results might also be a consequence of some hidden latent variable that was simply not considered within any empirical approach. Those constructs could be e.g., corporate reputation (AMBLEE and BUI, 2008, p. 11), perceived quality and value (STEPHEN and TOUBIA, 2010, p. 226), or new product launches (MCALISTER et al., 2011, p. 9). Taking into account that the majority of empirical attempts works with fixed or random effects, they are to some extent able to mitigate correlations with unobservable variables in the background (HARTMANN et al., 2008, p. 294). Interestingly, hand-coded valence measures show no effect on product performance measures and market prices (GODES and MAYZLIN, 2004, LIU, 2006). Consumers do not process all information but tend to rely on simpler heuristics like rating systems. Volume seems to be the more stable influencing factor across all studies and methods. One reason for this finding might be that *"[...] when the valence does not convey enough information to differentiate products, the volume becomes a significant factor in consumers' purchase decisions"* (ETZION and AWAD, 2007, p. 11). Nevertheless, CHINTAGUNTA et al. (2010, p. 956) emphasize that their findings about a positive influence of valence and no effect of volume reverses previously established findings in this domain. This especially highlights the importance to academically continue the ongoing discussion.

The effects of the prevoius chapter, of course, cannot be seen as generalizable across all industries and product categories. The majority of studies uses classical experience goods (e.g., books, TV-series, movies, video-games) to analyze eWOM effects. The influence of eWOM differs, when e.g., search or credence qualities come into play or different shopping goals (e.g., utilitarian vs. hedonistic) of consumers are taken into account. Chapter 4.3 will present these moderating effects in more detail.

4.2.3 EWOM and Financial Performance

The effects of eWOM on financial performance measures form the last step of the investigation along the value chain. Financial performance measures, as *how financial markets react*, are of crucial interest to CFOs or CEOs unlike the majority of marketing metrics (KELLER and LEHMANN, 2006, p. 754, GUPTA and ZEITHAML, 2006, p. 719). Fifteen articles could be identified that treat eWOM as an exogenous construct and analyze effects on financial performance measures. The majority of studies in this paragraph use eWOM about stocks extracted from stock message boards (e.g., Yahoo! Finance or Raging Bull) as independent variable. As stock-eWOM follows a similar logic like e.g., analyst forecasts and other information sources about the stock market, the effect of buy/hold/sell recommendations on these platforms follows a different rationale than UGC within a purchase decision or product choice. To enable comparison possibilities to previous and following chapters, pure stock-eWOM shall be neglected in this paragraph. Nevertheless, Table 6 presents all 15 papers sorted by their dependent financial performance measure and splits up regarding their eWOM type used. Due to the comprehensiveness of studies, many papers have to be displayed multiple times.

Financial Performance Measure	Illustrative Dependent Variables	Illustrative Studies	Empirical Findings
Stock Return/ Firm Value	Abnormal stock returns, stock price, excess return	Stock eWOM WYSOCKI (1999); THAPA and BIRD (2010); TUMARKIN and WHITELAW (2001); COOK and LU (2009); ANTWEILER and FRANK (2004); DAS and CHEN (2007); OH and LIU SHENG (2011); BIRD and THAPA (2011)	Positive effect of eWOM volume, no effect of eWOM volume, negative effect of eWOM volume, positive effect of eWOM valence (ratio/IT), negativity effect was found
		General eWOM HU et al. (2011); MCALISTER et al. (2011); TIRUNILLAI and TELLIS (2012); LUO and ZHANG (2013); LUO et al. (2013b); CHEN et al. (2012); HU et al. (2012)	Positive effect of volume and blog visibility, negativity effect (IT), positive effect for eWOM volume and valence (ratings), strongest pre-release, low blog visibility leads to higher stock returns
Stock Volatility/ Risk	Idiosyncratic risk, conditional volatility	Stock eWOM DAS and CHEN (2007); BIRD and THAPA (2011); ANTWEILER and FRANK (2004)	Positive effect of eWOM volume
		General eWOM TIRUNILLAI and TELLIS (2012); LUO and ZHANG (2013); LUO et al. (2013b); CHEN et al. (2012)	Positive effect of volume and competitor chatter, negative effect of nWOM (IT), positive predictive power of eWOM valence (ratings) and volume
Trading Volume	Daily turnover	Stock eWOM TUMARKIN and WHITELAW (2001); ANTWEILER and FRANK (2004); DAS and CHEN (2007)	Positive effect of eWOM volume, negative and no effect of dispersion
		General eWOM HU et al. (2011); TIRUNILLAI and TELLIS (2012)	Positive effect of eWOM volume, nWOM (IT), and blog visibility

Table 6: Effects of eWOM on Financial Performance Measures

Stock Return/Firm Value. MCALISTER et al. (2011) did not focus on stock message boards but scraped the whole internet in order to extract general, stock-unrelated eWOM messages. They find that the volume of total and neutral chatter both have a positive effect on stock returns. TIRUNILLAI and TELLIS (2012) extracted company and product related UGC from online shopping platforms and found that pure volume measures have the strongest relationship with stock returns both in the short and long term. Furthermore, they confirmed the asymmetric impact of valence measures on stock returns. The negative effect of nWOM, again, is stronger than the positive consequences of pWOM. Interestingly, this assumption only holds true for the IT-coded valence measures and is non-existent for numerical ratings (i.e., Amazon star ratings). LUO et al. (2013b) also confirm those results using a panel-dataset of nine IT hard and software companies. They argue that eWOM volume and valence (ratings) are leading indicators for firm equity value. EWOM is found to be superior to other social media metrics like Google searches or web traffic (cf. also LUO and ZHANG, 2013). Especially valence ratings show high predictive power. By means of an event study in the movie industry, CHEN et al. (2012) confirm that eWOM exerts significant impact on stock returns in the direction of their valence (ratings). The effect is strongest pre-release. As soon as sales data become available, the eWOM effect diminishes. Furthermore, HU et al. (2011) found that the visibility of a company across blogs is positively associated with the respective firm's value. However, one year later, HU et al. (2012) report different results. Using a similar dataset they argue that companies with low blog visibility actually realize higher returns than do companies with a comparably higher blog visibility. The effect holds true even when controlling for other risk factors and traditional media coverage and is more prominent for stocks with low institutional ownership. They argue that the blog effect can be attributed to the limited attention theory and cannot be arbitraged due to investors' self-attribution and short-sale constraints.

Stock Volatility/Risk. TIRUNILLAI and TELLIS (2012) show that eWOM volume positively influences stock volatility. In addition, negative valence information in IT-coded UGC messages causes a significant increase in idiosyncratic risk. The authors also showed that chatter about a competitor is capable to influence a firm's risk measures. These results are confirmed by LUO et al. (2013b) and LUO and ZHANG (2013) with very similar datasets.

Trading Volume. Again, eWOM volume induces subsequent trading. The more people talk about a specific company's products and services, the more shares will be traded. In addition, IT-coded nWOM messages also elevate trading quantity in both the short and long term (TIRUNILLAI and TELLIS, 2012). HU et al. (2011) report that trading volume is also caused by a company's blog visibility.

In summary, stock-unrelated eWOM has the potential to predict stock returns. Due to the lack of perfect information, investors use the information on different platforms and on the web in general (TIRUNILLAI and TELLIS, 2012, p. 213). Again, nWOM has higher predictive accuracy than pWOM (TIRUNILLAI and TELLIS, 2012, p. 213). In addition, pWOM and nWOM were found to be highly correlated which might be a symptom of the nature of online communication, where praise can be met swiftly with scorn and vice versa (MCALISTER et al., 2011, p. 10). It is still questionable if blog visibility shows a positive or a negative effect on firm value. Further clarification of the discussion raised by HU et al. (2011) and HU et al. (2012) is needed and a replication seems promising.

4.3   Moderators of the Main Effects

CHEUNG and THADANI (2012, p. 464) provide an overview of eWOM communication by the application of a classical stimulus response model adapted from HOVLAND (1948). They argue that the process of eWOM communication consists of the communicator (i.e., the sender), the stimulus (i.e., the message transmitted), the receiver (i.e., the individual who responds to the communication), and the response itself that is triggered by the respective message. Three arguments make it necessary to adjust the proposed framework for the paper at hand. First, the authors see the communicator as independent from the respective stimulus he sends. This remains doubtful taking into account that social media users decide themselves what they write or review about. Second, CHEUNG and THADANI (2012) state that platform effects (e.g., Facebook vs. blog vs. forum) only influence the degree of eWOM adoption. As it can be assumed that platforms, especially discussion boards or forums are mostly topic specific (cf. e.g., DE VALCK et al., 2009, NAMBISAN and WATT, 2011), the contextual factors have to be considered much earlier than in the stage of the actual response measure. Third, the authors use the framework to sort both, moderator effects and actual eWOM outcomes, whereas in this paper only moderator effects shall be categorized. And fourth, they only focus on individual-level eWOM research as a directed interpersonal approach. The paper at hand uses both, individual and market-level studies as its source for systematization. Thus, the proposed framework of CHEUNG and THADANI cannot be transferred directly to systematize the identified moderators of the main effects in the upper chapters. It has to be customized to fit this paper's approach. Figure 2 provides an overview of the proposed classification.

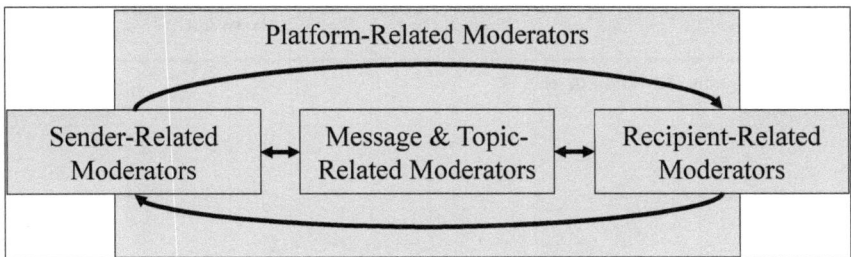

Figure 2: Framework for Moderator-Effects

Table 7 provides an overview of the identified moderators of eWOM effects along the social media value chain sorted by the types of moderators presented in Figure 2. The articles in this paragraph come from the research area of consumer mindset metrics and product market performance. Because of their major focus on stock-chatter, financial performance literature does not add to the moderators extracted in this chapter.

Type of Moderator	Illustrative Moderators	Illustrative Studies	Empirical Findings
Sender-Related	Expertise & Trustworthiness	SENECAL and NANTEL (2004); SMITH et al. (2005); ADJEI et al. (2009)	↑expertise and trust→↑eWOM effect
	Product Experience	GARNEFELD et al. (2010)	↓experience→↑ eWOM effect of sending
	Credibility	COOK and LU (2009)	↑credibility→↑eWOM effect
	Information disclosure	FORMAN et al. (2008)	↑disclosure→↑eWOM effect
Relationship of Sender & Receiver	Tie strength	DE BRUYN and LILIEN (2008); PAN and CHIOU (2011) SMITH et al. (2005)	↑tie strength →↑eWOM effect
	Demographic similarity	DE BRUYN and LILIEN (2008)	↑dissimilarity→↑eWOM effect
	Geographical proximity	FORMAN et al. (2008)	↑proximity→↑eWOM effect
Recipient-Related	Consumption goal (regulatory focus)	ZHANG et al. (2010)	↑promotion (prevention) focus→ ↑pWOM (↑nWOM) effect
	Product/Brand experience	ADJEI et al. (2009); CHAKRAVARTY et al. (2010)	↓product and brand experience→ ↑eWOM effect; ADJEI et al. (2009) report opposite
	Gender	BICKART and SCHINDLER (2001)	eWOM effect higher for females
	Internet proficiency	DE VALCK et al. (2009); THORBJØRNSEN et al. (2002)	↑internet proficiency→↓eWOM effect
	Need for cognition	GUPTA and HARRIS (2010)	↑higher NFC→↑eWOM effect
	Need for uniqueness	WANG et al. (2012)	↓lower NFU→↑ eWOM effect
	Product involvement	PARK et al. (2007)	↓involvement→↑eWOM volume rather than review quality
	Shopping goal	SMITH et al. (2005)	↑utilitarian shopping goal (↑hedonistic)→↑effect of eWOM (↓eWOM effect)

Table 7: Moderators of eWOM Effects

Type of Moderator	Illustrative Moderators	Illustrative Studies	Empirical Findings
Message & Topic-Related	Product complexity	ADJEI et al. (2009)	↑complexity→↑eWOM effect
	Product types	PAN and CHIOU (2011); PARK and LEE (2009); SEN and LERMAN (2007); SENECAL and NANTEL (2004); BENLIAN et al. (2012); JIMÉNEZ and MENDOZA (2013)	↑eWOM effect for hedonic, and experience goods. Negativity effect ↑for credence and experience goods ↑eWOM effect for experience goods ↑eWOM detail→↑ effect for search than experience goods
	Consumption type → symbolic/social	PARRY et al. (2012)	↑eWOM effect when product is consumed socially visible (Iphone)
	Recency and obscurity of recommendation	PATHAK et al. (2010) SHIN et al. (2011)	↑recency & ↑obscurity→↑eWOM effect ↑price→↑ nWOM effect
	Price of product/brand Brand and product popularity	SHIN et al. (2011); ZHU and ZHANG (2010); DEWAN and RAMAPRASAD (2012)	↑popularity→↑nWOM effect & ↓pWOM effect ↑eWOM effect for niche vs. mainstream products
	Brand equity	HO-DAC et al. (2013)	↑eWOM effect for brands with low brand equity
Platform-Related	Platform type (user vs. corporate initiated)	ADJEI et al. (2009); BICKART and SCHINDLER (2001); JANG et al. (2008); SENECAL and NANTEL (2004)	User (company) initiated→↑(↓) eWOM effect; ADJEI et al. (2009) and SENECAL and NANTEL (2004) report no difference
	Website reputation	PARK and LEE (2009)	↑reputation→↑eWOM effect
	Brand community size	SCARPI (2010)	↓size→↑eWOM effect
	EWOM source	GU et al. (2011)	External > internal eWOM

Table 7 continued: Moderators of eWOM Effects

Sender-Related. As eWOM messages are produced by other consumers and social media users, characteristics of the sender play a huge role in influencing the strength of a respective eWOM message. Certain information about the sender can increase or decrease the penetrating power. Perceived expertise/trustworthiness of an eWOM sender increases the effect on consumer mindset metrics like uncertainty reduction, trust, or product choice decision (cf. ADJEI et al., 2009, SMITH et al., 2005, MAYZLIN, 2006). The more information is disclosed about an eWOM creator by a specific social media platform, or by the sender himself, the higher the perceived source credibility which also transfers into aggregated sales data (FORMAN et al., 2008). GARNEFELD et al. (2010) report, sending out eWOM messages also enhances the sender's affective commitment and behavioral loyalty to a brand or company. This effect is stronger for eWOM senders with low product or brand experience.

Relationship of Sender & Receiver. Sender and receiver of eWOM messages are not isolated from each other (e.g., Facebook friends) in the social media environment. A strong social relationship in an online setting between eWOM creator and receiver can be a result of their connection in the offline world or a strong established connection in the specific online setting. Social tie strength exerts a positive influence on the strength of eWOM recommendations. The stronger the tie between sender and receiver, the higher the identified effect on product awareness measures (DE BRUYN and LILIEN, 2008), credibility and helpfulness of messages (PAN and CHIOU, 2011), and product choices (SMITH et al., 2005). DE BRUYN and LILIEN (2008) add, that when it comes to demographic similarities, it is not always the most similar person that has the highest influence on recipients. Dissimilar ties are found to be more influential than demographically similar ones across different stages of the decision-making process. Book recommendations collected from Amazon proved to be more effective when sent by a consumer that shows geographical proximity to the eWOM receiver (FORMAN et al., 2008). It makes eWOM messages more helpful and transfers more strongly into actual online sales data. Information given about eWOM senders may be used to develop social categorizations such as those based on geographic location, which enhances common identity (FORMAN et al., 2008, p. 309).

Recipient-Related. The heterogeneousness of eWOM receivers within the social media environment feeds the discussion about recipient related moderators. Personality traits and attitudes form the most important attribute used to operationalize these individual differences. Messages that confirm prior attitudes, experiences, abilities, and beliefs enhance the influence of UGC. Within laboratory experiments this could be shown for the regulatory focus as consumption goal (ZHANG et al., 2010), need for cognition (GUPTA and HARRIS, 2010), or internet proficiency (DE VALCK et al., 2009, THORBJØRNSEN et al., 2002)[13]. The experiment of BICKART and SCHINDLER (2001) revealed a slight tendency that the effects of UGC on the consumer mindset are stronger for female participants. The actual previous experience with a product or brand was also found to negatively moderate the effect of UGC. Three laboratory experiments of CHAKRAVARTY et al. (2010) using simulated movie review platforms reveal that movie going frequency as proxy for product experience negatively moderates the effect of user generated movie reviews. The less experienced people are with a specific product or brand, the higher the influence of eWOM on perceived pre-release product value. Surprisingly, ADJEI et

---

[13] Note that even though DE VALCK et al. (2009) do not use an experimental setup, they report a weak, significant, and negative effect of internet proficiency (p < 0.1) on different decision making phases in their regression analysis.

al. (2009) report the contrary. Using survey data from two woodworking equipment forums, they find that perceived eWOM quality leads to more uncertainty reduction for those with higher personal expertise. The authors reason this effect with the high specificity of the equipment and a better ability of experienced users to sift through large amounts of information. Dependent from receivers' shopping goal, SMITH et al. (2005) show that the influence of sender's expertise and rapport between sender and receiver changes. Consumers with a utilitarian shopping goal put more weight on a sender's expertise, whereas hedonistic shoppers prefer eWOM from strong ties. By means of a structural equation model using Chinese social media users, WANG et al. (2012) investigate the moderating effect of need for uniqueness. People that score low in their need for uniqueness are found to be influenced more strongly by eWOM messages. People who emphasize uniqueness want to differentiate themselves more and realize consumption decisions that are less dependent on sources like eWOM, but based on their own preferences.

Message & Topic-Related. EWOM metrics like volume, length, valence, or dispersion can essentially be seen as a classical moderator of social media communication where e.g., the valence of a post positively moderates the subsequent effects of eWOM. As chapter 4.1 specifically deals with different ways to operationalize eWOM, this paragraph contains exceeding factors beyond classical UGC metrics. PATHAK et al. (2010) report a significantly higher effect of eWOM taken from Amazon.com and Barnesandnoble.com when the recommended item is new. They add that the obscurity of a recommended product also positively moderates the influence of online recommendations on online sales ranks. ADJEI et al. (2009) find that eWOM about a more complex product has a higher influence on receivers' consumer mindset than UGC about less complex goods or services. The use of eWOM as quality signal reduces inherent choice complexity and acts as information surrogate for a product's hardly observable quality. Negative discussions show a larger effect-size when the product is higher priced or more popular (ZHU and ZHANG, 2010, SHIN et al., 2011). However, DEWAN and RAMAPRASAD (2012) and HO-DAC et al. (2013) find the contrary. Using large scale datasets they find that the effect of eWOM discussions and messages is higher for niche products in the music industry (DEWAN and RAMAPRASAD, 2012) and consumer electronic brands that show a lower level of brand equity (HO-DAC et al., 2013). As an interim conclusion, the majority of studies still apply UGC from the experience-good sector (e.g., computer games, restaurant guide). More generally speaking, the eWOM effect for both volume and valence measures is found to be higher when users exchange information about experience goods than search goods (SENECAL and NANTEL, 2004, BENLIAN et al., 2012). Especially nWOM is more important in the case of experience than search goods (PARK and LEE, 2009). However, the laboratory experiment of JIMÉNEZ and MENDOZA (2013) revealed that the level of detail inherent in eWOM messages shows a higher effect in case of search goods as consumers specifically investigate different sources for in-depth information. The negativity bias is also stronger for hedonic products compared to utilitarian goods (SEN and LERMAN, 2007). SEN and LERMAN find this effect within their experimental setup with five utilitarian (i.e., PDAs) and five hedonic (i.e., movie videos) goods. They add that consumers engage more with nWOM posts in the case of a hedonic product category. Product category, thus, moderates the effect on consumers' attitude towards the product. PARRY et al. (2012) find that the type of consumption associated with a certain product plays an important role regarding the eWOM effectiveness. In their sample of Japanese consumer electronic customers they found that the eWOM effect is higher for products that are socially visible and are consumed in a symbolic way (i.e., smart phone).

Platform-Related. Contradictory results were found regarding the moderator influence of platform types. Authors hypothesize that UGC on consumer generated platforms is more relevant to consumers, can carry more empathy, and has more credibility than corporate owned vehicles (BICKART and SCHINDLER, 2001). BICKART and SCHINDLER (2001) find positive evidence that UGC creates higher product awareness and interest than company websites. JANG et al. (2008) confirm that UGC on consumer initiated brand communities shows higher information quality and has higher commitment and loyalty consequences than corporately owned forums. Contrary to those findings, ADJEI et al. (2009) and SENECAL and NANTEL (2004) report no significant difference between the eWOM effect on company-generated platforms and consumer generated platforms. PARK and LEE (2009) unveil a positive moderator effect of website reputation. They state that the effect of eWOM on established websites is higher than on unestablished websites. SCARPI (2010) adds that the size of a social media platform and its connected community negatively influences the eWOM effect on brand loyalty. He argues that small communities do operate more like a group of friends which evokes attachment and belongingness emotions that put more weight on community eWOM exchange (cf. also JAHN et al., 2011). By analyzing eWOM discussions from two different online retailers, GU et al. (2011) found that eWOM discussions also show spill-over effects. The authors extracted UGC about digital cameras from multiple product review platforms. The effect of eWOM from external platforms turned out to be more effective in predicting sales ranks on Amazon than internal consumer recommendations extracted from Amazon itself. For this reason, monitoring eWOM discussions across a broader range of platforms seems promising.

In summary, the proposed framework of Figure 2 offers a good way to classify the moderators tested along the social media value chain. Interestingly, most moderator-effects are again found within laboratory experimental setups. It still remains questionable if the proposed effects also hold true in field studies and the more complex online environment. The role of size or popularity moderators is still unanswered. The question if eWOM is more predictive for performance measures of popular products (e.g., SHIN et al., 2011) or rather unknown products (e.g., DEWAN and RAMAPRASAD, 2012) demands further clarification.

4.4 The Company and its Dual Role

Whereas in the offline environment advertising and communication about products and brands was solely induced by the respective company, the web 2.0 landscape opens up a powerful tool for customers to independently contribute to discussions and express their opinion about product, brand, company, or service related factors. This constant and independent level of buzz makes it necessary to monitor and moderate ongoing discussions (GODES et al., 2005, p. 421). Questions of who, when, what, and where a company should respond or engage in eWOM dicussions are of key interest for marketing managers. Within the 28 papers identified in this section only two analyze possibilities for companies to moderate ongoing nWOM discussions. The majority of works, however, focuses on the importance of eWOM for viral marketing campaigns and try to answer the question of how companies can purposefully create eWOM (e.g., BERGER and MILKMAN, 2012). Furthermore, studies give advice on how social media can be implemented in corporate marketing strategies (e.g., VAN DER LANS et al., 2009, WINER, 2009). Even though there are plenty of articles with empirical backgrounds, the amount of theoretical contributions and game theoretical approaches is slightly dominating. This chapter follows the dual role of companies and presents results sorted by how companies can moderate ongoing eWOM discussions and how they can stimulate UGC through viral marketing campaigns. In one last stanza, the chapter at hand will present different views of how social media marketing beneficially ties into a company's overall marketing strategy.

The Company as Moderator. VAN LAER and DE RUYTER (2010) present results from three experimental studies with a main focus on corporate response strategies for nWOM communications on blogs. They investigate effects of response format (i.e., narrative vs. analytical), response content (i.e., denial vs. apology), and replying person (i.e., responsible employee vs. company's spokesperson) on the dependent variables of "intention to switch" and "perceived integrity". When a company chooses an analytical response format, consumers perceive greater integrity and switch less often if the response content is denial rather than apology. In case of a narrative response format, the integrity is higher and the intention to switch is lower if the response content is apology rather than denial. Consumers also perceive greater integrity if the responsible employee, rather than a company's spokesperson issues the apology. To show empathy in a reply also turned out to be highly important. It, therefore, has a significant, positive impact on perceptions of the integrity of the accused party. Even though the authors created their scenarios only within the automobile, healthcare, and public railway context, they derive clear implications for practitioners. The approach of VAN LAER and DE RUYTER (2010) should be expanded to different industries and other settings to test the robustness of their empirical findings. The second study about effective means for companies to counteract nWOM was conducted by VAN NOORT and WILLEMSEN (2012). They also use ficticious blog posts and apply a scenario of a car recall in the automotive industry. They focus on the role of webcare intervention strategies (i.e., proactive vs. reactive) and investigate the effects on "overall brand evaluation" moderated by platform type. The authors report that proactive intervention strategies engenders more positive brand evaluations on a brand-generated than consumer-generated platform. Further, they differentiate the perceived "corporateness" and "human voice" of a respective post. It is found that proactiveness is perceived as higher in natural human voice on a brand than consumer-generated platform. Reactive intervention strategies, however, create positive brand evaluations, irrespective of the platform and are also perceived as high in natural human voice. As the authors only look at one industry and provide scarce infromation about the experimental treatment, their approach has to be enhanced to other industries and settings. Also, a retrospective look at company engagements within archived nWOM discussions (e.g., on Facebook) seems promising.

The Company as Creator. Applying customer-leverage possibilities for corporate communication aspects has long been of interest for marketing managers (DE BRUYN and LILIEN, 2008, p. 151). Viral marketing can be seen as a technique which utilizes the internet to transmit and spread messages among individuals who will filter and forward the messages to their peers. The goal is to capture attention, triggering interest, and eventually cause product adoption or create sales (DE BRUYN and LILIEN, 2008, p. 152, WOERNDL et al., 2008, p. 34). By means of virally generated sales, higher revenues can be generated compared to traditional advertising efforts. VILLANUEVA et al. (2008) show that eWOM-induced customers add nearly twice as much long-term value to the respective firm. But it is still difficult to identify substantial evidence to explain why and how viral marketing works. This is why viral campaigns are currently viewed as more of an art than a science (DE BRUYN and LILIEN, 2008, p. 152). Articles in this section focus on the investigation of two major aspects of viral campaigns: Content deliberations and seeding strategies.

Content. The content is of crucial importance for viral marketing campaigns. BERGER and MILKMAN (2012) show that positive content is more viral than negative content. The authors add that marketing managers should target activating emotions (e.g., awe, anxiety, and anger) because they are linked to a higher virality. Emotions characterized by deactivation (e.g., sadness) are negatively linked to a campaigns success. Closely connected to these message characteristics, HO and DEMPSEY (2010) provide insight into what motivates people to process and forward online content. They report that a viral campaign is more successful when the communication strategy fits key motivations of the receivers. Opinion leaders' inclusion, altruism, and need for personal growth should be addressed to enhance virality of marketing messages. The content of a viral message has to further consider the current atmosphere within the target group (e.g., scandals/topics in society) to be successful. Furthermore, content should be humorous, creatively executed (BAMPO et al., 2008), have a high originality, and should create desire (LIN and HUANG, 2006). KOZINETS et al. (2010) conclude that blogs are highly suitable for viral campaigns. However, it has to be kept in mind that the content of viral messages has to fit in the system of character narratives, communication forms, and communal norms inherent on a respective platform. Importantly for marketers, the number of blogs about a product is also capable of predicting market outcomes (ONISHI and MANCHANDA, 2012). However, DROGE et al. (2010) add that only measuring the volume of positive mentions across blogs is too short. The posts and reactions following a viral message bear valuable information that should be extracted by the respective company for at least three days after the message was seeded on the specific blog.

Seeding. BAMPO et al. (2008) report that in general the reach is proportional to the number of seeds used. When resources allow contacting a high number of seeds, the structure of underlying networks is less important. But with limited resources, the network structure has a marked impact. The authors find that in particular, scale-free networks are efficient for viral campaigns. Thus, higher numbers of seeds can be exchanged trough identifying influential customers who might then function as hubs. Within their game theoretical study, GALEOTTI and GOYAL (2009) also report that knowing the underlying network structure is of crucial importance for viral campaign's success. However, they state that it is not always the most connected individual within a network that should be contacted at first hand. When a company wants to increase the strength of influence on each particular individual, it is the best option to target poorly connected individuals. HINZ et al. (2011) find that the highest number of referrals can be created if a message is sent to hubs or bridges of the underlying network. Hubs naturally have a multitude of connections. Bridges allow a viral message to spread across different subpopulations of the network that would not be connected without them. It is also not always the most loyal customer who should be targeted. It has to be kept in mind that less loyal customers are more likely to attract less experienced and less informed people that are harder to reach for marketing managers (GODES and MAYZLIN, 2009). DE BRUYN and LILIEN (2008) add that given the importance of tie strength and perceptual affinity it is the network of friends and acquaintances rather than the network of professionals and colleagues that is most likely to generate awareness. However, not using very close social ties among the actors within the seeding process also proves inefficiency.

Besides the advice regarding viral content and seeding strategies, research also provides further insights about social media phenomena and marketing practice. In his theoretic contribution, KOZINETS (2002) introduces "Netnography" as a fast, simple, and cheap tool for marketing research. Highly relevant marketing information can be extracted much easier compared to the traditional method of ethnography by using brand communities and forums to conduct targeted marketing research. Research not only looks at the positive aspects of brand fan communities. KRISHNAMURTHY and KUCUK (2009) provide evidence that especially for successful brands with high brand value, the presence of anti-brand sites is a logical consequence. The number of anti-brand sites on the internet is directly associated with a decrease in brand value reported in the Business Week's top 100 brand list of the years 2004 and 2005. However, CLEMONS et al. (2006) use data from eWOM discussions of a beer-rating platform in the USA to show that eWOM dispersion is positively associated with sales growth. It is thus more important to have some customers who love you than a huge number of customers who merely like you. Products targeted at consumers who tend to have extreme reactions will grow faster. To simply use eWOM as an external source of information is also not enough in today's online environment. Companies also try to disguise corporate product ratings as UGC. In his game theoretic paper, DELLAROCAS (2006) finds that in a broad class of settings, firms of all types as well as society would be strictly better off if a manipulation of posts would not be possible. However, he adds that the current situation is similar to a "rat race". Companies have to manipulate consumer generated eWOM messages to not suffer a strategic disadvantage.

How Social Media Ties into the Overall Marketing Strategy. Marketing by the directed activation of viral chains can be seen as more persistent compared to traditional advertising vehicles. TRUSOV et al. (2009) report that the effects of viral campaigns remain for approximately three weeks. Traditional tools of media and events wear off after just a few days. A similar effect on long term customer equity measures could be empirically shown by VILLANUEVA et al. (2008). EWOM induced customers add twice as much long-term value to the firm than traditional marketing induced customers. Financial incentives should be used to boost the generation of eWOM and forwarding behavior. Following the argument of viral marketing's supremacy, many articles argue that social media marketing will substitute traditional vehicles because social networks are an unbiased milieu where peoples voluntarily and freely congregate and exchange information. Traditional push advertising itself is constantly losing credibility and impact (CLEMONS, 2009b, pp. 48, 52). In their game theoretical contribution, GALEOTTI and GOYAL (2009) show that for a firm with heavy advertising, eWOM and advertising are indeed substitutes. A boost in eWOM lowers optimal advertising spending and vice versa if a firm undertakes only little advertising to start with. MAYZLIN (2006) constrains the substitutional point of view in her game theoretical article and states that both can only be seen as equal when advertising messages are also anonymous. In her scenario, advertising messages are disguised as consumer generated eWOM messages and are, thus, indistinguishable to receiving consumers. However, on a market with inferior and superior products, this leads to the necessity for companies to spend more resources promoting inferior products. A unique equilibrium could be identified where eWOM is still a persuasive force regardless of promotional chat activities from competing firms. CHEN and XIE (2008) restrict the commutability of social media marketing and traditional advertising, too. They report that both are only substitutes when product costs are high and/or there are sufficient novice product users. In other words, a seller has to reduce advertising efforts after eWOM reviews become available. There is a complementary relationship when product costs are low and/or product users are more sophisticated. The sellers have to increase advertising expenditures when eWOM posts become available to combine eWOM and advertising effects for a superior outcome. By looking into data from an actual viral marketing campaign of a financial service provider, VAN DER LANS et al. (2009) found that marketing activities directly connected with a viral campaign show a stronger long-term effect. Targeted supportive advertising online and offline delays the wear-out effect of campaigns. Looking at blogs, ONISHI and MANCHANDA (2012) also conclude that both have a complementary relationship because pre-launch advertising spurs blogging activities but becomes less effective post-launch. An integration of viral marketing into existing marketing strategies as enhancer of traditional marketing seems to be the logical consequence due to its inexpensiveness and potential to quickly reach a large target audience. However, WINER (2009, p. 116) states that due to social media's interactivity and the sheer uncountable number of alternative ways to communicate with customers, the availability and integration of web 2.0 marketing opportunities has created both opportunities and problems for managers and academics. Being "the new hybrid element of the promotional mix" (MANGOLD and FAULDS, 2009) and changing the marketing landscape to a "pinball like environment" (HENNIG-THURAU et al., 2010) exhibits the fact that customers and consumers have extremely strengthened their position in the web 2.0 environment. Only those companies who accept this new shift in powers and the necessary integration of new media into their marketing toolbox will survive the next 50 years (BREAZEALE, 2009, p. 313).

5   Conclusion, Limitations, and Implications

Appendices 1 — 4 provide a short evaluation of the studies used as input for the conducted narrative review. Nevertheless, some aspects of the selected studies shall be discussed in more detail. Overall, the quality of studies is rather high. Empirical analyses as well as theoretical contributions all show a superior level of quality that, of course, can be seen as a result of the article selection process described in chapter 3. Even though measurement techniques widely vary among the studies, they can be seen as consistently positive. Thus, criticism can only be made on a very high level, however, some general aspects regarding data bases, prevalent methods, and sampling characteristics have to be mentioned. With regard to eWOM effects on consumer mindset metrics, the majority of studies apply experimental setups mostly in laboratory settings. The use of mainly student samples as representatives of the general population may slightly bias the results regarding their different levels of income, education, age, and knowledge. Especially when taking into account that the average social media and network user for example in Germany is in his late thirties (BITKOM, 2011, p. 6)[14]. Social Media research needs subsequent field studies to investigate eWOM effects in real-life settings with a multitude of distracting information sources to judge the external validity of evinced results (cf. also LUO et al., 2013b, ARAL and WALKER, 2012). A challenging question for further research is also given by the endogeneity of eWOM discussions and its interconnection with previous performance measures as well as previous posting volume. Even though the narrative review at hand does not take inherent endogeneity into account, it provides a first framework for a classification of different eWOM research areas. I encourage further research to pick up the classification of my paper and conduct quantitative meta-analysis with a main focus on methodologies and data used to identify a quality label for major contributions in the field. Also, the focus of target journals for a quantitative approach should not only be limited to top-tier journals of the field but comprehensively collect contributions to the research stream. The multitude and highly diverse approaches, methodologies, and datasets, of course, make quantitative meta-analysis a truly challenging task. But academics as well as researchers still strive to answer the question if the overall effect of social media is generalizable, stable, and comparable across studies conducted. Besides these methodological and sample aspects, the applied industries in the papers at hand also raise minor doubts about the generalization of the reported effects. A major part of studies applies eWOM and UGC data from the movie and book sector. This might be mainly for data availability reasons. However, the application of mostly experience goods in eWOM literature positively biases reported effects and has to be extended to other industries and product categories (e.g., service industry). Further, the conducted literature search was not limited to studies with a focus on eWOM created by consumers. It is interesting that only two studies could be identified with a focus on how companies can moderate negative consumer complaints and discussions. Strategies for counteracting negative consumer posts should be developed further to provide a broader toolbox for the social media responsible (e.g., MUNZEL and MEYER, 2011). The paper at hand also wants to encourage research to take the lack of eWOM escalation models as a starting point

---

[14] This number is calculated on the basis of both private and professional social networks (e.g. XING).

for further investigation. The question of what makes a negative post critical for brands is only partially answered (cf. e.g., DECKER and TRUSOV, 2010). The still blurred picture of valence and the strong influence of pure eWOM volume, so far, make it difficult to derive clear guidelines if and how valence of chatter and buzz shall be tracked for a superior monitoring of potential eWOM effects. It has to be considered if other classification schemes of UGC might be more efficient than a pure separation in positive, neutral, and negative chatter. Beyond that, social media platforms like Facebook or Google+ are underrepresented in today's top tier journals. Whereas plenty of research is available supporting practitioners within viral marketing campaigns, little is known about the right application, design, or posting activity of companies on corporate or brand fan pages, even though similarities to viral campaigns can be observed (cf. e.g., JAHN and KUNZ, 2011, p. 105). Practitioners seem to follow a trial-and-error strategy on their brand pages mostly guided by simple reach metrics as number of likes or number of comments (cf. e.g., DE VRIES et al., 2012). Research has to extend these awareness-like metrics and investigate if and how it is possible to move consumers further down the brand funnel. Questions like "are targeted company-generated posts on e.g., Facebook able to strengthen a consumer's attitude towards a brand, purchase intention, or brand image" have to be put on research agendas. In addition, brand image effects of eWOM have not been investigated in any study of the sample at hand.

This paper provides a road map for practitioners showing effects of social media metrics on corporate performance measures along the value chain. The integration of social media and especially eWOM marketing can be seen as an elementary requirement of web 2.0 developments as traditional push marketing will become more and more limited (KOZINETS et al., 2010, p. 87, CLEMONS, 2009b, p. 55). The interactive involvement of the customer and a constant engagement in social media communications is unavoidable (HENNIG-THURAU et al., 2010, p. 324). This does not mean that companies only have to produce content in a creative, humorous, and original way to entertain customers, users, or fans (BAMPO et al., 2008, LIN and HUANG, 2006). It also means to be informed about a company's current temperature in the web 2.0 environment. This paper shows that eWOM volume measures already enable a prediction of subsequent effects along the social media value chain. It becomes obvious that discussions on the internet indeed influence key firm performance metrics. A regular tracking of key social media metrics like level/volume of chatter and buzz with a parallel valence coding is a key issue for today's marketers. Even though there are some tendencies that information given within

UGC posts is not completely processed by consumers, a pure extraction of simple rating measures would fall short. IT-coded valence algorithms are a cost effective alternative to hand-coding, but flaws in language processing algorithms have to be kept in mind. Firms should further implement social media metrics into early warning systems and marketing dashboards. By doing so, companies are able to use the real-time communication of web 2.0 to their advantage, be up-to-date, and able to counteract negative developments immediately. Defining guidelines of how to answer and handle negative consumer posts on social media platforms is also a key success factor. Taking into account that corporate social media actions again form a touch-point with customers, which itself is again an important antecedent for eWOM creation, also fosters high relevancy for marketers today. A good management of UGC as well as a good communications strategy for brand pages does not necessarily boost firm performance measures right away. However, it provides a base for a constant positive development of a company or brand and forms an important precursor for consumer mindset metrics and corporate performance measures.

References

ADJEI, M. T., NOBLE, S. M. & NOBLE, C. H. 2009. The Influence of C2C Communications in Online Brand Communities on Customer Purchase Behavior. *Journal of the Academy of Marketing Science,* 38(5), 634-653.

AGARWAL, R., GUPTA, A. K. & KRAUT, R. 2008. Editorial Overview - The Interplay Between Digital and Social Networks. *Information Systems Research,* 19(3), 243-252.

AGGARWAL, R. & SINGH, H. 2013. Differential Influence of Blogs across Different Stages of Decision Making: The Case of Venture Capitalists. *MIS Quarterly,* 37(4), 1093-1112.

AHLUWALIA, R. 2002. How Prevalent Is the Negativity Effect in Consumer Environments? *Journal of Consumer Research,* 29(2), 270-279.

ALJUKHADAR, M., SENECAL, S. & OUELLETTE, D. 2010. Can the Media Richness of a Privacy Disclosure Enhance Outcome? A Multifaceted View of Trust in Rich Media Environments. *International Journal of Electronic Commerce,* 14(4), 103-126.

AMBLEE, N. & BUI, T. 2008. Can Brand Reputation Improve the Odds of Being Reviewed On-Line? *International Journal of Electronic Commerce,* 12(3), 11-28.

AMBLER, T., BHATTACHARYA, C. B., EDELL, J., KELLER, K. L., LEMON, K. N. & MITTAL, V. 2002. Relating Brand and Customer Perspectives on Marketing Management. *Journal of Service Research,* 5(1), 13-25.

ANDERSON, M. & MAGRUDER, J. 2012. Learning from the Crowd: Regression Discontinuity Estimates of the Effects of an Online Review Database. *The Economic Journal,* 122(563), 957-989.

ANTWEILER, W. & FRANK, M. Z. 2004. Is All That Talk Just Noise? The Information Content of Internet Stock Message Boards. *The Journal of Finance,* 59(3), 1259-1294.

ARAL, S. & WALKER, D. 2012. Identifying Influential and Susceptible Members of Social Networks. *Science,* 337(6092), 337-341.

ARNDT, J. 1967. Word of Mouth Advertising and Informal Communication. *In:* COX, D. F. (ed.) *Risk Taking and Information Handling in Consumer Behavior.* Harvard: University Press, 188-239.

BAMPO, M., EWING, M. T., MATHER, D. R., STEWART, D. & WALLACE, M. 2008. The Effects of the Social Structure of Digital Networks on Viral Marketing Performance. *Information Systems Research,* 19(3), 273-290.

BART, Y., SHANKAR, V., SULTAN, F. & URBAN, G. L. 2005. Are the Drivers and Role of Online Trust the Same for All Web Sites and Consumers? A Large-Scale Exploratory Empirical Study. *Journal of Marketing,* 69(4), 133-152.

BENLIAN, A., TITAH, R. & HESS, T. 2012. Differential Effects of Provider Recommendations and Consumer Reviews in E-Commerce Transactions: An Experimental Study. *Journal of Management Information Systems,* 29(1), 237-272.

BERGER, J. & SCHWARTZ, E. M. 2011. What Drives Immediate and Ongoing Word of Mouth? *Journal of Marketing Research,* 48(5), 869-880.

BERGER, J. & MILKMAN, K. L. 2012. What Makes Online Content Viral? *Journal of Marketing Research*, 49(2), 192-205.

BICKART, B. & SCHINDLER, R. M. 2001. Internet Forums as Influential Sources of Consumer Information. *Journal of Interactive Marketing*, 15(3), 31-40.

BIJMOLT, T. H. A. & PIETERS, R. G. M. 2001. Meta-Analysis in Marketing when Studies Contain Multiple Measurements. *Marketing Letters*, 12(2), 157-169.

BIRD, R. & THAPA, K. 2011. Stock Message Board and Investors' Reaction to Company News. *Working Paper.* http://www.afaanz.org/openconf/2011/modules/request.php? module=oc_proceedings&action=view.php&a=Accept+as+Paper&id=256 [Accessed 2013-06-13].

BITKOM, 2011. *Soziale Netzwerke - Eine repräsentative Untersuchung zur Nutzung sozialer Netzwerke im Internet* [Online]. Berlin: Bundesverband Informationswirtschaft, Telekommunikation und neue Medien e. V. Available: http://www.bitkom.org/files/ documents/BITKOM_Publikation_Soziale_Netzwerke.pdf [Accessed 2013-06-13].

BONE, P. F. 1992. Determinants of WOM Communication during Product Consumption. *Advances in Consumer Research*, 19(1), 579-583.

BREAZEALE, M. 2009. Word of Mouse – An Assessment of Electronic Word-of-Mouth Research. *International Journal of Market Research*, 51(3), 297-318.

BRIGGS, R., KRISHNAN, R. & BORIN, N. 2005. Integrated Multichannel Communication Strategies: Evaluating the Return on Marketing Objectives - The Case of the 2004 Ford F-150 Launch. *Journal of Interactive Marketing*, 19(3), 81-90.

BRODIE, R. J., ILIC, A., JURIC, B. & HOLLEBEEK, L. 2011. Consumer Engagement in a Virtual Brand Community: An Exploratory Analysis. *Journal of Business Research*, 66(1), 105-114.

BROWN, J. J. & REINGEN, P. H. 1987. Social Ties and Word-of-Mouth Referral Behavior. *Journal of Consumer Research*, 14(3), 350-362.

BROWN, T. J., BARRY, T. E., DACIN, P. A. & GUNST, R. F. 2005. Spreading the Word: Investigating Antecedents of Consumers' Positive Word-of-Mouth Intentions and Behaviors in a Retailing Context. *Journal of the Academy of Marketing Science*, 33(2), 123-138.

CABLE, D. M., AIMAN-SMITH, L., MULVEY, P. W. & EDWARDS, J. R. 2000. The Sources and Accuracy of Job Applicants' Beliefs about Organizational Culture. *Academy of Management Journal*, 43(6), 1076-1085.

CHAKRAVARTY, A., LIU, Y. & MAZUMDAR, T. 2010. The Differential Effects of Online Word-of-Mouth and Critics' Reviews on Pre-release Movie Evaluation. *Journal of Interactive Marketing*, 24(3), 185-197.

CHEN, B. Y., HARPER, F. M., KONSTAN, J. & LI, S. X. 2010. Social Comparisons and Contributions to Online Communities: A Field Experiment on MovieLens. *American Economic Review*, 100(4), 1358-1398.

CHEN, P.-Y., WU, S.-Y. & YOON, J. 2004. The Impact of Online Recommendations and Consumer Feedback on Sales. *Twenty-Fifth International Conference on Information Systems*.

CHEN, Y. & XIE, J. 2008. Online Consumer Review: Word-of-Mouth as a New Element of Marketing Communication Mix. *Management Science,* 54(3), 477-491.

CHEN, Y., FAY, S. & WANG, Q. 2011a. The Role of Marketing in Social Media: How Online Consumer Reviews Evolve. *Journal of Interactive Marketing,* 25(2), 85-94.

CHEN, Y., WANG, Q. I. & XIE, J. 2011b. Online Social Interactions: A Natural Experiment on Word of Mouth Versus Observational Learning. *Journal of Marketing Research,* 48(2), 238-254.

CHEN, Y., LIU, Y. & ZHANG, J. 2012. When Do Third-Party Product Reviews Affect Firm Value and What Can Firms Do? The Case of Media Critics and Professional Movie Reviews. *Journal of Marketing,* 76(2), 116-134.

CHEUNG, C. M. K. & THADANI, D. R. 2012. The Impact of Electonic Word-of-Mouth Communication: A Literature Analysis and Integrative Model. *Decision Support Systems,* 54(1), 461-470.

CHEVALIER, J. A. & MAYZLIN, D. 2006. The Effect of Word of Mouth on Sales: Online Book Reviews. *Journal of Marketing Research,* 43(3), 345-354.

CHINTAGUNTA, P. K., GOPINATH, S. & VENKATARAMAN, S. 2010. The Effects of Online User Reviews on Movie Box Office Performance: Accounting for Sequential Rollout and Aggregation Across Local Markets. *Marketing Science,* 29(5), 944-957.

CHUI, M., MANYIKA, J., BUGHIN, J., DOBBS, R., ROXBURGH, C., SARRAZIN, H., SANDS, G. & WESTERGREN, M. 2012. The Social Economy: Unlocking Value and Productivity through Social Technologies. *McKinsey Global Institute,* 2012(7), 1-13.

CLEMONS, E. K., GAO, G. & HITT, L. 2006. When Online Reviews Meet Hyperdifferentiation: A Study of the Craft Beer Industry. *Journal of Management Information Systems,* 23(2), 149-171.

CLEMONS, E. K. 2009a. Business Models for Monetizing Internet Applications and Web Sites: Experience, Theory, and Predictions. *Journal of Management Information Systems,* 26(2), 15-41.

CLEMONS, E. K. 2009b. The Complex Problem of Monetizing Virtual Electronic Social Networks. *Decision Support Systems,* 48(1), 46-56.

CMOSURVEY. 2014. *The CMO Survey from Duke University's Fuqua School of Business and the American Marketing Association - Topline Results February 2014* [Online]. Available:https://faculty.fuqua.duke.edu/cmosurveyresults/The_CMO_Survey-Topline_Report-Feb-2014.pdf [Accessed 2014-02-21].

COOK, D. O. & LU, X. 2009. Noise, Information, and Rumors: Internet Board Messages Affect Stock Returns. *Working Paper.* http://69.175.2.130/~finman/Reno/Papers/Information_Matters_Noises_Donnt_Internet_Message_Boards_Affect_Stock_Return s.pdf [Accessed 2013-06-13].

DAS, S. R. & CHEN, M. Y. 2007. Yahoo! for Amazon: Sentiment Extraction from Small Talk on the Web. *Management Science,* 53(9), 1375-1388.

DE BRUYN, A. & LILIEN, G. L. 2008. A Multi-Stage Model of Word-of-Mouth Influence through Viral Marketing. *International Journal of Research in Marketing,* 25(3), 151-163.

DE VALCK, K., VAN BRUGGEN, G. H. & WIERENGA, B. 2009. Virtual Communities: A Marketing Perspective. *Decision Support Systems,* 47(3), 185-203.

DE VRIES, L., GENSLER, S. & LEEFLANG, P. S. H. 2012. Popularity of Brand Posts on Brand Fan Pages: An Investigation of the Effects of Social Media Marketing. *Journal of Interactive Marketing,* 26(2), 83-91.

DECKER, R. & TRUSOV, M. 2010. Estimating Aggregate Consumer Preferences from Online Product Reviews. *International Journal of Research in Marketing,* 27(4), 293-307.

DEIGHTON, J. & KORNFELD, L. 2009. Interactivity's Unanticipated Consequences for Marketers and Marketing. *Journal of Interactive Marketing,* 23(1), 4-10.

DELLAROCAS, C. 2003. The Digitization of Word of Mouth: Promise and Challenges of Online Feedback Mechanisms. *Management Science,* 49(10), 1407-1424.

DELLAROCAS, C. 2006. Strategic Manipulation of Internet Opinion Forums: Implications for Consumers and Firms. *Management Science,* 52(10), 1577-1593.

DELLAROCAS, C., ZHANG, X. & AWAD, N. F. 2007. Exploring the Value of Online Product Reviews in Forcasting Sales: The Case of Motion Pictures. *Journal of Interactive Marketing,* 21(4), 23-46.

DEWAN, S. & RAMAPRASAD, J. 2012. Research Note - Music Blogging, Online Sampling, and the Long Tail. *Information Systems Research,* 23(3), 1056-1067.

DHAR, V. & CHANG, E. A. 2009. Does Chatter Matter? The Impact of User-Generated Content on Music Sales. *Journal of Interactive Marketing,* 23(4), 300-307.

DOBNI, D. & ZINKHAN, G. M. 1990. In Search of Brand Image: A Foundation Analysis. *In:* GOLDBERG, M. E., GORN, G. & POLLAY, R. W. (eds.) *Advances in Consumer Research Volume 17.* Provo, UT: Association for Consumer Research, 110-119.

DROGE, C., STANKO, M. A. & POLLITTE, W. A. 2010. Lead Users and Early Adopters on the Web: The Role of New Technology Product Blogs. *Journal of Product Innovation Management,* 27(1), 66-82.

DUAN, W., GU, B. & WHINSTON, A. B. 2008a. Do Online Reviews Matter? - An Empirical Investigation of Panel Data. *Decision Support Systems,* 45(4), 1007-1016.

DUAN, W., GU, B. & WHINSTON, A. B. 2008b. The Dynamics of Online Word-of-Mouth and Product Sales - An Empirical Investigation of the Movie Industry. *Journal of Retailing,* 84(2), 233-242.

EAST, R., HAMMOND, K. & LOMAX, W. 2008. Measuring the Impact of Positive and Negative Word of Mouth on Brand Purchase Probability. *International Journal of Research in Marketing,* 25(3), 215-224.

ENGEL, J. F., BLACKWELL, R. D. & KEGERREIS, R. J. 1969. How Information is Used to Adopt an Innovation. *Journal of Advertising Research,* 9(4), 3-8.

ERDEM, T. & SWAIT, J. 1998. Brand Equity as a Signaling Phenomenon. *Journal of Consumer Psychology,* 7(2), 131-157.

ETZION, H. & AWAD, N. F. 2007. Pump up the Volume? Examining the Relationship between Number of Online Reviews and Sales: Is More Necessarily Better? *Twenty Eighth International Conference on Information Systems.* Montreal.

EYRICH, N., PADMAN, M. L. & SWEETSER, K. D. 2008. PR Practitioners' Use of Social Media Tools and Communication Technology. *Public Relations Review*, 34(4), 412-414.

FARLEY, J. U., HOENIG, S., LEHMANN, D. R. & SZYMANSKI, D. M. 2004. Assessing the Impact of Marketing Strategy Using Meta-Analysis. *In:* MOOREMAN, C. & LEHMANN, D. R. (eds.) *Assesing Marketing Strategy Performance.* Cambridge MA, 145-164.

FORMAN, C., GHOSE, A. & WIESENFELD, B. 2008. Examining the Relationship Between Reviews and Sales: The Role of Reviewer Identity Disclosure in Electronic Markets. *Information Systems Research*, 19(3), 291-313.

FRANKE, G. R. 2001. Applications of Meta-Analysis for Marketing and Public Policy: A Review. *Journal of Public Policy & Marketing*, 20(2), 186-200.

FREEDMAN, L. 2011. *The 2011 Social Shopping Study* [Online]. Available: http://www.powerreviews.com /assets/download/Social_Shopping_2011_Brief1.pdf [Accessed 2013-06-13].

GALEOTTI, A. & GOYAL, S. 2009. Influencing the Influencers: A Theory of Strategic Diffusion. *The RAND Journal of Economics*, 40(3), 509-532.

GARNEFELD, I., HELM, S. & EGGERT, A. 2010. Walk Your Talk: An Experimental Investigation of the Relationship Between Word of Mouth and Communicators' Loyalty. *Journal of Service Research*, 14(1), 93-107.

GENSLER, S., VÖLCKNER, F., LIU-THOMPKINS, Y. & WIERTZ, C. 2013. Managing Brands in the Social Media Environment. *Journal of Interactive Marketing*, 27(4), 242-256.

GODES, D. & MAYZLIN, D. 2004. Using Online Conversations to Study Word-of-Mouth Communication. *Marketing Science*, 23(4), 545-560.

GODES, D. & MAYZLIN, D. 2009. Firm-Created Word-of-Mouth Communication: Evidence from a Field Test. *Marketing Science*, 28(4), 721-739.

GODES, D., MAYZLIN, D., CHEN, Y., DAS, S., DELLAROCAS, C., PFEIFFER, B., LIBAI, B., SEN, S., SHI, M. & VERLEGH, P. 2005. The Firm's Management of Social Interactions. *Marketing Letters*, 16(3/4), 415-428.

GRUEN, T. W., OSMONBEKOV, T. & CZAPLEWSKI, A. J. 2006. eWOM: The Impact of Customer-to-Customer Online Know-How Exchange on Customer Value and Loyalty. *Journal of Business Research*, 59(4), 449-456.

GU, B., PARK, J. & KONANA, P. 2011. Research Note - The Impact of External Word-of-Mouth Sources on Retailer Sales of High-Involvement Products. *Information Systems Research*, 23(1), 182-196.

GU, B., TANG, Q. & WHINSTON, A. B. 2013. The Influence of Online Word-of-Mouth on Long Tail Formation. *Decision Support Systems*, 56, 474-481.

GUPTA, S. & ZEITHAML, V. 2006. Customer Metrics and Their Impact on Financial Performance. *Marketing Science*, 25(6), 718-739.

GUPTA, P. & HARRIS, J. 2010. How e-WOM Recommendations Influence Product Consideration and Quality of Choice: A Motivation to Process Information Perspective. *Journal of Business Research*, 63(9-10), 1041-1049.

HALL, J. A. & ROSENTHAL, R. 1995. Interpreting and Evaluating Meta-Analysis. *Evaluation & the Health Professions*, 18(4), 393-407.

HARTMANN, W. R., MANCHANDA, P., NAIR, H., BOTHNER, M., DODDS, P., GODES, D., HOSANAGAR, K. & TUCKER, C. 2008. Modeling Social Interactions: Identification, Empirical Methods and Policy Implications. *Marketing Letters*, 19(3-4), 287-304.

HENNIG-THURAU, T. & WALSH, G. 2004. Electronic Word-of-Mouth: Motives for and Consequences of Reading Customer Articulations on the Internet. *International Journal of Electronic Commerce*, 8(2), 51-74.

HENNIG-THURAU, T., GWINNER, K. P., WALSH, G. & GREMLER, D. D. 2004a. Electronic Word-of-Mouth via Consumer-Opinion Platforms: What Motivates Consumers to Articulate Themselves on the Internet? *Journal of Interactive Marketing*, 18(1), 38-52.

HENNIG-THURAU, T., WALSH, G. & SCHRADER, U. 2004b. VHB-JOURQUAL : Ein Ranking von betriebswirtschaftlich-relevanten Zeitschriften auf der Grundlage von Expertenurteilen. *Schmalenbachs Zeitschrift für betriebswirtschaftliche Forschung*, 56(6), 520-545.

HENNIG-THURAU, T., MALTHOUSE, E. C., FRIEGE, C., GENSLER, S., LOBSCHAT, L., RANGASWAMY, A. & SKIERA, B. 2010. The Impact of New Media on Customer Relationships. *Journal of Service Research*, 13(3), 311-330.

HINZ, O., SKIERA, B., BARROT, C. & BECKER, J. U. 2011. Seeding Strategies for Viral Marketing: An Empirical Comparison. *Journal of Marketing*, 75(6), 55-71.

HO, J. Y. C. & DEMPSEY, M. 2010. Viral Marketing: Motivations to Forward Online Content. *Journal of Business Research*, 63(9-10), 1000-1006.

HO-DAC, N. N., CARSON, S. J. & MOORE, W. L. 2013. The Effects of Positive and Negative Online Customer Reviews: Do Brand Strength and Category Maturity Matter? *Journal of Marketing*, 77(6), 37-53.

HOVLAND, C. I. 1948. Social Communication. *Proceedings of the American Philosophical Society*, 92(5), 371-375.

HU, N., LIU, L., TRIPATHY, A. & YAO, L. J. 2011. Value Relevance of Blog Visibility. *Journal of Business Research*, 64(12), 1361-1368.

HU, N., DONG, Y., LIU, L. & YAO, L. J. 2012. Not All That Glitters Is Gold: The Effect of Attention and Blogs on Investors' Investing Behaviors. *Journal of Accounting, Auditing & Finance*, 28(1), 4-19.

IRIBERRI, A. & LEROY, G. 2009. A Life-Cycle Perspective on Online Community Success. *ACM Computing Surveys*, 41(2), 1-29.

JAHN, B. & KUNZ, W. 2011. Does Social Media Work? - Evidence of the Impact of Fan Pages on the Consumer-Brand Relationship. *International Colloquium in Relationship Marketing*. Rochester, New York: Saunders College of Business.

JAHN, B., BRUDLER, B. & MEYER, A. 2011. Members Only! - Nutzen von geschlossenen Social Networking Sites aus Nutzer- und Betreibersicht. *Marketing ZFP*, 33(4), 317-327.

JANG, H., OLFMAN, L., KO, I., KOH, J. & KIM, K. 2008. The Influence of On-Line Brand Community Characteristics on Community Commitment and Brand Loyalty. *International Journal of Electronic Commerce*, 12(3), 57-80.

JANSEN, B. J., ZHANG, M., SOBEL, K. & CHOWDURY, A. 2009. Twitter Power: Tweets as Electronic Word of Mouth. *Journal of the American Society for Information Science*, 60(11), 2169-2188.

JIMÉNEZ, F. R. & MENDOZA, N. A. 2013. Too Popular to Ignore: The Influence of Online Reviews on Purchase Intentions of Search and Experience Products. *Journal of Interactive Marketing*, 27(3), 226-235.

KANE, G. C. & ALAVI, M. 2008. Casting the Net: A Multimodal Network Perspective on User-System Interactions. *Information Systems Research*, 19(3), 253-272.

KAPLAN, A. M. & HAENLEIN, M. 2010. Users of the World, Unite! The Challenges and Opportunities of Social Media. *Business Horizons*, 53(1), 59-68.

KATZ, E. & LAZARFELD, P. F. 1955. *Personal Influence: The Part Played by People in the Flow of Mass Communication*, Glencoe, IL: Free Press.

KELLER, K. L. & LEHMANN, D. R. 2003. How Do Brands Create Value? *Marketing Management*, 12(3), 26-31.

KELLER, K. L. & LEHMANN, D. R. 2006. Brands and Branding: Research Findings and Future Priorities. *Marketing Science*, 25(6), 740-759.

KELLER, E. & LIBAI, B. 2009. A Holistic Approach to the Measurement of WOM. *ESOMAR Worldwide Media Measurement Conference 2009*. Stockholm, Sweden.

KIETZMANN, J. H., HERMKENS, K., MCCARTHY, I. P. & SILVESTRE, B. S. 2011. Social Media? Get Serious! Understanding the Functional Building Blocks of Social Media. *Business Horizons*, 54(3), 241-251.

KOZINETS, R. V. 2002. The Field Behind the Screen: Using Netnography for Marketing Research in Online Communities. *Journal of Marketing Research*, 39(1), 61-72.

KOZINETS, R. V., DE VALCK, K., WOJNICKI, A. C. & WILNER, S. J. S. 2010. Networked Narratives: Understanding Word-of-Mouth Marketing in Online Communities. *Journal of Marketing*, 74(2), 71-89.

KRISHNAMURTHY, S. & KUCUK, S. U. 2009. Anti-Branding on the Internet. *Journal of Business Research*, 62(11), 1119-1126.

LABRECQUE, L. I., VOR DEM ESCHE, J., MATHWICK, C., NOVAK, T. P. & HOFACKER, C. F. 2013. Consumer Power: Evolution in the Digital Age. *Journal of Interactive Marketing*, 27(4), 257-269.

LEE, J., PARK, D.-H. & HAN, I. 2008. The Effect of Negative Online Consumer Reviews on Product Attitude: An Information Processing View. *Electronic Commerce Research and Applications*, 7(3), 341-352.

LEE, J. & LEE, J.-N. 2009. Understanding the Product Information Inference Process in Electronic Word-of-Mouth: An Objectivity–Subjectivity Dichotomy Perspective. *Information & Management*, 46(5), 302-311.

LEVIN, J. & MILGROM, P. 2010. Online Advertising: Heterogeneity and Conflation in Market Design. *American Economic Review*, 100(2), 603-607.

LI, L. I. 2010. Reputation, Trust, and Rebates: How Online Auction Markets Can Improve their Feedback Mechanisms. *Journal of Economics & Management Strategy*, 19(2), 303-331.

LI, X. & HITT, L. M. 2008. Self-Selection and Information Role of Online Product Reviews. *Information Systems Research,* 19(4), 456-474.

LIBAI, B., MULLER, E. & PERES, R. 2009. The Role of Within-Brand and Cross-Brand Communications in Competitive Growth. *Journal of Marketing,* 73(3), 19-34.

LIN, Y.-S. & HUANG, J.-Y. 2006. Internet Blogs as a Tourism Marketing Medium: A Case Study. *Journal of Business Research,* 59(10-11), 1201-1205.

LIPSEY, M. W. & WILSON, D. B. 2001. *Practical Meta-Analysis,* Thousand Oaks, CA: Sage Publications.

LIU, Y. 2006. Word of Mouth for Movies: Its Dynamics and Impact on Box Office Revenue. *Journal of Marketing,* 70(3), 74-89.

LUO, X. & ZHANG, J. 2013. How Do Consumer Buzz and Traffic in Social Media Marketing Predict the Value of the Firm? *Journal of Management Information Systems,* 30(2), 213-238.

LUO, X., RAITHEL, S. & WILES, M. A. 2013a. The Impact of Brand Rating Dispersion on Firm Value. *Journal of Marketing Research,* 50(3), 399-415.

LUO, X., ZHANG, J. & DUAN, W. 2013b. Social Media and Firm Equity Value. *Information Systems Research,* 24(1), 146-163.

MA, M. & AGARWAL, R. 2007. Through a Glass Darkly: Information Technology Design, Identity Verification, and Knowledge Contribution in Online Communities. *Information Systems Research,* 18(1), 42-67.

MANGOLD, W. G. & FAULDS, D. J. 2009. Social media: The New Hybrid Element of the Promotion Mix. *Business Horizons,* 52(4), 357-365.

MATOS, C. A. & ROSSI, C. A. V. 2008. Word-of-Mouth Communications in Marketing: A Meta-Analytic Review of the Antecedents and Moderators. *Journal of the Academy of Marketing Science,* 36(4), 578-596.

MAYZLIN, D. 2006. Promotional Chat on the Internet. *Marketing Science,* 25(2), 155-163.

MCALISTER, L., SONNIER, G. & SHIVELY, T. 2011. The Relationship Between Online Chatter and Firm Value. *Marketing Letters,* 23(1), 1-12.

MOE, W. W. & TRUSOV, M. 2011. The Value of Social Dynamics in Online Product Ratings Forums. *Journal of Marketing Research,* 48(3), 444-456.

MUNOZ, T. & KUMAR, S. 2004. Brand Metrics: Gauging and Linking Brands with Business Performance. *Journal of Brand Management,* 11(5), 381-387.

MUNZEL, A. & MEYER, A. 2011. Sorry Seems to Be the Hardest Word: The Power of Social Accounts in Reducing Effects of Negative eWOM. *International Colloquium in Relationship Marketing.* Rochester, New York: Saunders College of Business.

NAMBISAN, P. & WATT, J. H. 2011. Managing Customer Experiences in Online Product Communities. *Journal of Business Research,* 64(8), 889-895.

NARAYAN, V., RAO, V. R. & SAUNDERS, C. 2011. How Peer Influence Affects Attribute Preferences: A Bayesian Updating Mechanism. *Marketing Science,* 30(2), 368-384.

OH, C. & LIU SHENG, O. R. 2011. Investigating Predictive Power of Stock Micro Blog Sentiment in Forecasting Future Stock Price Directional Movement. *Thirty Second International Conference on Information Systems.* Shanghai.

OINAS-KUKKONEN, H., LYYTINEN, K. & YOO, Y. 2010. Social Networks and Information Systems: Ongoing and Future Research Streams. *Journal of the Association for Information Systems,* 11(2), 61-68.

OLIVER, R. L. 1999. Whence Consumer Loyalty? *Journal of Marketing,* 63(Special issue 1999), 33-44.

ONISHI, H. & MANCHANDA, P. 2012. Marketing Activity, Blogging and Sales. *International Journal of Research in Marketing,* 29(3), 221-234.

PAN, L.-Y. & CHIOU, J.-S. 2011. How Much Can You Trust Online Information? Cues for Perceived Trustworthiness of Consumer-generated Online Information. *Journal of Interactive Marketing,* 25(2), 67-74.

PARK, C. & LEE, T. M. 2009. Information Direction, Website Reputation and eWOM Effect: A Moderating Role of Product Type. *Journal of Business Research,* 62(1), 61-67.

PARK, D.-H., LEE, J. & HAN, I. 2007. The Effect of On-Line Consumer Reviews on Consumer Purchasing Intention: The Moderating Role of Involvement. *International Journal of Electronic Commerce,* 11(4), 125-148.

PARRY, M. E., KAWAKAMI, T. & KISHIYA, K. 2012. The Effect of Personal and Virtual Word-of-Mouth on Technology Acceptance. *Journal of Product Innovation Management,* 29(6), 952-966.

PATHAK, B., GARFINKEL, R., GOPAL, R. D., VENKATESAN, R. & YIN, F. 2010. Empirical Analysis of the Impact of Recommender Systems on Sales. *Journal of Management Information Systems,* 27(2), 159-188.

PATTERSON, A. 2012. Social-Networkers of the World, Unite and Take Over: A Meta-Introspective Perspective on the Facebook Brand. *Journal of Business Research,* 65(4), 527-534.

REUBER, A. R. & FISCHER, E. 2011. International Entrepreneurship in Internet-Enabled Markets. *Journal of Business Venturing,* 26(6), 660-679.

ROSENTHAL, R. 1995. Writing Meta-Analytic Reviews. *Psychological Bulletin,* 118(2), 183-192.

SCARPI, D. 2010. Does Size Matter? An Examination of Small and Large Web-Based Brand Communities. *Journal of Interactive Marketing,* 24(1), 14-21.

SCHAU, H. J. & GILLY, M. C. 2003. We are what We Post? Self-Presentation in Personal Web Space. *Journal of Consumer Research,* 30(3), 385-404.

SEN, S. & LERMAN, D. 2007. Why are you Telling me this? An Examination into Negative Consumer Reviews on the Web. *Journal of Interactive Marketing,* 21(4), 76-94.

SENECAL, S. & NANTEL, J. 2004. The Influence of Online Product Recommendations on Consumers' Online Choices. *Journal of Retailing,* 80(2), 159-169.

SHIN, H. S., HANSSENS, D. M. & GAJULA, B. 2011. Positive vs. Negative Online Buzz as Leading Indicators of Daily Price Fluctuation. *Working Paper.* http://www.anderson.ucla.edu/faculty/dominique.hanssens/content/e-Sentiment%20

as%20a%20Leading%20Indicator%20of%20Price%20Fluctuation.pdf   [Accessed 2013-06-13].

SMITH, D., MENON, S. & SIVAKUMAR, K. 2005. Online Peer and Editorial Recommendations, Trust, and Choice in Virtual Markets. *Journal of Interactive Marketing*, 19(3), 15-37.

SONNIER, G. P., MCALISTER, L. & RUTZ, O. J. 2011. A Dynamic Model of the Effect of Online Communications on Firm Sales. *Marketing Science*, 30(4), 702-716.

SRINIVASAN, S. & HANSSENS, D. M. 2009. Marketing and Firm Value: Metrics, Methods, Findings, and Future Directions. *Journal of Marketing Research*, 46(3), 293-312.

SRINIVASAN, S., VANHUELE, M. & PAUWELS, K. 2010. Mind-Set Metrics in Market Response Models: An Integrative Approach. *Journal of Marketing Research*, 47(4), 672-684.

STEPHEN, A. T. & GALAK, J. 2012. The Effects of Traditional and Social Earned Media on Sales: A Study of a Microlending Marketplace. *Journal of Marketing Research*, 49(5), 624-639.

STEPHEN, A. T. & TOUBIA, O. 2010. Deriving Value from Social Commerce Networks. *Journal of Marketing Research*, 47(2), 215-228.

SUN, M. 2012. How Does the Variance of Product Ratings Matter? *Management Science*, 58(4), 696-707.

SUNDARAM, D. S., KAUSHIK, M. & WEBSTER, C. 1983. Word-of-Mouth Communications: A Motivational Analysis. *Advances in Consumer Research*, 25(1), 527-531.

THAPA, K. & BIRD, R. 2010. Reading Stock Message Board: Do Your Own Research. *New Horizons in Finance for Asia and the Region*. Hong Kong: Asian Finance Association.

THOMPSON, S. A. & SINHA, R. K. 2008. Brand Communities and New Product Adoption: The Influence and Limits of Oppositional Loyalty. *Journal of Marketing*, 72(6), 65-80.

THORBJØRNSEN, H., SUPPHELLEN, M., NYSVEEN, H. & PEDERSEN, P. E. 2002. Building Brand Relationships Online: A Comparison of Two Interactive Applications. *Journal of Interactive Marketing*, 16(3), 17-34.

TIRUNILLAI, S. & TELLIS, G. J. 2012. Does Chatter Really Matter? Dynamics of User-Generated Content and Stock Performance. *Marketing Science*, 31(2), 198-215.

TRUSOV, M., BUCKLIN, R. E. & PAUWELS, K. 2009. Effects of Word-of-Mouth Versus Traditional Marketing: Findings from an Internet Social Networking Site. *Journal of Marketing*, 73(5), 90-102.

TUMARKIN, R. & WHITELAW, R. F. 2001. News or Noise? Internet Message Board Activity and Stock Prices. *Financial Analysts Journal*, 57(3), 41-51.

TUMASJAN, A., SPRENGER, T. O., SANDNER, P. G. & WELPE, I. M. 2011. Election Forecasts With Twitter: How 140 Characters Reflect the Political Landscape. *Social Science Computer Review*, 29(4), 402-418.

VAKRATSAS, D. & AMBLER, T. 1999. How Advertising Works: What Do We Really Know? *Journal of Marketing*, 63(1), 26-43.

VAN DER LANS, R., VAN BRUGGEN, G., ELIASHBERG, J. & WIERENGA, B. 2009. A Viral Branching Model for Predicting the Spread of Electronic Word of Mouth. *Marketing Science*, 29(2), 348-365.

VAN LAER, T. & DE RUYTER, K. 2010. In Stories We Trust: How Narrative Apologies Provide Cover for Competitive Vulnerability after Integrity-Violating Blog Posts. *International Journal of Research in Marketing,* 27(2), 164-174.

VAN NOORT, G. & WILLEMSEN, L. M. 2012. Online Damage Control: The Effects of Proactive Versus Reactive Webcare Interventions in Consumer-generated and Brand-generated Platforms. *Journal of Interactive Marketing,* 26(3), 131-140.

VILLANUEVA, J., YOO, S. & HANSSENS, D. M. 2008. The Impact of Marketing-Induced Versus Word-of-Mouth Customer Acquisition on Customer Equity Growth. *Journal of Marketing Research,* 45(1), 48-59.

WANG, W. & BENBASAT, I. 2008. Attributions of Trust in Decision Support Technologies: A Study of Recommendation Agents for E-Commerce. *Journal of Management Information Systems,* 24(4), 249-273.

WANG, X., YU, C. & WEI, Y. 2012. Social Media Peer Communication and Impacts on Purchase Intentions: A Consumer Socialization Framework. *Journal of Interactive Marketing,* 26(4), 198-208.

WEBSTER, J. & WATSON, R. T. 2002. Analyzing the Past to Prepare for the Future: Writing a Literature Review. *MIS Quarterly,* 26(2), xiii-xxiii.

WEISS, A. M., LURIE, N. H. & MACINNIS, D. J. 2008. Listening to Strangers: Whose Responses Are Valuable, How Valuable Are They, and Why? *Journal of Marketing Research,* 45(4), 425-436.

WESTBROOK, R. A. 1987. Product/Consumption-Based Affective Responses and Postpurchase Processes. *Journal of Marketing Research,* 24(3), 258-270.

WILSON, J. H., GUINAN, P. J., PARISE, S. & WEINBERG, B. D. 2011. What's Your Social Media Strategy? *Harvard Business Review,* 89(7/8), 23-25.

WINER, R. S. 2009. New Communications Approaches in Marketing: Issues and Research Directions. *Journal of Interactive Marketing,* 23(2), 108-117.

WOERNDL, M., PAPAGIANNIDIS, S., BOURLAKIS, M. & LI, F. 2008. Internet-Induced Marketing Techniques: Critical Factors in Viral Marketing Campaigns. *Journal of Business,* 3(1), 33-45.

WYSOCKI, P. D. 1999. *Cheap Talk on the Web: The Determinants of Postings on Stock Message Boards* [Online]. Available: http://www.ssrn.com/abstract=160170 [Accessed 2013-06-13].

YUN, G. W., PARK, S.-Y. & HA, L. 2008. Influence of Cultural Dimensions on Online Interactive Review Feature Implementations: A Comparison of Korean and U.S. Retail Web Sites. *Journal of Interactive Marketing,* 22(3), 40-50.

ZHANG, J. Q., CRACIUN, G. & SHIN, D. 2010. When does Electronic Word-of-Mouth Matter? A Study of Consumer Product Reviews. *Journal of Business Research,* 63(12), 1336-1341.

ZHU, F. & ZHANG, X. 2010. Impact of Online Consumer Reviews on Sales: The Moderating Role of Product and Consumer Characteristics. *Journal of Marketing,* 74(2), 133-148.

Markus Kick

IV Corporate Brand Posts on Facebook - The Role of Interactivity, Vividness, and Involvement

Abstract

Brand presences on social network sites (SNSs) like Facebook, Twitter, or Google[+] form important communication tools for marketers in the social media environment. Engaging the consumer in an ongoing dialogue via brand fan pages, especially on Facebook, becomes more and more important. However, evidence about what drives a successful Facebook brand post is scarce. By means of a field experimental study over a two week treatment period, I study the effect of corporate brand posts on brand fans' post recall capability, attitude toward the brand, and purchase intention. I manipulate the degree of brand post interactivity and vividness and the underlying degree of product involvement by posting on two different brand fan pages. Results indicate that Facebook brand posts are able to positively influence fans' attitude toward the brand. The degree of interactivity and vividness positively moderates the main effect as posts with a high degree of interactivity and vividness cause a higher change in attitudinal measures than low interactive and vivid posts. Further, Facebook brand fans are able to better recall posts from high involvement brands due to selective perception effects in the distractive Facebook environment. On the contrary, posts are more effective on fans' attitude toward the brand when posted from a fan page with a comparably lower involvement level. Facebook brand posts activate peripheral routes of information processing which are in favor for communication needs of low involvement products. In addition, a significant interaction effect between the level of involvement and the degree of interactivity and vividness is found. Highly interactive and vivid brand posts are more successful when posted by a low involvement product or brand. Implications for marketing research and practitioners are discussed.

1   Motivation

Researchers as well as practitioners more and more realize the tremendous potential inherent in "Social Media". Especially "Social Network Sites" (SNSs) like Facebook, Twitter, LinkedIn, or Google⁺ form one of the key tools within the new interactive environment. Facebook, as the largest SNS (HOLLENBECK and KAIKATI, 2012, p. 395), connects over one billion people around the globe with about 700 million daily users (FACEBOOK, 2013, p. 1). Not surprisingly, marketers follow their customers into the social network environment and shift their marketing budgets more and more toward social media and SNSs. With a current level of 7.4% of total marketing expenses, social media spendings are expected to even increase to about 18.1% within the upcoming five years (CMOSURVEY, 2014, p. 25). The fact that 49% of marketing managers see Facebook as the most important social media platform for corporate engagements (STELZNER, 2013, p. 27), underpins the crucial role of Facebook within today's marketing landscape.

Branded content on Facebook appears in multiple forms and marketing campaigns are executed in many ways. However, the marketing game has drastically changed. Marketers, to a certain degree, have lost control over their brands (HENNIG-THURAU et al., 2010, p. 313). Today, consumers can respond to marketing efforts immediately and even attack companies or brands with invectives or parodies (DEIGHTON and KORNFELD, 2009, p. 4). Rather than pushing a brand's message at its consumers, it is one of the main tasks for corporate social media engagements to involve consumers into an ongoing dialogue to foster the brand-consumer relationship (cf. e.g., THORBJØRNSEN et al., 2002, p. 17, HENNIG-THURAU et al., 2010, p. 313). The most common possibility to realize this goal are brand communities in form of brand fan pages where customers can actively interact with the company through liking or commenting corporate brand posts. They can take part in interactive discussions about brand related topics with both, corporate representatives and other consumers (cf. e.g., MCALEXANDER et al., 2002, p. 38, ADJEI et al., 2009, pp. 634-635, ZAGLIA, 2013, pp. 217-218, NAMBISAN and WATT, 2011, p. 889).

However, preliminary research on brand fan pages on Facebook is still in its infancy (JAHN and KUNZ, 2012, p. 344). Especially, evidence on the effects of corporate brand post on Facebook is scarce. Most studies are descriptive, lack a theoretical foundation (e.g., PUGSLEY, 2012), and do not provide clear empirical guidelines about what makes a good brand post on the Facebook platform (HOFFMANN and FODOR, 2010, p. 41). Thus, companies seem to follow a trial and error strategy with their brand fan pages due to the lack of empirical evidence (SHANKAR and BATRA, 2009, p. 285). DE VRIES et al. (2012) are the first to provide empirical evidence about the factors influencing brand post popularity. They find that posts with a high degree of interactivity and vividness are more popular (i.e., measured by the number of likes and comments of historic brand posts) than their low degree counterparts. As the design of interactive and vivid content as well as the maintenance of brand pages consume a lot of resources and are costly, marketers strive to know more about the effectiveness of corporate brand posts. Questions like: *Are Facebook posts generally able to guide recipients through the purchase funnel? Is the effectiveness of brand posts on Facebook independent of consumers' product involvement? Does the degree of post-interactivity and post-vividness interact with the level of product involvement?* are still unanswered and demand further clarification.

By answering these questions, the paper at hand contributes to the current literature in the following ways. First, this paper uses a field experiment in order to extract information about the effectiveness of Facebook brand posts. While social media literature mainly uses historical posts to retrospectively look at posting effects (e.g., DE VRIES et al., 2012, RAUSCHNABEL et al., 2012) or applies laboratory settings (e.g., NELSON-FIELD et al., 2013, ZHANG et al., 2010), this paper wants to explicitly extract results with high external validity in the distracting Facebook environment. Second, I change perspective away from simple reach measures (i.e., likes and comments) and apply metrics of the purchase funnel (i.e., brand post recall, attitude toward the brand, purchase intent) to assess brand post effectiveness (cf. KELLER and LEHMANN, 2006). Third, I extend the work of DE VRIES et al. (2012) by adding different involvement levels to my experimental approach. And fourth, I propose and show that there is an interaction effect between product involvement and the degree of interactivity and vividness regarding the effectiveness of brand posts.

The remainder of this paper is organized as follows. First, I describe the role of brand pages in today's social media environment and then develop a theoretical framework to derive hypotheses for the proposed effects of product involvement, interactivity, and vividness on brand post effectiveness. Subsequently, the methodological deliberations and the execution of the experimental setup are discussed, before moving on to the empirical results. I conclude the paper with practical implications and propose some limitations that may act as starting point for further research.

2   Conceptual Framework and Hypotheses

2.1   Brand Fan Pages and the Purchase Funnel

Starting as a simple catchphrase after the web 2.0 breakthrough, social media "grew up" and gained a lot of public attention in the past years (RICHTER et al., 2011, p. 89). Especially SNSs have become extremely popular. They can be seen as a mean to allow users to build and host their individual profiles and build and maintain a network of friends for social (e.g., Facebook) or professional (e.g., LinkedIn) interaction. Users acquire new contacts by searching and browsing the network or screening networks of existing contacts and send "friend requests" to connect to other users (TRUSOV et al., 2009, pp. 92-93). It is up to each individual user, how many details he discloses to the social network community and how much content he shares with his social network friends (BOYD and ELLISON, 2007, p. 211, ELLISON et al., 2007, p. 1143). Next to connections between private individuals, profile holders can also become fans of companies or brands on dedicated brand fan pages. They click the "Like" button on the fan page and, thus, enable the brand's posts to show up in their newsfeed. Similar to status updates and content posted from their peers, they can now like, comment, share, and interact with the content posted by brands. Facebook brand pages, thus, are quite similar to online brand communities where fans interact with the brand and other consumers at the same time (ADJEI et al., 2009, p. 634).

In the past two decades, research about SNSs and online brand communities has grown constantly and applied a multitude of perspectives to shed light on the new phenomenon. Behavioral studies provide evidence on people's motivations to participate in SNSs and the drivers and motives behind their disclosing behavior. RAACKE and BONDS-RAACKE (2008) find that making new friends, locating old friends, and being up-to-date are the main reasons for participants to use SNSs. Participation behavior in SNSs and brand communities itself can be explained by informational value, entertainment value, altruism, and purposive values that all form a common social network identity (DHOLAKIA et al., 2004). Similar uses and gratifications approaches are also applied in other studies (e.g., DUNNE et al., 2010, SMOCK et al., 2011, JOINSON, 2008, HENNIG-THURAU et al., 2004). They all find that SNSs and brand communities facilitate the participants to execute personal aims (e.g., identity creation and management), social goals (e.g., social interaction and companionship), and help to build group identities with common values and norms. Within brand communities, people strive to create, discuss, and negotiate meaning (MCALEXANDER et al., 2002, p. 38) through sharing information, cementing the history and culture of a brand or providing assistance to other consumers (MUNIZ and O'GUINN, 2001, pp. 419-426).

Research also sheds light on the effects of a brand community engagement with regards to corporate performance measures and consumer mindset metrics along the purchase funnel. NAMBISAN and WATT (2011) show an increase in attitude toward the brand and products when consumers were engaged in brand related discussions on IT-forums. BRODIE et al. (2013) demonstrate that trust measures could be increased when consumers were highly engaged in virtual brand communities. The authors identify the sharing of knowledge and content, the learning through consuming information, and simple socializing factors as the main drivers for the elevated level of trust across community members. THOMPSON and SINHA (2008) elaborate community messages from four major IT brand communities. They find that the level of community engagement is positively associated with the adoption and choice of new products and even reduces adoption time. Even brand loyalty measures, as the "Holy Grail" of the marketing profession (MCALEXANDER et al., 2002, p. 38), are found to be driven by brand community participation. LAROCHE et al. (2013) report that brand communities show positive effects on the consumers' relationship with the product, the brand, and the company itself, which in turn have positive effects on brand trust and loyalty dimensions (cf. also SCHAU et al., 2009).

Taking a closer look at the studies mentioned above reveals that they mostly derive their implications based on the interpersonal communications between consumers on the respective brand community websites. The company or brand itself is left out and treated like a pure observer of social media discussions not taking over an active role on the brand community platform (GODES et al., 2005, p. 422).

However, Facebook is a highly effective communication and distribution channel and demands the active participation of brands and company representatives (KAPLAN and HAENLEIN, 2010, pp. 64-65, DHOLAKIA and DURHAM, 2010, p. 26). The options for firms to engage are basically threefold. First, companies can develop social games or applications (RAUSCHNABEL et al., 2012, p. 153). Second, they can promote their brands through simple advertising measures similar to online banner ads (e.g., CHANG et al., 2012, p. 634, CHU, 2011, p. 30, LIPSMAN et al., 2012, p. 40). And third, they can get in touch with their consumers through their brand fan pages (GOH et al., 2013, p. 88). They can post photos, videos, quizzes, or any kind of brand related information users can interact with. By using the underlying social network structures, branded content sent out through brand fan pages spreads across the social network and can reach not only fans, but also the network of friends of fans as an interaction with brand posts is also displayed in the newsfeed of friends (LIPSMAN et al., 2012, p. 44)[1]. As people increasingly use brand fan pages to also learn about unfamiliar brands (NAYLOR et al., 2012, p. 105), the question of how the ideal brand posts should look like becomes crucial.

The success of corporate brand posts is often assessed using simple popularity measures. A post is, for example, seen as popular when it gets a high number of likes, creates high impressions, has a high number of comments, or is shared by many users (LIPSMAN et al., 2012, p. 46, HOFFMANN and FODOR, 2010, p. 44, DE VRIES et al., 2012, p. 84). Even though these metrics are easy to access and provide a solid approximation of how many people appreciate a certain post, they do not necessarily reflect beneficial effects on a brand's image, reputation, or on people's attitude toward the brand. Moreover, many likes and comments can be generated by simply posting humorous content (BAMPO et al., 2008), that has a high degree of originality (LIN and HUANG, 2006), or just fits the current atmosphere within the target group (HO and DEMPSEY, 2010). However, just using the styles above to quickly generate a high number of likes and comments falls short. It implies the danger of neglecting other factors like a suitable post-brand-link and a unique brand positioning (RAITHEL and TAYLOR, 2013, p. 6). This can also be harmful as the initial interest fades quickly and can even cause inferior long term effectiveness (BERGER and SCHWARTZ, 2011, p. 871).

For a successful and persuasive communication, not only on Facebook, it is necessary to guide the recipients through a hierarchical sequence by creating awareness, facilitate knowledge about the brand and products and create attitudes and feelings that might be able to trigger a purchase act and could ultimately result in loyal customer behavior (cf. e.g., LAVIDGE and STEINER, 1961, pp. 59-61, YOO et al., 2004, p. 50, AMBLER et al., 2002, pp. 14-16, KELLER and LEHMANN, 2006, p. 745). As the long-term value of loyal customers together with a farsighted return on invest calculation has become evident in today's marketing landscape (cf. e.g., RUST et al., 2004, p. 110), I move away from assessing brand posts' effectiveness by simple reach metrics.

---

[1]   Please note that not all activities of a user show up in the newsfeed of his/her friends. The Facebook newsfeed uses an algorithm to rank content based upon the likely interest to a specific Facebook member (LIPSMAN et al., 2012, p. 44).

I herewith support the proposition of LIPSMAN et al. (2012, p. 40), who claims that a good Facebook brand fan page with effective corporate brand posts is able to create a deeper engagement, shapes positive attitudes, enhances customer loyalty and increases purchase intentions amongst the fan base.

I consequently formulate the following hypotheses about the effects of corporate brand posts on metrics along the purchase funnel[2]:

Corporate brand posts on Facebook show a positive effect on consumers'...
> H_{1b} ... *attitude toward the brand*
> H_{1c} ... *purchase intention.*

Figure 1 shows the conceptual framework, hypotheses, and moderating effects of the paper at hand. I argue that corporate brand posts on Facebook are able to positively influence metrics along the purchase funnel (H_1). Additionally, I propose a positive moderator effect of the degree of interactivity and vividness (H_2), a mixed moderator effect of the level of product involvement (H_3), and a significant interaction between the two moderators (H_4). The dependent variables of interest along the purchase funnel are post recall, attitude toward the brand, and purchase intention.

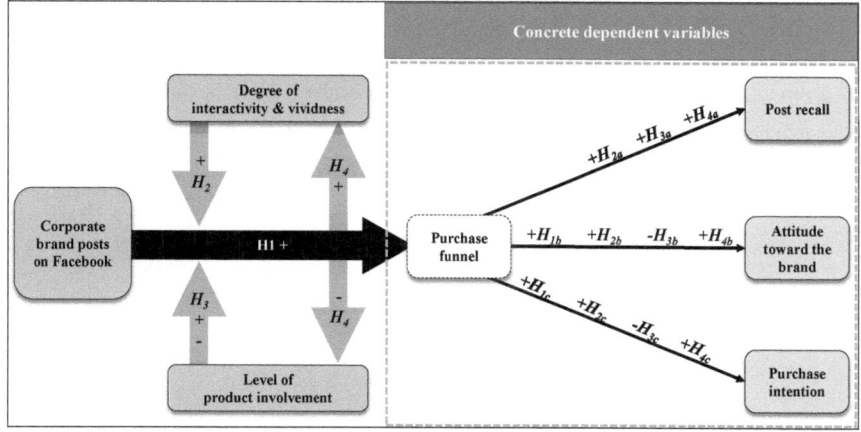

Figure 1: Conceptual Framework and Hypotheses

---

[2]   Please note that I do not postulate H_{1a}, since a positive post recall of participants is a natural consequence of any posting activity on Facebook brand pages (cf. also Figure 1).

2.2   The Moderating Role of Interactivity and Vividness

Today, users like approximately 40 brand fan pages that communicate 36 times per month with their respective fan base. On average, each Facebook user sees 1,440 status updates from brand fan pages every month in his newsfeed (SEABROOK, 2013). Given this fact, it becomes obvious that the competition amongst brand fan pages for the attention of Facebook users has long begun. Social media managers have to create content that differs from others, shows a good brand-post fit, and catches the respondent's attention. However, research about what companies should post to achieve these goals is scarce and further insights are needed (JAHN and KUNZ, 2012, p. 344, JAHN et al., 2011, p. 326).

Interactivity

One way of enhancing brand posts' effectiveness is to use interactive brand post characteristics. The level of interactivity of corporate communication efforts is not predefined by the respective medium (i.e., the internet) or the platform (i.e., Facebook). It is rather the individual execution of communication efforts that creates different levels of interactivity (RAFAELI, 1990, p. 126). Interactivity can be defined as "[t]*he degree to which two or more communication parties can act on each other, on the communication medium, and on the messages and the degree to which such influences are synchronized*" (LIU and SHRUM, 2002, p. 54)[3]. Further, interactivity on brand fan pages comes along with a real time, two-way communication between participants all given by the internet in general and Facebook in particular (GOLDFARB and TUCKER, 2011). Research has shown many beneficial aspects that come along with a high level of interactivity regarding corporate communication efforts. Table 1 provides an overview of the state of research.

---

[3]   For a more comprehensive overview of definitions and concepts of interactivity, please refer to the works of FORTIN and DHOLAKIA (2005, p. 388) and MCMILLAN and HWANG (2002, pp. 31-33).

Study	Methodological Approach	Major Findings
LIU and SHRUM (2002)	Theoretical Contribution	Interactivity shows positive effect on user satisfaction
GOLDFARB and TUCKER (2011)	Field Experiment	Interactivity of ad increases its intrusiveness
FORTIN and DHOLAKIA (2005)	Experiment and SEM	Interactivity has a positive effect on social presence
HOFFMAN and NOVAK (2012)	Theoretical Contribution	Interactivity enhances a flow experience
SICILIA et al. (2005)	Experiment	Interactivity leads to higher information processing and higher favorability toward the brand and product
MACIAS (2003)	SEM	Interactivity has positive influence on perceptions of brands and the respective advertisement
MADDOX et al. (1997)	Descriptive Analysis	Interactivity leads to more favorable evaluations of the brand and its products
JEE and LEE (2002)	Experiment	Interactivity increases attitude toward the website
JO and KIM (2003)	Experiment	Interactivity shows positive effects on relationship building (e.g., positivity, trust, commitment etc.)

Table 1: State of Research - Interactivity

By introducing a modified Elaboration Likelihood Model, CHO (1999) adds that high interactive online advertisements provide superior peripheral cues that result in a more enduring, peripheral shift in the recipients' attitude that is predictive of their subsequent behavior. As the Facebook environment is highly distractive by nature, interactivity of brand posts plays an important role to stimulate peripheral cues to achieve advanced brand post effectiveness. Based on the deliberations above, it can be concluded that posts with a high degree of interactivity enhance the positive influence of brand posts on purchase funnel metrics (i.e., brand post recall, attitude toward the brand, purchase intention).

Vividness

Another way to enrich brand posts is the inclusion of vivid characteristics into communication efforts of the brand fan page. STEUER (1992) defines vividness as the representational richness of a mediated environment by its formal features. It is the way, in which an environment presents the information to the senses. Facebook brand pages allow marketers to include many vivid characteristics into their posts. Including videos, presenting pictures, adding animations, or using different colors are just some examples how vividness can be created (CHO, 1999, GOLDFARB and TUCKER, 2011, FORTIN and DHOLAKIA, 2005). But it is, again, not only the ability of a communication medium that influences the degree of vividness. It is also the depth or quality of the sensory information that is presented (STEUER, 1992). Even though, vividness, also referred to as "media richness" (DAFT and LENGEL, 1986), is correlated with interactivity, the both can occur without each other (FORTIN and DHOLAKIA, 2005, p. 389). Research shows that the level of vividness on commercial websites increases users' attitudes toward the website and brand (COYLE and THORSON, 2001). The observed attitudinal change is also found to be more persistent compared to websites with a low degree of vividness. FORTIN and DHOLAKIA (2005) add that the perceived social presence of a web-based advertisement is increased, when vividness features are used. By means of their experimental approach, they could subsequently show an increase of arousal across participants which transfers into a superior advertising effectiveness. I therefore conclude that more vivid brand posts are also able to enhance the positive effects of Facebook brand posts on purchase funnel metrics.

DE VRIES et al. (2012), for the first time, tested the effects of both, interactivity and vividness in the Facebook environment. They find that especially posts with a high degree of interactivity and vividness get more likes and comments and are, thus, more popular among brand fans. As a result of their analysis on post individual level, they looked at interactivity and vividness separately. For the purpose of the field experiment at hand, this approach has to be changed. I conducted extensive desk research and screened 20 Facebook brand fan pages of the Top 100 Facebook Brands (SOCIALBAKERS, 2013) and their respective posting behavior. It became obvious that there is no single brand fan page that uses exclusively high (low) interactive or exclusively high (low) vivid brand posts[4]. To keep the field experiment and its treatment realistic, the compilations of brand posts cannot be purely interactive or vivid — it is rather a mix between both elements. For this reason, I will not separate the two dimensions but formulate common hypotheses for both, interactivity and vividness:

Highly interactive and vivid brand posts on Facebook are more effective than posts with a low degree of interactivity and vividness regarding their effect on consumers'...

H_{2a} ... *post recall capability*

H_{2b} ... *attitude toward the brand*

H_{2c} ... *purchase intention.*

2.3   The Moderating Role of Product Involvement

For many decades, product involvement has played a crucial role in advertising research. Defined as "[a] person's perceived relevance of the object based on inherent needs, values, and interests" (ZAICHKOWSKY, 1985, p. 342), people with different levels of product involvement

---

[4]   Please note that a detailed overview of different brand posts and their assigned level of vividness and interactivity will be presented and discussed in chapter 3.1.

will vary in the extensiveness of their purchase decision process. People with higher involvement will need more attributes to compare alternatives, need more time for the decision process, have a higher willingness to reach a maximum or a threshold level of satisfaction within their decision process, and need a higher degree of information (KRUGMAN, 1966). Based on these deliberations, LAURENT and KAPFERER (1985, p. 42) state that product involvement is a consequence of antecedents like personal interest, hedonic value, sign value, and perceived importance of a specific product. CELSI and OLSON (1988, p. 211) add that the personal relevance or importance is represented by the perceived link between one's personal goals and values and their respective product knowledge. In addition, the authors state that individuals are more attentive and more cognitively activated when processing information regarding a high involvement product. Thus, research demands corporate communication to consequently adjust their actions along the requirements of recipients' involvement level to increase advertising or communication effectiveness (FU et al., 2012, p. 195, DE PELSMACKER et al., 2002, p. 51). People demand detailed product information and high quality arguments in case of high product involvement and, thus, use more cognitive resources for information processing. People focus more on peripheral cues like the attractiveness of a message or pure design and layout aspects when it comes to the low involvement product category (e.g., PETTY et al., 1983, DENS and DE PELSMACKER, 2009, DENS and DE PELSMACKER, 2010, BAUER et al., 2006). For this reason I propose a difference in brand post effectiveness along the purchase funnel for brand pages of high versus low involvement products.

Branded content on Facebook is primarily consumed within the newsfeed of users. Users are up to 150 times more likely to consume branded content in the newsfeed than to visit the brand fan page itself (LIPSMAN et al., 2012, p. 40). Given the fact that Facebook users are confronted with a huge number of brand messages and status updates of their peers on their newsfeed, they are simply not able to fully process all information presented. Rather, people sift through their newsfeed and apply cognitive filtering mechanisms to reduce the complexity of the Facebook environment. Messages from high involvement products, characterized by peoples' higher product knowledge (PARK and MOON, 2003, pp. 982-987), higher interest in the product/brand (ZAICHKOWSKY, 1985, p. 347), and a superior conformity with consumers' personal values and norms (CELSI and OLSON, 1988, p. 221), are, therefore, more likely to be perceived and should be recalled more often:

H₃ₐ: *Facebook brand posts are more effective for companies in the high involvement*
          product category than for comparably low involvement product companies with
          respect to their effect on consumers' post recall capability.

The involvement construct also shows positive moderating effects on other variables along the purchase funnel. Advertising shows a higher influence on recipients' attitude toward the brand/product/company under a high compared to a low involvement condition (e.g., ANDREWS and SHIMP, 1990, p. 210, SPIELMANN and RICHARD, 2013, p. 499). Similar effects could also be shown on trust, satisfaction, and commitment measures (e.g., MARTÍN et al., 2011, pp. 148-152, GNEPA, 2012, p. 42), as well as for purchase related variables like purchase intention or willingness to pay (e.g., WIESEKE and HAUMANN, 2010, pp. 178-179). The argumentations of these studies almost exclusively follow the logic of the elaboration likelihood model. The elaboration likelihood model suggests that recipients of brand communication engage in more effortful cognitive processing of the messages in case of a high involvement situation or product. They process the presented information in more detail and form new cognitive structures based on the evaluation of the respective content. Information about low involvement products is processed in a more superficial way. Peripheral cues like source attractiveness, music, humor, or visual stimuli play the dominant role and result in a temporary attitudinal change (PETTY and CACIOPPO, 1986, PETTY et al., 1983, PETTY et al., 2004). Having said this, one could argue that Facebook brand posts work better under a high involvement condition. However, the central route of cognitive processing can only be activated when recipients have the ability to process the information in depth consistent with their involvement state (PETTY et al., 1983, p. 143, PETTY et al., 2004, p. 69). Two main reasons support the fact that social network users do not have the possibility to systematically process the information presented by brands. First, even though Facebook allows messages up to 60,000 characters to distribute detailed information, most brands stick to messages of about 80 characters to achieve the best interaction rates (WIESE, 2013). The necessary depth of information that high involvement fans demand can hardly be transferred through 80 character messages. Second, through the tremendously high number of status updates from peers and brands (cf. also chapter 2.2), the Facebook page and especially a fan's newsfeed form a highly complex environment that is bounded by the problem of information overload. KOROLEVA et al. (2011) confirm the inherent information overload and state that users constantly try to reduce complexity though applying perceptional filters and heuristics. The authors further confirm that Facebook mainly activates affective and more superficial ways of information processing that are in line with the peripheral routes of the elaboration likelihood model. Especially, attitudinal measures and behavioral intentions seem to be driven by a more emotional and superficial way of information processing that argues in favor of a higher effectiveness of brand related Facebook communication in case low involvement brands, products, or situations. Following these arguments, I propose that Facebook posts better fit the communication goals of low involvement products and formulate the following two hypotheses:

Facebook brand posts are more effective for companies in the low involvement product category than for comparably high involvement product companies with respect to their effect on consumers'...
> *H_{3b} ... attitude toward the brand*
> *H_{3c} ... purchase intention.*

The Interplay of Interactivity, Vividness and Involvement

Advertising research defines peripheral cues as the attractiveness of a message (PETTY et al., 1983, p. 137). These attention-getting and curiosity-generating visual cues like size, animation or color can be seen as closely related to the levels of interactivity and vividness (CHO, 1999, p. 37). CHO (1999, p. 39) also confirms that people indeed are more likely to interact with interactive and vivid banner ads in case of low involvement situations. Both dimensions fit the peripheral route of the Facebook environment. I therefore hypothesize:

High interactive & vivid brand posts are more effective for low involvement products than high involvement products with regards to their effect on consumers'...
> *H_{4a} ... post recall capability*
> *H_{4b} ... attitude toward the brand*
> *H_{4c} ... purchase intention.*

3   Research Design

As one of the main contributions of this paper is to test whether Facebook brand posts are able to influence fans' mindset metrics along the purchase funnel in a realistic setting, I conduct an online field experiment to elevate the external validity of the paper at hand. The study design consists of an online Facebook experiment over a two week treatment period. I set up brand fan pages for two brands. One is representing a high involvement product and one shows a comparably low product involvement. Furthermore, I designed two compilations of Facebook brand posts. One consists of mainly high interactive and vivid brand posts where the other shows a lower degree of interactivity and vividness.

3.1   Choice of Brands and Treatment

To minimize preexisting knowledge and affect due to a prior familiarity and exposure with the content presented in the field experiment, fictitious brands from the product categories relevant to our student biased sample population were created — a young fashion label *attraction*, a sports drink *ISOPOWA*®, and a fixed gear bicycle manufacturer *BikeBelow*. Online research revealed that the brand names were not preallocated or connected to any existing companies. In line with the deliberations and findings of TILL and SHIMP (1998), I expect the bicycle manufacturer *BikeBelow* to be the representative of the high involvement product category, whereas *ISOPOWA*® and *attraction* should be located in the lower involvement segment.

Pretest I

To assure a correct manipulation of the different product involvement levels, the three fictitious brand profiles[5] were fed into a pretest. Product involvement was measured by applying the 20-item semantic differential scale suggested by ZAICHKOWSKY (1985)[6] as it has been applied to a myriad of different setting and studies and has proven high reliability (e.g., SPIELMANN and RICHARD, 2013, KIM et al., 2008, DE PELSMACKER et al., 2002). A total of 60 respondents answered the questionnaire. 46.9% were female and the ages ranged between 19 and 30. Table 2 gives a detailed overview of the generated results.

---

[5] The detailed brand profiles can be found in Appendix 1.
[6] Please note that the full 20-item scale was only used in pretest I. For efficiency reasons, the further experimental procedure relied on a subset of seven involvement items (cf. chapter 3.2).

Brands	Involvement Mean	N	Post-Hoc-Comparison Bonferroni	Conclusion
(1) attraction	2.400 (1.075)	20	(1) vs. (2): p = .039 (1) vs. (3): p < .001	**Comparably Low Involvement**
(2) ISOPOWA®	3.265 (1.538)	21	(2) vs. (1): p = .039 (2) vs. (3): p = .024	Excluded
(3) BikeBelow	4.203 (0.758)	19	(3) vs. (1): p < .001 (3) vs. (2): p = .024	**Comparably High Involvement**

Note: Involvement means are scores on seven-point Likert-scales; Standard deviations in parentheses; Cronbach's α of involvement scale = 0.966;Alternative post-hoc-tests revealed similar results

Table 2: Pretest Involvement - ANOVA

Analysis of variance revealed that there is a significant difference between the involvement level of the three brands ($F(2,58) = 13.568$; $p < .001$). The post-hoc test indicates that the bicycle as rather high and the fashion label as comparably low involvement product are significantly different from each other. However, it has to be noted that *BikeBelow* did not reach a high involvement level on the seven point Likert scale. With its mean score of 4.203 it rather ranges in the middle of the involvement spectrum. As the difference between the two brands is close to two scale points, I still consider the two brands appropriate to be used as vehicles in the subsequent field experiment. For clarity reasons, I will still address the two brands as representatives of the "high" and "low" involvement category, even though they can only be seen in relation to each other representing a "comparably high" and a "comparably low" involvement level. The sports drink *ISOPOWA®* also proved to be significantly different but ranged between *attraction* and *BikeBelow*. It was, therefore, excluded from the subsequent field experiment.

Pretest II

In order to design actual Facebook brand posts for the two selected companies (i.e., *BikeBelow* and *attraction*) and to properly manipulate the degree of interactivity and vividness, it is necessary to understand what posting options companies have and how they can be classified regarding their interactivity and vividness. DE VRIES et al. (2012) provide an overview of different posting styles and their respective classifications. The grouping of DE VRIES et al. (2012) shall also be the basis for the post compilations used in the study at hand. Table 3 shows that textual and pure pictorial posts show a low degree of vividness, whereas videos address multiple senses and, therefore, belong to the high vividness category. A company can further increase the degree of interactivity by e.g., not posting simple links to websites, but asking questions or announcing quizzes.

Level	Vividness	Interactivity
Low	Textual posts	Link to website (mainly news sites, blogs, but not to company website)
	Pictorial (photo or image)	Voting (brand fans are able to vote for alternatives, e.g., design or taste)
Medium	Event (application at the brand page and announces an upcoming event)	Call to act (urges brand fans to do something)
		Contest (brand fans are requested to do something for which they can win prizes)
High	Video (mainly videos from YouTube)	Question
		Quiz (similar to question, but now brand fans can win prizes)

Table 3: Interactivity and Vividness Classification of DE VRIES 2012

Desk research revealed that brands — again referring to the Top 100 Facebook Brands (SOCIALBAKERS, 2013) — mostly do not post on a daily base. To assure a realistic environment for the field experiment, I leave four days without a post in the two-week treatment period and designed two post compilations (i.e., high interactivity/vividness and low interactivity/vividness) for both brands, each consisting of ten posts.

Next to the posting frequency, important deliberations regarding the posting content have to be made. SNSs are often used for promotional means by posting special offers, social media vouchers and discounts, or launching product based advertising campaigns (e.g., SZABO and HUBERMAN, 2010, p. 80, SMITH et al., 2012, p. 102). As the field experiment at hand is based on fictitious brands, a focus on product-advertisement or promotion goals would fall short. Rather than posting purely product related posts, I focus on corporate brand posts that do not center on a pure selling aspect but represent the corporate brand's self image. The respective style and content is kept constant across the two brands to assure a high degree of comparability. Of course, content is different in that the bicycle content is transferred over to comparable topics in the fashion industry. I hereby also control for a similar mix of informative and entertaining posts in all treatment groups. Further, it has to be noted, that each post comes with a short text to keep posting activities realistic. Table 4 shows the post compilations for both brands. The compilation for the high interactive/vividness treatment group of each brand mainly consists of videos and questions. Following the classification of DE VRIES et al. (2012), they both represent the highest manifestation in the interactivity and vividness category.

Post Number	High Interactivity/Vividness	Low Interactivity/Vividness
1	Video + Question (information product category)	Photo (product picture)
2	Question (fans' expectations)	Photo (product picture)
3	Video + Question (fans' vacation plans)	Link (product category expert blog)
4	Question (design trends)	Vote (use of product)
5	Video + Question (use of product)	Photo (product picture)
6	Question (where to buy the product)	Photo (new designs)
7	Question (how to enjoy weather with product)	Link (product category expert blog)
8	Video (passion with product category)	Vote (most important attribute of product)
9	Question (favorite city to use/buy product)	Link (newspaper article about product category)
10	Video & Contest (image video about the company)	Vote (product picture in action)

Table 4: Overview of Post Compilations[7]

To validate the correct manipulation of the different interactivity and vividness levels, a second pretest was conducted. An online questionnaire was designed which presented all posts of the compilations. Each respondent was randomly assigned to one of the four compilations (high and low interactivity/vividness for *attraction* and *BikeBelow*) and was confronted with the short brand profile. Subsequently, all posts of the respective compilation where shown and participants were asked to indicate the perceived level of vividness and interactivity. To assess the perceived level of interactivity, I applied six items[8] of the perceived interactivity scale by MCMILLAN and HWANG (2002, p. 37). Respondents were asked to indicate their level of appreciation of each statement on a seven point Likert scale with 1 = "do not agree at all" to 7 = "fully agree". Vividness was measured by means of a four item seven-point semantic differential of KRISHNAMURTHY and SUJAN (1999)[9]. Participants were only part of one treatment group pretest to avoid learning effects. Again, in total, 60 respondents took part in the pretest. 27 participants rated posts from *attraction* and 33 from *BikeBelow*. Table 5 shows the results of the interactivity and vividness pretest.

---

[7]   The different post compilations together with the pictures and videos used can be found on the data-CD handed in together with this thesis.

[8]   i.e. enable concurrent communication, enable tow-way communication, are interactive, primarily enable one-way communication, are interpersonal, and enabled conversations.

[9]   i.e. abstract/concrete, dull/vivid, vague/clear, and not figurative/figurative.

Interactivity/Vividness Levels	Interactivity Mean	Vividness Mean	N	ANOVA Results
High Interactive/Vivid	5.229	5.225	30	Interactivity:
Compilation	(0.685)	(0.764)		**F(1,59) = 59.984; p < .001**
Low Interactive/Vivid	4.014	4.475	30	Vividness:
Compilation	(0.518)	(0.781)		**F(1,59) = 14.149; p < .001**

Note: Interactivity and vividness means are scores on seven-point Likert-scales; Standard deviations in parentheses; Cronbach's α of interactivity-scale = .804 and of vividness-scale α = .724

Table 5: Pretest Interactivity and Vividness

As intended, the designed post compilations are perceived more interactive and more vivid in the high interactivity and vividness posting compilations (i.e., interactivity: $F(1,59) = 59.984$, $p < .001$; vividness: $F(1,59) = 14.149$, $p < .001$). There are no significant differences between the two brands. This confirms that the differences in interactivity and vividness are caused by the posting compilations. The posts are, therefore, sufficient to be included into the field experiment.

3.2   Design and Measurement

Design

The field experiment is conducted as a before-and-after 2 (interactivity/vividness: high or low) × 2 (involvement: high or low) between- and within-subjects design. The whole experimental procedure includes an initial survey, a treatment period of two weeks on Facebook, and a posttest. The treatments are posted on the Facebook brand fan pages of *attraction* and *BikeBelow*. For this reason, the whole experimental procedure is carried out as an online field experiment. To receive the treatments, participants had to become fan of the created brand fan pages on Facebook. As each brand appears in the experimental procedure twice (i.e., low and high interactivity and vividness), it had to be assured that participants from one experimental group are not connected to participants from the other treatment group of the brand. In other words, if two Facebook friends are part of the experimental set up in the different treatment groups of one brand, their newsfeed would show any liking, sharing, or commenting activity of their friend connected to the other group. Therefore, the experimental treatments would not be mutually exclusive to the treatment group anymore. For this reason, I execute the experiment in two stages. The treatment groups of high interactive and vivid brand posts for *BikeBelow* and *attraction* are launched and completed first. Subsequently, the low interactivity and vividness counterparts are fielded. Figure 2 shows the design and execution of the field experiment with the respective timeframes from April to May 2013. Consequently, the experiment shows two recruiting stages before stage 1 and 2. Thus, I conducted two initial surveys, two experimental stages, and two posttests.

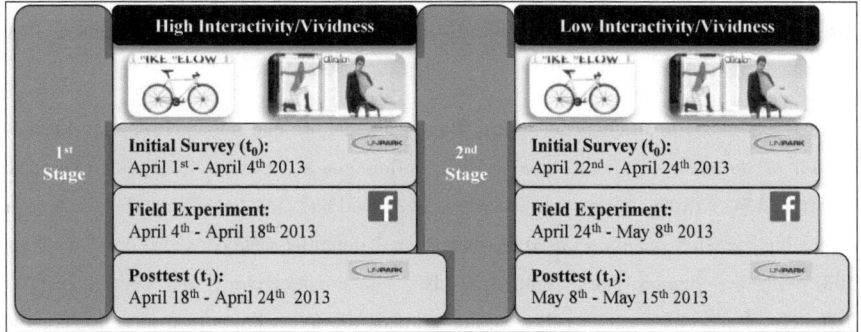

Figure 2: Design and Execution of the Field Experiment

Initial Survey

Participants were invited to the initial survey[10] and had to indicate their email address. Email addresses were used to match respondents' answers of the initial survey with posttest responses. Afterwards, participants were led through the demographic block which concluded with the screener-question: *"Do you have an own Facebook profile?"*. The next part of the questionnaire dealt with people's internet experience. To assess participants' internet usage behavior measured in time intervals, I used five categories from "0-1 hour per day" up to "over 4 hours per day" (cf. also THORBJØRNSEN et al., 2002, p. 26). The Facebook usage behavior measured in hours spent per day[11] and the number of Facebook friends were further questioned (cf. ELLISON et al., 2007, p. 1150). Those who indicated to be a fan of a company or brand on Facebook were asked additional questions about how many posts they consciously realize and how they interact with these corporate communication efforts. The next set of questions asked respondents to indicate their attitude toward Facebook, again, taken from ELLISON et al. (2007, p. 1150). Following, trust toward Facebook was surveyed by a single item (cf. LIN and LU,

---

[10] Please note that the initial survey and the posttest in t_1 are conducted with EFS survey from Unipark. The language throughout the whole experiment is German. If not indicated otherwise, all items are measured on seven-point Likert scales.

[11] The intervals were questioned on a per day basis. Six categories were used from "less than 10 minutes" up to "more than 3 hours".

2011, p. 568). In addition, I asked respondents to indicate their privacy concerns toward Facebook, also by means of the single item introduced by HOY and MILNE (2010, p. 33). At this point, respondents are assigned randomly to either *attraction* or *BikeBelow* and confronted with the respective brand profiles. Similar to pretest I, the level of product involvement is assessed by using seven items[12] of the 20-item semantic differential scale suggested by ZAICHKOWSKY (1985).

Next, the t_0-values of the dependent variables of interest are questioned. I measure *attitude toward the brand* by applying three semantic differential scale items of MACKENZIE et al. (1986, p. 134) with the anchors: positive/negative, good/bad, and favorable/unfavorable. For evaluating *purchase intention* I used the three-item differential scale of WANG et al. (2012, p. 203) with the bipolar pairs "unlikely/likely", "uncertain/certain", and "definitely not/ definitely"[13]. The final page in this section explains the following course of action for the experimental procedure. Further, it questions respondents' Facebook aliases to track if they become fan of the respective brand page. Finally, participants are forwarded to the brand fan page on Facebook of either *attraction* or *BikeBelow* and are asked to become fan of the brand.

Posttest

After the two week treatment period, participants are invited by email to take part in the posttest of the experiment. To match the dataset of the posttest with the initial survey, email addresses are questioned first and checked with initial responses. Respondents are further questioned if they became fan of the respective brand to screen out people that did not click the like button. Subsequently, the posttest assessed the number of perceived brand posts as the third dependent variable. To ensure that participants really perceived at least one post, an open text field asked them to name the topic or content of one or more brand posts. To match the open answers with actual postings allowed controlling for the actual perception of Facebook fans in the study set up and generated a reliable variable of *post recall*. The procedure was necessary due to the fact

---

[12] i.e. important/unimportant, matters to me/doesn't matter, means a lot to me/means nothing to me, useless/useful, of no concern/of concern to me, uninterested/interested, and essential/nonessential.

[13] At this point it has to be noted that developing purchase intention toward a brand's product, of course, is dependent from many aspects other than Facebook posts. However, as already stated in chapter 2.1, people more and more use brand fan pages to also learn about unfamiliar brands (NAYLOR et al., 2012, p. 105). Therefore, the experimental stimulation of brand page interaction seems appropriate as it reflects Facebook users' information search behavior regarding new and rather unfamiliar brands. As the positive effect of brand posts on attitude toward the brand can be expected, it will be interesting to see if the attitudinal effect caused by posts of the fictitious brands is strong enough to also influence respondents' purchase intention.

that Facebook fans are able to hide status updates from brands, friends, or apps in their newsfeed anytime. In addition, there is no reliable source of information, if and how long participants have been interacting with Facebook during the experimental procedure.

The following part involves the identical questions and scales posed in the initial survey to generate t_1 data for the dependent variables of *attitude toward the brand* and *purchase intention*. Changes of the dependent variables are determined by the difference between the t_1 means and the respective t_0 values. The questionnaire concluded with manipulation checks regarding the effect of the respective treatments. Again, the perceived level of interactivity and vividness of the brand posts was measured using the scales of MCMILLAN and HWANG (2002) and KRISHNAMURTHY and SUJAN (1999) similar to the second pretest. To assure the reliability of the applied scales, Cronbach's-alpha values are calculated. Table 6 provides an overview of the α-values. They all exceed the recommended threshold of .70, show a good level of reliability, and are, therefore, sufficient for the study at hand (cf. NUNALLY, 1978, KIM and KO, 2012, p. 1484).

Cronbach's Alpha Values of Scales					
Attitude toward the Brand	Purchase Intention	Interactivity	Vividness	Involvement	Attitude toward Facebook
.901	.883	.840	.825	.903	.805

Table 6: Reliability Scores

4   Analysis and Results

4.1   Sample, Manipulation Checks, and Covariates

Sample

The initial survey was completed by a total of 212 respondents from a convenience sample. They were randomly assigned to one of the four treatments groups. To motivate participation, respondents that completed the whole experiment over the two week period automatically took part in a lottery in which ten €20 Amazon vouchers were raffled. I had to exclude 44 participants that did not take part in the posttest survey and an additional 25 respondents that did not become fan of the brand pages on Facebook. Even though generalized linear models would allow answering the hypotheses derived in this paper without a balanced group size, for pragmatic reasons and to increase the robustness of the statistical analyses, I decided to randomly exclude three of the remaining 143 participants. This resulted in a group size of n = 35 in all four treatment groups. A total of 140 complete responses were fed into the conducted (co-)variance-analytical analyses.

Participants were between 16 and 47 years old with an average age of 24.91. 53.6% were female (n = 75) and 46.4% were male (n = 65). The predominant educational background was A-level with 56.4% of the sample[14]. Taking a closer look at respondents' internet usage behavior reveals, that one half is online up to three hours a day, whereas the other half even exceeds those numbers. Regarding people's Facebook usage behavior, close to fifty percent indicated to spend up to half an hour on Facebook daily. The other half clearly invests more time. The average participant in the sample is connected to about 350 peers and exactly 70% (n = 98) are already fan of one or more brands on Facebook. When people interact with brand posts, they mostly "like" a status update (M = 3.429, SD = 1.492 on a seven-point Likert scale from 1 = "never" to 7= "very frequently"). Participants further state that they rarely use the "commenting" (M = 1.745, SD = 1.087) or "sharing" (M = 1.806, SD = 1.081) functions to interact with brand posts on Facebook.

Manipulation Checks

To assure a proper perception of the experimental manipulations among participants, two different manipulation checks are built into the posttest. First, the involvement level for the two brands *attraction* and *BikeBelow* is assessed, again using seven items of the scale suggested by ZAICHKOWSKY (1985). As intended, Table 7 shows that *BikeBelow* is perceived higher in product involvement than the fashion label *attraction*. The results from the conducted ANOVA confirm the findings from pretest I and verify a successful manipulation of the involvement level. However, *BikeBelow*, again, only shows a medium involvement level on the seven point scale. As this study relies on fictitious brand profiles, simulating a high involvement level among participants was not successful. However, working with real brands would have led to different problems that also counteract the feasibility of the experimental design (e.g. preexisting attitudes toward real brands, no right for posting content on real brand fan pages etc.). Thus, it has to be kept in mind that the inherent involvement level of *attraction* has to be

---

[14] Please note that there are no significant differences in demographic measures across the single treatment groups that could bias the study's results (ANOVA$_{interactivity/vividness}$: age $F(1,138) = 3.720$, p > .05; gender $F(1,138) = 2.332$, p > .05; education $F(1,138) = .926$, p > .05 and ANOVA$_{involvement}$: age $F(1,138) = 2.986$, p > .05; gender $F(1,138) = 3.512$, p > .05; education $F(1,138) = 1.537$, p > .05).

interpreted as comparably low and the level of *BikeBelow* as comparably high for the remainder of this paper (cf. also chapter 3.1).

Brands	Involvement Mean	N	ANOVA Results
Comparably High Involvement (BikeBelow)	3.922 (1.097)	70	F(1,138) = 8.585; p < .01
Comparably Low Involvement (attraction)	3.045 (1.174)	70	

Note: Involvement means are scores on seven-point, Likert-scales; Standard deviations in parentheses; Involvement was measured in t₁ after the two week treatment period

Table 7: Manipulation Check Involvement

Second, the experimental manipulation of the different interactivity and vividness levels is also challenged. The posttest, again, assesses the perceived interactivity and vividness (cf. MCMILLAN and HWANG, 2002, KRISHNAMURTHY and SUJAN, 1999) of posting compilations among experimental participants. Following Pretest II, the manipulation check shows a statistically significant difference between the two experimental groups regarding respondents' perceived level of interactivity and vividness (cf. Table 8). Therefore, the manipulation of the vividness and interactivity level proved to be successful for the study's purposes. However, respondents' assessments about the different interactivity and vividness levels are more similar than indicated in pretest II. Embedding the posts in a real Facebook setting might have led to a different perception of posts' interactivity and vividness levels compared to the stand alone presentation in the online survey of pretest II (cf. chapter 3.1).

Treatment Groups	Interactivity/Vividness Mean	N	ANOVA Results
High Interactive/Vivid Group	4.057 (1.197)	70	F(1,138) = 3.944; p < .05
Low Interactive/Vivid Group	3.852 (1.144)	70	

Note: Interactivity/vividness means are scores on seven-point, Likert-scales; Standard deviations in parentheses

Table 8: Manipulation Check Interactivity/Vividness

Covariates

To control for effects that might bias the results of the paper at hand, I also measured covariates as potential controls. GOLDFARB and TUCKER (2011) argue that privacy concerns play a huge role within the online environment. People react more sensitive to postings on social networks when their privacy concerns are high. For this reason I include a single item in the initial survey stating "*I am concerned regarding the private information that can be found about me on Facebook*" with 1 = "do not agree at all" and 7 = "fully agree" (cf. HOY and MILNE, 2010). The covariate privacy concerns is split after the neutral scale point four and sums up 55.7% of respondents that show lower privacy concerns compared to 44.3% with higher privacy concerns.

Again following GOLDFARB and TUCKER (2011), I use the average time spent on Facebook to control for effects that stem from experiences through heavy use of the highly distracting Facebook environment. Especially attitudinal changes can differ drastically when experienced and non-experienced users are treated equally (cf. COYLE and THORSON, 2001, p. 72). Therefore, I split the variable "On average, how much time do you spend on Facebook per day?" into 44.7% of the sample using Facebook up to 30 minutes a day and contrast them to the remaining 55.3% of more frequent users.

4.2   Results

Table 9 presents the mean values for the dependent variables of the study at hand.

n = 140	High Involvement (BikeBelow, n = 70)				Low Involvement (attraction, n = 70)			
	High Interactive & Vivid (n = 35)		Low Interactive & Vivid (n = 35)		High Interactive & Vivid (n = 35)		Low Interactive & Vivid (n = 35)	
Dependent Variable	t_0	t_1	t_0	t_1	t_0	t_1	t_0	t_1
Perceived Number of Posts	---	3.200 (1.876)	---	2.830 (1.774)	---	2.460 (2.119)	---	2.140 (2.158)
Attitude Toward the Brand	5.141 (0.684)	5.253 (1.054)	4.794 (1.111)	4.995 (1.149)	3.983 (1.152)	4.840 (0.962)	4.271 (1.047)	4.349 (1.064)
Purchase Intention	3.779 (1.117)	3.750 (1.291)	3.142 (1.582)	2.960 (1.387)	3.333 (1.207)	3.571 (1.312)	3.294 (1.374)	3.168 (1.405)

Note: Cells are mean scores across items on seven-point, Likert-scales; Standard deviations in parentheses

Table 9: Overview of Mean-Values for Dependent Variables in Treatment-Groups

The mean values reveal that the triggered movements within the dependent variables attitude toward the brand and purchase intention between t_0 and t_1 are rather small. Participants purchase intention does not seem to be influenced by the posting activities in the experimental setup, whereas the attitude toward the brand measure was slightly increased in all groups. However, the movement in the group of highly interactivity and vivid brand posts of the low involvement product *attraction* seems to not fit the pattern of the overall experiment. The delta of almost one scale point indicates that participants seem to be distinctly influenced by the high interactive and vivid brand posts in the low involvement category which appears to be rather high compared to the overall experiment. To comprehend this phenomenon, one of the first thoughts goes to a measurement error in the respective group. Respondents in this group could be systematically biased regarding their demographics, attitudes toward the experimental procedure, or other unobserved characteristics. Nevertheless, two arguments speak in favor of the experimental approach and the suitability of the collected data. First, as already shown in footnote 14, there are no significant differences across groups regarding the collected demographic variables. I further tested for differences regarding other variables that might differentiate the treatment groups. The variables attitude toward Facebook ($F(1, 136) = 2.477$, $p > .05$), trust toward Facebook ($F(1, 136) = .956$, $p > .05$), internet experience ($F(1, 136) = .670$, $p > .05$), and time on Facebook ($F(1, 136) = 2.235$, $p > .05$) did not reveal any significant differences that might explain the high sensitivity to the highly interactive and vivid brand posts in the low involvement treatment group. Second, two recruitment stages were used to collect participants for the experiment. It has to be noted that participants were not exclusively collected for one treatment group. As figure 2 already showed, both groups using highly interactive and vivid brand posts (i.e. *attraction* and *BikeBelow* as representatives of rather high and rather low involvement) were recruited at the same time and use the same convenience sampling procedure through campus mailing lists and snowballing. As participants were randomly assigned to either *BikeBelow* or *attraction*, a possible bias of the recruiting process would also be reflected in the high interactive and vivid treatment group of *BikeBelow*. As the delta value in the highly interactive and vivid posting group of the high involvement product did not react in the same way, a measurement error can at least partly be ruled out. Of course, all results in the following have to be seen as only derived from the findings of this study under the assumption that the results are unbiased for the above reasons. For further analyses, I calculate the deltas of the dependent variables *attitude toward the brand* and *purchase intention* as t_1 minus t_0 to reduce the design's dimensionality. As the *perceived number of posts* is only assessed in t_1, I use the posttest values for statistical evaluation.

General Effectiveness of Facebook Brand Posts

Hypothesis 1 predicts that Facebook brand posts are generally able to positively influence people's attitude toward the brand and purchase intention irrespective of the involvement situation or the level of post interactivity and vividness. To test this assumption, I use all 140 responses because all are part of the experimental manipulation at hand. Every participant received ten Facebook brand posts of either high or low interactivity/vividness in either a high or low involvement setting in the two-week treatment period. Thus, I conduct a one-sample t-test, testing the respective delta values against zero to assure there is a significant main effect. Table 10 provides the corresponding test statistics.

One Sample T-Test - Testing Value = 0; n = 140						
Dependent Variable	t_0	t_1	Δ	T	sig.	Hypothesis
Attitude Toward the Brand	4.547 (1.101)	4.859 (1.099)	+0.312 (1.019)	3.626	p < .001	H_{1b} supported
Purchase Intention	3.387 (1.338)	3.362 (1.372)	-0.0245 (1.286)	-0.226	n.sig	H_{1c} not supported

Note: Values represent the mean scores across items on seven-point, Likert-scales; Standard deviations in parentheses; all respondents did see ten posts in the two-week period

Table 10: Effectiveness of Corporate Brand Posts on Facebook

Within the experimental manipulation it was possible to positively influence respondents' attitude toward the brand ($\Delta_{attitude}$ = +0.312, p < .001) independently of the posting style or product involvement group. The results support H_{1b} and confirm that Facebook postings are indeed able to influence attitudinal measures of the fan popularity. In contrast, purchase intention almost stayed constant and could not be influenced through posting activities ($\Delta_{purchase\ intention}$ = -0.0245, n.sig.). The attitudinal change over the two week treatment period was too small to trigger any subsequent movement in purchase intention. One reason might, again, be the use of fictitious brand profiles and the awareness of participants that they cannot purchase the products presented anyway. Moreover, I relied on more general brand posts not having a special sales or promotion focus. H_{1c} is, thus, not supported.

The Moderating Role of Interactivity and Vividness

To examine the moderating effect of post interactivity and vividness on the general effectiveness of Facebook brand posts, I conduct analysis of covariance (ANCOVA) using the covariates of chapter 4.1. Time spent on Facebook (F(1,137) = 6.064, p < .05) and privacy concerns $(F(1,137) = 4.350, p < .05)$ indeed show a significant influence on the dependent variables and confirm the prior deliberations based on GOLDFARB and TUCKER (2011) and COYLE and THORSON (2001). The sample is split up into two groups. One summarizes the high interactive and vivid posting groups from both *attraction* and *BikeBelow*, the other sums up their low interactive and vivid counterparts. Table 11 shows the results of the conducted ANCOVA.

		Perceived Number of Posts	Attitude Toward the Brand	Purchase Intention	N
Level of Interactivity and Vividness	High	2.829 (2.021)	Δ +0.485 (1.236)	Δ +0.105 (1.379)	70
	Low	2.486 (1.991)	Δ +0.140 (0.709)	Δ -0.154 (1.181)	70
ANCOVA Results		$F(1,137) = 0.754$ n.sig.	$F(1,137) = 3.096$ $p < .081, \eta^2 = 0.024$	$F(1,137) = 0.672$ n.sig.	
Hypothesis		H_{2a} not supported	H_{2b} weak support	H_{2c} not supported	

Note: Δ-values calculated out of the mean scores across items t_1-t_0; Number of perceived posts calculated as mean from open answers in t_1 (0-10 posts); Standard deviations in parentheses

Table 11: The Moderating Effect of Interactivity and Vividness

The manipulation of interactivity and vividness in the posting compilations causes a slight movement in the number of perceived posts and, therefore, post recall capability among participants ($M_{high} = 2.829$ vs. $M_{low} = 2.486$). However, ANCOVA results reveal that there is no statistical evidence for this effect to be significantly different from chance. Therefore, H_{2a} is not supported. Nevertheless, high interactive and vivid brand posts show a superior effect on respondents' attitude toward the brand compared to their low interactive and vivid equivalents ($\Delta_{high} = +0.485$ vs. $\Delta_{low} = +0.140$ with $p < .10$). Posting in an interactive and vivid manner is, therefore, superior when corporate social media responsible try to influence attitudinal measure in consumers' heads. An $\eta^2 = 0.024$ reveals a small to medium effect size which is comparable to other experimental studies (cf. e.g., VAN NOORT and WILLEMSEN, 2012) and meaningful for field experimental setups (COHEN, 1988, p. 355). Thus, results weakly support H_{2b}. With regard to the effects of interactive and vivid postings on participants' purchase intent, the same constellation as for the perceived number of posts is identified. Even though purchase intention is influenced in the intended direction ($\Delta_{high} = +0.105$ vs. $\Delta_{low} = -0.154$), no significant results could be found. Therefore, I find no support for H_{2c}.

The Moderating Role of Product Involvement

Similar to the approach in the upper paragraph, I also conduct ANCOVAs to investigate the moderating effect of product involvement on Facebook post effectiveness. For this purpose, the sample is again split up into two groups. The first group sums up the respondents from the two treatments groups of the high involvement brand *BikeBelow,* independent from the respective posting style. The second group pools both groups from *attraction* as representatives of a comparably lower product involvement level. Table 12 shows the respective results.

		Perceived Number of Posts	Attitude Toward the Brand	Purchase Intention	N
Level of Product Involvement	High (BikeBelow)	3.014 (1.822)	Δ +0.157 (0.873)	Δ -0.105 (1.297)	70
	Low (attraction)	2.300 (2.129)	Δ +0.468 (1.131)	Δ +0.056 (1.278)	70
ANCOVA Results		$F_{(1,137)} = 3.884$ $p = .05, \eta^2 = 0.028$	$F_{(1,137)} = 5.041$ $p < .05, \eta^2 = 0.036$	$F_{(1,137)} = 1.269$ n.sig.	
Hypothesis		H_{3a} supported	H_{3b} supported	H_{3c} not supported	

Note: *Δ-values calculated out of the mean scores across items t_1-t_0;Number of perceived posts calculated as mean from open answers in t_1 (0-10 posts); Standard deviations in parentheses*

Table 12: The Moderating Effect of Product Involvement

Hypothesis *3a* suggests that, due to selective perception filters applied to the Facebook environment, brand fans perceive more posts from brands with a higher level in product involvement. This coherence could be supported by the experimental results at hand. Whereas respondents in the *attraction* groups on average can recall M = 2.300 posts, *BikeBelow* fans are able to recall on average M = 3.014 posts (p = .05, $\eta^2 = 0.028$). Users indeed apply perceptional filters when confronted with status updates and brand posts on Facebook and tend to perceive posts from high involvement brands that fit their interest (cf. also ZAICHKOWSKY, 1985, p. 347) and their personal values and norms (cf. also CELSI and OLSON, 1988, p. 221). Thus, a moderating effect of product involvement on fans' post recall capability is found and H_{3a} supported. However, the brand posts used might not have been perceived equally across the two brands. Even though the posting compilations of *BikeBelow* and *attraction* were arranged carefully, were pretested regarding their interactivity and vividness level, and the content as well as the execution style was kept constant across the treatment groups, there still might be unobservable quality differences in the posting compilations that could have led to the higher perception in the high involvement group of *BikeBelow.*

In contrast to the superior effect of the high involvement product on brand post recall, H_{3b} proposes an opposite effect as the distracting Facebook environment does not allow for an in depth information processing needed to trigger an attitudinal change in the high involvement product category. The prevalence of peripheral cues, therefore, better fits the communication efforts of low involvement products. ANCOVA results confirm the suggested effect as participants in the low involvement groups show a significantly higher change in attitude toward the brand than their high involvement counterparts (Δ_{high} = +0.157 vs. Δ_{low} = +0.468, p < .05, η^2 = 0.036). Hypothesis *3b* is supported. However, the involvement literature consistently states that involvement is not only product or service specific. Moreover, the involvement level is influenced by situational factors, a respective person's personality traits and attitudes, as well a preexisting knowledge regarding a specific situation, product, or brand (e.g., ZAICHKOWSKY, 1985, CELSI and OLSON, 1988, LAURENT and KAPFERER, 1985). To also test if personal or situative factors influence the dependent variables independently from the presented product or brand, I divided participants into high and low involvement regarding their individual reported involvement score. A median split was conducted separating 50 % of the 140 participants with high (i.e., > 3.82 on a seven point scale) from the remaining half with low involvement. Results of the conducted ANCOVAs reveal that there are no significant influences of the personal or situative involvement level across all three dependent variables[15]. For this reason, the manipualtion of the involvement levels through the brand profiles at the beginning of the experiment can be seen as succesfull which further argues in favor of Hypothesis *3b*.

With regard to the effect of Facebook brand posts on brand fans' purchase intention, Hypothesis *3c* expects the same cohesion. Although a slight tendency toward the desired effect can be observed (Δ_{high} = -0.105 vs. Δ_{low} = +0.056), the effect of Facebook brand post on purchase intention is not significant and Hypothesis *3c*, consequently, not supported.

The Interplay of Interactivity, Vividness and Involvement

To test the final set of Hypothesis *4*, the experimental groups are now looked at separately. Each experimental group with n = 35 is fed into the ANCOVA to identify the potential interaction effect between the two categories manipulated in the experimental setup. The

---

[15] The respective test statistics are: post recall - M_{high} = 2.57 vs. M_{low} = 2.74 ($F(1,137)$ = .316, n.sig.); attitude toward the brand - Δ_{high} = .220 vs. Δ_{low} = .405 ($F(1,137)$ = 1.484, n.sig.); purchase intention - Δ_{high} = -.102 vs. Δ_{low} = .053 ($F(1,137)$ = 1.179, n.sig.).

analysis of covariance is calculated including both factors — interactivity/vividness and product involvement. Again, the two covariates time on Facebook and privacy concerns are included and both showed a significant effect on the dependent variables. Table 13 presents the results of the analyses.

Dependent Variable	High Involvement (BikeBelow, n = 70)		Low Involvement (attraction, n = 70)		ANCOVA Results	Hypothesis
	High Interactive & Vivid	Low Interactive & Vivid	High Interactive & Vivid	Low Interactive & Vivid		
Perceived Number of Posts	3.200 (1.876)	2.830 (1.774)	2.460 (2.119)	2.140 (2.158)	$F(3,135) = 0.041, p = .84$	H_{4a} not supported
Attitude Toward the Brand	Δ +0.112 (1.029)	Δ +0.201 (0.697)	Δ +0.857 (1.326)	Δ +0.079 (0.727)	$F(3,135) = 5.426, p < .05, \eta^2 = 0.039$	H_{4b} supported
Purchase Intention	Δ -0.029 (1.416)	Δ -0.182 (1.182)	Δ +0.238 (1.348)	Δ -0.126 (1.196)	$F(3,135) = 0.070, p = .79$	H_{4c} not supported

Note: Δ-values calculated out of the mean scores across items t1-t0; Number of perceived posts calculated as mean from open answers in t_1 (0-10 posts); Standard deviations in parentheses

Table 13: The Interplay of Interactivity, Vividness and Involvement

When perceived number of posts is the dependent variable, product involvement and the level of interactivity and vividness do not interact ($F(1,135) = 0.041$, p = .84). Moreover, respondents' purchase intention was also not influenced by the interaction term ($F(3,135) = 0.070$, p = .79). Therefore, Hypothesis *4a* and *4c* are not supported. On the contrary, the ANCOVA with attitude toward the brand as dependent variable reveals a clear interaction between product involvement and the respective level of post interactivity/vividness ($F(3,135) = 5.426$, p < .05, $\eta^2 = 0.039$). Following Hypothesis *4b*, highly interactive and vivid brand posts on Facebook are more effective when distributed by the comparably low involvement brand *attraction*. Postings that show high interactivity and vividness do not cause a greater shift in attitude toward the brand in case of a high involvement product *BikeBelow*. Figure 3 illustrates the interaction effect of product involvement and interactivity/vividness on the dependent variable attitude toward the brand.

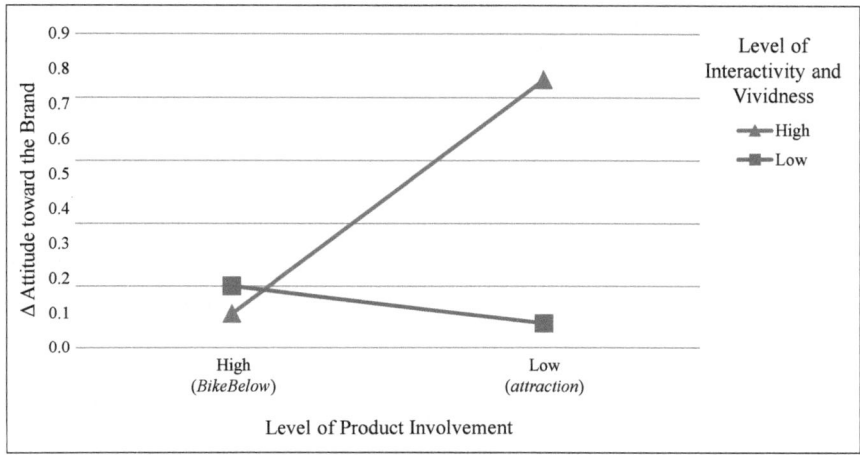

Figure 3: The Interaction between Interactivity/Vividness and Product Involvement

High and low interactive/vivid postings do not cause significantly different attitudinal changes in the high involvement group ($\Delta_{\text{high interactivity/vividness}}$ +0.112 and $\Delta_{\text{low interactivity/vividness}}$ +0.201). Thus, posting style seems to be less critical in case of a high involvement brand. Furthermore, the effect of low interactive/vivid posts does not differ much between the low and high involvement group ($\Delta_{\text{high involvement}}$ +0.201 and $\Delta_{\text{low involvement}}$ +0.079). However, a high degree of interactivity and vividness significantly increases Facebook fans' attitude toward the brand of the low involvement brand compared to their low interactive and vivid complements ($\Delta_{\text{high interactivity/vividness}}$ +0.857 vs. $\Delta_{\text{low interactivity/vividness}}$ +0.079). Hence, it is of high importance to post in an interactive and vivid manner in case of a low involvement product when aiming to positively influence fans' attitude toward the brand. Hypothesis *4b* is supported.

5   Conclusion, Limitations, and Implications

Conclusion

In the field experiment at hand, I manipulated the levels of interactivity/vividness and product involvement of Facebook brand fan pages and their respective posts over a two week treatment period. The dependent variables of interest (i.e., post recall, attitude toward the brand, and purchase intention) were chosen and aligned along the purchase funnel. Next to the fact that Facebook posts in general should be able to positively influence purchase funnel metrics independent from the conducted manipulations, it was expected that the positive influence of brand posts is higher when more interactive and vivid posts are used. Further, it was hypothesized that respondents perceive more posts in case of a high involvement situation, whereas the distracting Facebook environment leads to an inferior effectiveness of brand posts on people's attitude toward the brand and purchase intention compared to the low involvement setting. In addition, I proposed an interaction effect between posts' degree of interactivity/vividness and the level of product involvement. It is assumed that high interactive and vivid posts are more effective in case of a low involvement product as the necessary depth of information transmitted through Facebook brand posts better fits the communicational setting of low involvement products (cf. e.g., PETTY et al., 1983, p. 137, CHO, 1999, p. 39).

I found that Facebook brand posts are able to drive attitude toward a brand. This effect could be shown irrespectively of the degree of interactivity and vividness as well as the product involvement level at hand. As I chose corporate brand post content that focuses on the (fictitious) company's overall self image and not sales and product related promotion activities, purchase intention could not be increased significantly throughout the whole experiment. However, slight tendencies in the intended directions could be observed. I also found that participants who saw the Facebook brand pages with highly interactive and vivid brand posts developed a stronger attitude toward the brand than those who saw the comparably low interactivity and vivid brand fan page communication. This finding is in line with the findings of DE VRIES et al. (2012). Contrary to my expectations, the same effect could not be found for the number of posts recalled. Further, participants that were assigned to the Facebook fan pages of the high involvement product were able to recall a higher number of Facebook brand post than those in the comparably low product involvement groups. On the contrary, the positive effect on attitude toward the brand was confirmed to be superior in the low involvement product setting as hypothesized in H_{3b}. Finally, I found support for the hypothesis that high interactive and vivid brand posts help to create a greater attitudinal increase when posted from companies that are connected to a lower level of product involvement.

Before drawing further implication for research and practitioners, it has to be stated that due to the limitations already stated in chapters 4.1 and 4.2, the results and implications derived in the section at hand have to be treated with caution. Even though the experiment was conducted thoroughly, the following four points became evident. First, the manipulation of involvement levels did not result in a clear distinction between high and low involvement. Second, the application of fictitious brand profiles as base for the experimental manipulation could have been problematic. Third, the perceived differences in interactivity and vividness across the treatment groups were rather small. And fourth, posting compilations could have been perceived differently with regards to their (entertainment) qualities in the different treatment groups. Summarizing, the reported results are solely based on the study at hand and do not claim to be representative for the overall Facebook environment. Further research, outlined at the end of this paper, is necessary to counteract the current limitations and strengthen the robustness of the findings at hand. Nevertheless, this paper provides a valuable first step in field experimental literature on Facebook and encourages replications and subsequent works following the outlined approach.

Implications

The field experiment confirms that Facebook brand posts are able to influence consumer mindset metrics along the purchase funnel. Independently of posting style or the underlying brand, corporate brand posts are able to influence attitudinal measures toward the brand. This is consistent with the findings of LIPSMAN et al. (2012). Marketers, therefore, should see social media communication via brand posts as means to engage consumers in an ongoing dialogue often claimed by current research (e.g., HENNIG-THURAU et al., 2010, p. 313). Posting seems to be the superior strategy versus no posting activities. Solely communicating image related corporate brand information can drive attitude toward the brand, but falls short when aiming at an increase in purchase intention. A posting strategy that combines corporate and product/sales related information seems promising to also trigger purchase intention.

Findings regarding the ideal posting style reveal that the magnitude of the attitudinal change is indeed dependent on the posts' level of interactivity and vividness. The experiment revealed that the magnitude is over three times bigger for highly interactive and vivid brand posts (Δ_{high} + 0.485 / Δ_{low} + 0.140) than for posts of the low interactivity/vividness category. This finding is in line with JAHN et al. (2013) who state that interactivity of members and the companies themselves are crucial success factors of Facebook brand pages. Nevertheless, highly interactive and vivid brand posts do not come without costs. Highly vivid posts like image videos about the brand or highly interactive quizzes and contests in which prizes are given away consume a lot of resources and, therefore, create cost that have to be kept in mind. Not every post has to be highly interactive and vivid to be successful. As the experiment at hand used realistic compilations of ten Facebook posts that, in sum, consisted of rather high or low interactive and vivid posts, the overall picture of the company's posting activities has to be considered.

The effectiveness of Facebook brand communication is also moderated by the underlying product involvement of a specific product or category. Comparably high involvement products do not benefit from Facebook postings in the same way low involvement products do. Whereas people that see posts of a high involvement product show a better recall rate due to selective perception effects in the distractive Facebook environment (cf. also PARK and MOON, 2003, pp. 982-987, ZAICHKOWSKY, 1985, p. 347, CELSI and OLSON, 1988, p. 221), the positive effect on attitude toward the brand is higher in the low involvement category (cf. also ANDREWS and SHIMP, 1990, p. 210, SPIELMANN and RICHARD, 2013, p. 499). This stems from different information needs of customers regarding the product category and the superficial and distractive environment on the Facebook newsfeed. It emphasizes the peripheral route of information processing that better fits to low involvement products. With regard to low involvement products, customers do not require as detailed and as extensive information to develop attitude toward a brand or purchase intention as in high product involvement situations (cf. also PETTY et al., 1983, p. 143, PETTY et al., 2004, p. 69).

The combined evaluation of both moderators revealed, that there is a significant interaction effect between interactivity and vividness and the level of product involvement. High interactive and vivid posts are more effective when posted from low involvement product brand-fan pages. The peripheral cue of interactivity and vividness better matches the peripheral information processing sequence of low involvement products. In the high involvement category, interactivity and vividness do not make a significant difference regarding a change in attitude toward the brand. For marketers dealing with a comparably high involvement product this essentially means that it does not always have to be a highly interactive and vivid brand post to keep Facebook fans content. On the contrary, it is important for low involvement products to keep the interactivity and vividness-level of posts as high as possible to get the most out of Facebook posts concerning an optimal increase in attitude toward the brand. However, to not suffer a strategic disadvantage, high involvement product companies should also follow a strategy of rather high than low interactive and vivid brand posts but keep in mind that they probably won't reach the same effectiveness. This underlines the necessity for a solid benefit and cost rational of effectiveness and costs for interactivity and vividness for high involvement goods. Multi-brand companies should also follow a product based Facebook strategy along the involvement levels of their different goods and exploit the differences in effects described above.

Limitations

A number of limitations became apparent while conducting and analyzing the field experiment at hand that shall be starting point for further research. First, due to limits in budget, time, and participant recruiting only two fictitious brands represent the two levels of product involvement — a fashion label and a bicycle manufacturer. Research should further replicate the findings at hand and use at least two products representing one involvement dimension. A validation of the findings by means of other brand profiles representing the involvement levels seems promising. Second, it would be interesting to also transfer the experimental design over to Fanpages of already existing brand fan pages to increase external validity of the experimental design. Even though Facebook users more and more use the SNS to inform themselves about unfamiliar brands (cf. e.g., NAYLOR et al., 2012, BAIRD and PARASNIS, 2011, NEWMAN, 2011), the use of fictitious brands, of course, is dependent on the artificially created brand profiles used in the study at hand and suffers from a restricted sales and promotion focus. Third, financial resources did not allow for a proper simulation of the brand fan page interactivity between members. The experimental setup had to rely on the interaction of experimental participants with the fictitious brand fan pages. I did not pay fans to simulate interactivity through commenting and liking similar to an existing brand fan page. Even though the manipulation of interactivity was successful, the level of interactivity between experimental brand fans was still below average. As JAHN et al. (2013, p. 362) state that "*[...]member interactivity [is a] crucial success factor for driving customer engagement [...]*" on Facebook brand fan pages, the reported effects of the study at hand regarding the combination of interactivity and vividness probably originates more from the vividness dimension of the Facebook posts. Research should take this as starting point and replicate the findings with a realistic simulation of member interactions in the treatment groups. Forth and last, the number of posts representing the interactivity and vividness dimensions should be enhanced in future studies. The experiment at hand uses 20 posts per brand to simulate the interactivity and vividness levels. Other compilations and post variations have to be tried out to validate the findings of the paper at hand. Testing the different (entertainment) quality perceptions among participants of the compilations used seems promising. It allows keeping brand posts as comparable as possible even though different brand profiles are used. In addition, other timeframes exceeding the two week treatment period are worth an in depth look.

Appendix

Brand Profiles

Brand 1: Fashion Label - *attraction*

attraction — that's what it does! Das neue, innovative Label *attraction* vereint den Zeitgeist der aktuellen Modewelt und ermöglicht jungen Nachwuchsdesignern ihrer Kreativität freien Lauf zu lassen. Die Produkte des deutschen Nachwuchslabels sind im mittleren Preissegment angesiedelt. *attraction* bietet modernste und qualitativ hochwertige Fashion. Mode, gemacht von jungen Designern mit dem Ziel anzuziehen, anziehend zu sein, zu begeistern — *attraction*!

→ *attraction* - ist bald in Deutschland zu haben
→ *attraction* - gemacht für Mann & Frau
→ *attraction* - erscheint mit zwei neuen Kollektionen

Brand 2: Softdrink - *ISOPOWA®*

2012 revolutionierten Sportwissenschaftler den Markt der Energy-Drinks — *ISOPOWA®* wurde kreiert. *ISOPOWA®* ist ein innovatives isotonisches Sportgetränk, das Sie dabei unterstützt Elektrolyte aufzufüllen, die während der sportlichen Anstrengung verloren gegangen sind. *ISOPOWA®* hilft bei Ihrem Kampf um die Spitze im Sport. Hergestellt in Deutschland ohne künstliche Geschmacksstoffe, Farben und Süßungsmittel ist *ISOPOWA®* nun erhältlich – in drei Sorten: Black Currant, Orange und Lemon. Die *ISOPOWA®* GmbH entwickelt, produziert und vertreibt die Energy-Drinks und garantiert ein Höchstmaß an Qualität und Zufriedenheit.

Brand 3: Bicycle Manufacturer - *BikeBelow*

2012 war ein Jahr der Superlative für diejenigen, die an Dynamik, Design und Handling im Bereich des Fahrrads interessiert sind. *BikeBelow*, hat es sich zur Aufgabe gemacht qualitativ hochwertige, gut aussehende aber doch bezahlbare Stadtfahrräder zu entwickeln. Ein Team aus fahrradverrückten Ingenieuren, Wirtschaftlern und Studenten war daran federführend beteiligt, dass demnächst die ersten *BikeBelow*, Zweiräder präsentiert werden können. Egal ob im Alltag, auf dem Weg zur Schule, Universität oder Arbeitsplatz – mit einem *BikeBelow* kommt man immer mit Stil ans Ziel! Bald wird eine kleine aber feine Auswahl an Singlespeed Bikes auf den Markt gebracht, bei denen auf überflüssige, wartungsintensive Komponenten verzichtet wird. *BikeBelow* fährt mit nur einem Gang von A nach B — Back to basic!

References

ADJEI, M. T., NOBLE, S. M. & NOBLE, C. H. 2009. The Influence of C2C Communications in Online Brand Communities on Customer Purchase Behavior. *Journal of the Academy of Marketing Science,* 38(5), 634-653.

AMBLER, T., BHATTACHARYA, C. B., EDELL, J., KELLER, K. L., LEMON, K. N. & MITTAL, V. 2002. Relating Brand and Customer Perspectives on Marketing Management. *Journal of Service Research,* 5(1), 13-25.

ANDREWS, J. C. & SHIMP, T. 1990. Effects of Involvement, Argument Strength, and Source Characteristics on Central and Peripheral Processing of Advertising. *Psychology and Marketing,* 7(3), 195-214.

BAIRD, C. H. & PARASNIS, G. 2011. From Social Media to Social Customer Relationship Management. *Strategy & Leadership,* 39(5), 30-37.

BAMPO, M., EWING, M. T., MATHER, D. R., STEWART, D. & WALLACE, M. 2008. The Effects of the Social Structure of Digital Networks on Viral Marketing Performance. *Information Systems Research,* 19(3), 273-290.

BAUER, H. H., SAUER, N. E. & BECKER, C. 2006. Investigating the Relationship between Product Involvement and Consumer Decision-Making Styles. *Journal of Consumer Behaviour,* 5(4), 342-354.

BERGER, J. & SCHWARTZ, E. M. 2011. What Drives Immediate and Ongoing Word of Mouth? *Journal of Marketing Research,* 48(5), 869-880.

BOYD, D. M. & ELLISON, N. B. 2007. Social Network Sites: Definition, History, and Scholarship. *Journal of Computer-Mediated Communication,* 13(1), 210-230.

BRODIE, R. J., ILIC, A., JURIC, B. & HOLLEBEEK, L. 2013. Consumer Engagement in a Virtual Brand Community: An Exploratory Analysis. *Journal of Business Research,* 66(1), 105-114.

CELSI, R. L. & OLSON, J. C. 1988. The Role of Involvement in Attention and Comprehension Processes. *Journal of Consumer Research,* 15(2), 210-224.

CHANG, K. T. T., CHEN, W. & TAN, B. C. Y. 2012. Advertising Effectiveness in Social Networking Sites: Social Ties, Expertise, and Product Type. *IEEE Transactions on Engineering Management,* 59(4), 634-643.

CHO, C.-H. 1999. How Advertising Works on the WWW: Modified Elaboration Likelihood Model. *Journal of Current Issues & Research in Advertising,* 21(1), 33-50.

CHU, S.-C. 2011. Viral Advertising in Social Media : Participation in Facebook Groups and Responses among College-Aged Users. *Journal of Interactive Advertising,* 12(1), 30-43.

CMOSURVEY 2014. *The CMO Survey from Duke University's Fuqua School of Business and the American Marketing Association - Topline Results February 2014* [Online].

Available:https://faculty.fuqua.duke.edu/cmosurveyresults/The_CMO_Survey-Topline_Report-Feb-2014.pdf [Accessed 2014-02-21].

COHEN, J. 1988. *Statistical Power Analysis for the Behavioral Sciences*, Hillsdale, New Jersey: Lawrence Erlbaum Associates Publishers.

COYLE, J. & THORSON, E. 2001. The Effects of Progressive Levels of Interactivity and Vividness in Web Marketing Sites. *Journal of Advertising*, 30(3).

DAFT, R. L. & LENGEL, R. H. 1986. Organizational Information Requirements, Media Richness and Structural Design. *Management Science*, 32(5), 554-571.

DE PELSMACKER, P., GEUENS, M. & ANCKAERT, P. 2002. Media Context and Advertising Effectiveness : The Role of Context Appreciation and Context / Ad Similarity. *Journal of Advertising*, 31(2), 49-61.

DE VRIES, L., GENSLER, S. & LEEFLANG, P. S. H. H. 2012. Popularity of Brand Posts on Brand Fan Pages: An Investigation of the Effects of Social Media Marketing. *Journal of Interactive Marketing*, 26(2), 83-91.

DEIGHTON, J. & KORNFELD, L. 2009. Interactivity's Unanticipated Consequences for Marketers and Marketing. *Journal of Interactive Marketing*, 23(1), 4-10.

DENS, N. & DE PELSMACKER, P. 2009. Advertising for Extensions: Moderating Effects of Extension Type, Advertising Strategy, and Product Category Involvement on Extension Evaluation. *Marketing Letters*, 21(2), 175-189.

DENS, N. & DE PELSMACKER, P. 2010. Consumer Response to Different Advertising Appeals for New Products: The Moderating Influence of Branding Strategy and Product Category Involvement. *Journal of Brand Management*, 18(1), 50-65.

DHOLAKIA, U. M., BAGOZZI, R. P. & PEARO, L. K. 2004. A Social Influence Model of Consumer Participation in Network- and Small-Group-Based Virtual Communities. *International Journal of Research in Marketing*, 21(3), 241-263.

DHOLAKIA, U. M. & DURHAM, E. 2010. One Café Chain's Facebook Experiment. *Harvard Business Review*, 88(3), 26.

DUNNE, Á., LAWLOR, M.-A. & ROWLEY, J. 2010. Young People's Use of Online Social Networking Sites – a Uses and Gratifications Perspective. *Journal of Research in Interactive Marketing*, 4(1), 46-58.

ELLISON, N. B., STEINFIELD, C. & LAMPE, C. 2007. The Benefits of Facebook "Friends:" Social Capital and College Students' Use of Online Social Network Sites. *Journal of Computer-Mediated Communication*, 12(4), 1143-1168.

FACEBOOK. 2013. *Earnings Release - Facebook Reports Second Quarter 2013 Results* [Online]. Available: http://files.shareholder.com/downloads/AMDA-NJ5DZ/26812333 12x0x683496/a3bbb405-e82d-493a-a23ab3c5ade6e1b9/FB_Q213EarningsRelease.pdf [Accessed 2013-12-09].

FORTIN, D. R. & DHOLAKIA, R. R. 2005. Interactivity and Vividness Effects on Social Presence and Involvement with a Web-Based Advertisement. *Journal of Business Research*, 58(3), 387-396.

FU, J.-R., CHEN, J. H. F. & CHI, N. 2012. An Investigation of Factors that Influence Blog Advertising Effectiveness. *International Journal of Electronic Business Management*, 10(3), 194-203.

GNEPA, T. J. 2012. Product Involvement, Elaboration Likelihood and the Structure of Commercial Speech: A Tale of Two Print Advertisements. *International Journal of Business Research*, 12(5), 42-52.

GODES, D., MAYZLIN, D., CHEN, Y., DAS, S., DELLAROCAS, C., PFEIFFER, B., LIBAI, B., SEN, S., SHI, M. & VERLEGH, P. 2005. The Firm's Management of Social Interactions. *Marketing Letters*, 16(3/4), 415-428.

GOH, K. Y., HENG, C. S. & LIN, Z. 2013. Social Media Brand Community and Consumer Behavior: Quantifying the Relative Impact of User- and Marketer-Generated Content. *Information Systems Research*, 24(1), 88-107.

GOLDFARB, A. & TUCKER, C. 2011. Online Display Advertising: Targeting and Obtrusiveness. *Marketing Science*, 30(3), 389-404.

HENNIG-THURAU, T., GWINNER, K. P., WALSH, G. & GREMLER, D. D. 2004. Electronic Word-of-Mouth via Consumer-Opinion Platforms: What Motivates Consumers to Articulate themselves on the Internet? *Journal of Interactive Marketing*, 18(1), 38-52.

HENNIG-THURAU, T., MALTHOUSE, E. C., FRIEGE, C., GENSLER, S., LOBSCHAT, L., RANGASWAMY, A. & SKIERA, B. 2010. The Impact of New Media on Customer Relationships. *Journal of Service Research*, 13(3), 311-330.

HO, J. & DEMPSEY, M. 2010. Viral Marketing: Motivations to Forward Online Content. *Journal of Business Research*, 63(9-10), 1000-1006.

HOFFMANN, D. L. & FODOR, M. 2010. Can You Measure the ROI of Your Social Media Marketing? *MIT Sloan Management Review*, 52(1), 40-49.

HOFFMAN, D. L. & NOVAK, T. P. 2012. Toward a Deeper Understanding of Social Media. *Journal of Interactive Marketing*, 26(2), 69-70.

HOLLENBECK, C. R. & KAIKATI, A. M. 2012. Consumers' Use of Brands to Reflect their Actual and Ideal Selves on Facebook. *International Journal of Research in Marketing*, 29(4), 395-405.

HOY, M. G. & MILNE, G. 2010. Gender Differences in Privacy-Related Measures for Young Adult Facebook Users. *Journal of Interactive Marketing*, 10(2), 28-45.

JAHN, B., BRUDLER, B. & MEYER, A. 2011. Members Only! - Nutzen von geschlossenen Social Networking Sites aus Nutzer- und Betreibersicht. *Marketing ZFP - Journal of Research and Management*, 33(4), 317-328.

JAHN, B. & KUNZ, W. 2012. How to Transform Consumers into Fans of your Brand. *Journal of Service Management*, 23(3), 344-361.

JAHN, B., JAKIĆ, A. & KUNZ, W. 2013. The Importance of Perceived Interactivity for Customer Engagement on Social Media Brand Pages (funded by the UMass Healey Grant). *In:* KARAOSMANOĞLU, E. & ELMADAĞ BAŞ, A. B. (eds.) *Lost in Translation – Marketing in an Interconnected World, Proceedings of the 42nd Annual Conference - EMAC, 2013 Istanbul.* 362.

JEE, J. & LEE, W. 2002. Antecedents and Consequences of Perceived Interactivity: an Exploratory Study. *Journal of Interactive Advertising,* 3(1), 34-45.

JO, S. & KIM, Y. 2003. The Effect of Web Characteristics on Relationship Building. *Journal of Public Relations Research,* 15(3), 199-223.

JOINSON, A. 2008. Looking at, Looking up or Keeping up with People: Motives and Use of Facebook. *CHI 2008 Proceedings.* Florence, Italy.

KAPLAN, A. M. & HAENLEIN, M. 2010. Users of the World, Unite! The Challenges and Opportunities of Social Media. *Business Horizons,* 53(1), 59-68.

KELLER, K. L. & LEHMANN, D. R. 2006. Brands and Branding: Research Findings and Future Priorities. *Marketing Science,* 25(6), 740-759.

KIM, A. J. & KO, E. 2012. Do Social Media Marketing Activities Enhance Customer Equity? An Empirical Study of Luxury Fashion Brand. *Journal of Business Research,* 65(10), 1480-1486.

KIM, S., HALEY, E. & LEE, Y.-J. 2008. Does Consumers' Product-Related Involvement Matter When it Comes to Corporate Ads? *Journal of Current Issues & Research in Advertising,* 30(2), 37-48.

KOROLEVA, K., KRASNOVA, H. & GÜNTHER, O. 2011. Cognition or Affect? – Exploring Information Processing on Facebook. *In:* DATTA, A., SHULMAN, S., ZHENG, B., LIN, S.-D., SUN, A. & LIM, E.-P. (eds.) *Social Informatics – Proceedings of the Third International Conference SocInfo 2011 Singapore.* Heidelberg et al.: Springer, 171-183.

KRISHNAMURTHY, P. & SUJAN, M. 1999. Retrospection Versus Anticipation: The Role of the Ad Under Retrospective and Anticipatory Self-Referencing. *Journal of Consumer Research,* 26(1), 55-69.

KRUGMAN, H. E. 1966. The Measurement of Advertising Involvement. *Public Opinion Quarterly,* 30(4), 583-596.

LAROCHE, M., HABIBI, M. R. & RICHARD, M.-O. 2013. To Be or Not to Be in Social Media: How Brand Loyalty is Affected by Social Media? *International Journal of Information Management,* 33(1), 76-82.

LAURENT, G. & KAPFERER, J.-N. 1985. Measuring Consumer Involvement Profiles. *Journal of Marketing Research,* 22(1), 41-53.

LAVIDGE, R. J. & STEINER, G. A. 1961. A Model for Predictive Measurements of Advertising Effectiveness. *Journal of Marketing*, 25(6), 59-62.

LIN, K.-Y. & LU, H.-P. 2011. Intention to Continue Using Facebook Fan Pages From the Perspective of Social Capital Theory. *Cyberpsychology, Behavior and Social Networking*, 14(10), 565-570.

LIN, Y.-S. & HUANG, J.-Y. 2006. Internet Blogs as a Tourism Marketing Medium: A Case Study. *Journal of Business Research*, 59(10-11), 1201-1205.

LIPSMAN, A., MUDD, G., RICH, M. & BRUICH, S. 2012. The Power of "Like": How Brands Reach (and Influence) Fans through Social-Media Marketing. *Journal of Advertising Research*, 52(1), 40-52.

LIU, Y. & SHRUM, L. J. 2002. What Is Interactivity and Is It Always Such a Good Thing? Implications of Definition, Person, and Situation for the Influence of Interactivity on Advertising Effectiveness. *Journal of Advertising*, 31(4), 53-64.

MACIAS, W. 2003. A Preliminary Structural Equation Model of Comprehension and Persuasion of Interactive Advertising Brand Web Sites. *Journal of Interactive Advertising*, 3(2), 36-48.

MACKENZIE, S. B., LUTZ, R. J. & BELCH, G. E. 1986. The Role of Attitude toward the Ad as a Mediator of Advertising Effectiveness: A test of Competing Explanations. *Journal of Marketing Research*, 23(2), 130-143.

MADDOX, L. M., MEHTA, D. & DAUBEK, H. G. 1997. The Role and Effect of Web Addresses in Advertising. *Journal of Advertising Research*, 37(2), 47-59.

MARTÍN, S. S., CAMARERO, C. & JOSÉ, R. S. 2011. Does Involvement Matter in Online Shopping Satisfaction and Trust? *Psychology and Marketing*, 28(2), 145-167.

MCALEXANDER, J. H., SCHOUTEN, J. W. & KOENIG, H. F. 2002. Building Brand Community. *Journal of Marketing*, 66(1), 38-54.

MCMILLAN, S. J. & HWANG, J.-S. 2002. Measures of Perceived Interactivity: An Exploration of the Role of Direction of Communication, User Control, and Time in Shaping Perceptions of Interactivity. *Journal of Advertising*, 31(3), 29-42.

MUNIZ, J. A. M. & O'GUINN, T. C. 2001. Brand Community. *Journal of Consumer Research*, 27(4), 412-432.

NAMBISAN, P. & WATT, J. H. 2011. Managing Customer Experiences in Online Product Communities. *Journal of Business Research*, 64(8), 889-895.

NAYLOR, R. W., LAMBERTON, C. P. & WEST, P. M. 2012. Beyond the "like" Button: The Impact of Mere Virtual Presence on Brand Evaluations and Purchase Intentions in Social Media Settings. *Journal of Marketing*, 76(6), 105-120.

NELSON-FIELD, K., RIEBE, E. & SHARP, B. 2013. More Mutter About Clutter: Extending Empirical Generalizations to Facebook. *Journal of Advertising Research*, 53(2), 186-191.

NEWMAN, A. A. 2011. Brands Now Direct Their Followers to Social Media. *The New York Times.*

NUNALLY, J. C. 1978. *Psychometric Theory,* New York, McGraw-Hill.

PARK, C.-W. & MOON, B.-J. 2003. The Relationship between Product Involvement and Product Knowledge: Moderating Roles of Product Type and Product Knowledge Type. *Psychology and Marketing,* 20(11), 977-997.

PETTY, R. E., CACIOPPO, J. T. & SCHUMANN, D. 1983. Central and Peripheral Routes to Advertising Effectiveness: The Moderating Role of Involvement. *Journal of Consumer Research,* 10(2), 135-147.

PETTY, R. E. & CACIOPPO, J. T. 1986. *Communication and Persuasion: Central and Peripheral Routes to Attitude Change,* New York: Springer.

PETTY, R. E., RUCKER, D. D., BIZER, G. Y. & CACIOPPO, J. T. 2004. The Elaboration Likelihood Model of Persuasion. *In:* SEITER, J. S. & GASS, R. H. (eds.) *Perspectives on Persuasion, Social Influence, and Compliance Gaining.* Boston et al.: Pearson, 65-89.

PUGSLEY, S. 2012. *Six Ways to Make Your Facebook Posts Succeed* [Online]. ICROSSING. Available: http://www.icrossing.com/sites/default/files/Six%20Ways%20to%20Make %20Your%20Facebook%20Posts%20Succeed%20-%20iCrossing.pdf   [Accessed 2013-09-17].

RAACKE, J. & BONDS-RAACKE, J. 2008. MySpace and Facebook: Applying the Uses and Gratifications Theory to Exploring Friend-Networking Sites. *Cyberpsychology & Behavior,* 11(2), 169-174.

RAFAELI, S. 1990. Interacting with Media: Para-Social Interaction and Real Interaction. *In:* RUBEN, B. & LIEVROUW, L. (eds.) *Mediation, information and communication.* New Brunswick (NJ): Transaction Publishers, 125-183.

RAITHEL, S. & TAYLOR, C. R. 2013. Do Super Bowl Ads Build Brands? Working Papers at the Institute for Market-based Management, Munich/Philapdelphia.

RAUSCHNABEL, P. A., PRAXMARER, S. & IVENS, B. S. 2012. Social Media Marketing: How Design Features Influence Interactions with Brand Postings on Facebook. *In:* EISEND, M., LANGNER, T. & OKAZAKI, S. (eds.) *Advances in Advertising Research (Vol. III) – Current Insights and Future Trends.* Wiesbaden: Springer Gabler, 153-161.

RICHTER, D., RIEMER, K. & VOM BROCKE, J. 2011. Internet Social Networking. *Wirtschaftsinformatik,* 53(2), 89-103.

RUST, R. T., LEMON, K. N. & ZEITHAML, V. A. 2004. Return on Marketing: Using Customer Equity to Focus Marketing Strategy. *Journal of Marketing,* 68(1), 109-127.

SCHAU, H. J., MUÑIZ, A. M. & ARNOULD, E. J. 2009. How Brand Community Practices Create Value. *Journal of Marketing,* 73(5), 30-51.

SEABROOK, T. 2013. *Cutting Through the Crowds on Facebook News Feeds* [Online]. Socialbakers. Available: http://www.socialbakers.com/blog/1561-cutting-through-the-crowds-on-facebook-news-feeds [Accessed 2013-10-01].

SHANKAR, V. & BATRA, R. 2009. The Growing Influence of Online Marketing Communications. *Journal of Interactive Marketing,* 23(4), 285-287.

SICILIA, M., RUIZ, S. & MUNUERA, J. L. 2005. Effects of Interactivity in a Web Site: the Moderating Effect of Need for Cognition. *Journal of Advertising,* 34(4), 31-45.

SMITH, A. N., FISCHER, E. & YONGJIAN, C. 2012. How Does Brand-related User-generated Content Differ across YouTube, Facebook, and Twitter? *Journal of Interactive Marketing,* 26(2), 102-113.

SMOCK, A. D., ELLISON, N. B., LAMPE, C. & WOHN, D. Y. 2011. Facebook as a Toolkit: A Uses and Gratification Approach to Unbundling Feature Use. *Computers in Human Behaviour,* 27(6), 2322-2329.

SOCIALBAKERS. 2013. *TOP 100 Facebook Brands Social Media Stats* [Online]. Available: http://www.socialbakers.com/all-social-media-stats/facebook/ [Accessed 2013-10-30].

SPIELMANN, N. & RICHARD, M.-O. 2013. How Captive is your Audience? Defining Overall Advertising Involvement. *Journal of Business Research,* 66(4), 499-505.

STELZNER, M. A. 2013. *2013 Social Media Marketing Industry Report - How Marketers Are Using Social Media to Grow Their Businesses* [Online]. Social Media Examiner. Available: http://www.socialmediaexaminer.com/SocialMediaMarketingIndustry Report2013.pdf [Accessed 2013-09-16].

STEUER, J. 1992. Defining Virtual Reality: Dimensions Determining Telepresence. *Journal of Communication,* 42(4), 73-93.

SZABO, G. & HUBERMAN, B. A. 2010. Predicting the Popularity of Online Content. *Communications of the ACM,* 53(8), 80-88.

THOMPSON, S. A. & SINHA, R. K. 2008. Brand Communities and New Product Adoption: The Influence and Limits of Oppositional Loyalty. *Journal of Marketing,* 72(6), 65-80.

THORBJØRNSEN, H., SUPPHELLEN, M., NYSVEEN, H. & PEDERSEN, P. E. 2002. Building Brand Relationships Online: A Comparison of two Interactive Applications. *Journal of Interactive Marketing,* 16(3), 17-34.

TILL, B. D. & SHIMP, T. A. 1998. Endorsers in Advertising: The Case of Negative Celebrity Information. *Journal of Advertising,* 27(1), 67-82.

TRUSOV, M., BUCKLIN, R. E. & PAUWELS, K. 2009. Effects of Word-of-Mouth Versus Traditional Marketing: Findings from an Internet Social Networking Site. *Journal of Marketing,* 73(5), 90-102.

VAN NOORT, G. & WILLEMSEN, L. M. 2012. Online Damage Control: The Effects of Proactive Versus Reactive Webcare Interventions in Consumer-generated and Brand-generated Platforms. *Journal of Interactive Marketing,* 26(3), 131-140.

WANG, X., YU, C. & WEI, Y. 2012. Social Media Peer Communication and Impacts on Purchase Intentions: A Consumer Socialization Framework. *Journal of Interactive Marketing,* 26(4), 198-208.

WIESE, J. 2013. *"Cut my Post" hilft beim Texten von Statusupdates* [Online]. allfacebook.de. Available: http://allfacebook.de/features/cut-my-post-hilft-beim-texten-von-status updates [Accessed 2013-11-14].

WIESEKE, J. & HAUMANN, T. 2010. Prädiktoren der Preisbereitschaft von Kunden - Status-quo der aktuellen Sales- und Service- Forschung. *In:* KEUPER, F. & HOGENSCHURZ, B. (eds.) *Professionelles Sales & Service Management - Vorsprung durch konsequente Kundenorientierung.* Second updated edition. Bochum: Gabler Verlag/Springer Fachmedien, 170-205.

YOO, C., KIM, K. & STOUT, P. 2004. Assessing the Effects of Animation in Online Banner Advertising: Hierarchy of Effects Model. *Journal of Intertive Advertising,* 4(2), 49-60.

ZAGLIA, M. E. 2013. Brand Communities Embedded in Social Networks. *Journal of Business Research,* 66(2), 216-223.

ZAICHKOWSKY, J. 1985. Measuring the Involvement Construct. *Journal of Consumer Research,* 12(3), 341-352.

ZHANG, J. Q., CRACIUN, G. & SHIN, D. 2010. When does Electronic Word-of-Mouth matter? A Study of Consumer Product Reviews. *Journal of Business Research,* 63(12), 1336-1341.